Paddle the Lake District

A GUIDE TO EXPLORING THE LAKES BY CANOE, KAYAK OR PADDLEBOARD

Mark Rainsley

www.pesdapress.com

First published in Great Britain 2026 by Pesda Press

Tan y Coed Canol

Ceunant

Caernarfon

Gwynedd

LL55 4RN

© Copyright 2026 Mark Rainsley

ISBN: 9781917182041

Maps by Bute Cartographics.
Contains Ordnance Survey data © Crown copyright and database right 2026.

The Author has asserted his rights under the Copyright, Designs and Patents Act, 1988, to be identified as Author of this Work. All rights reserved. No part of this publication may be reproduced, stored in a retrieval system, or transmitted, in any form or by any means, electronic, mechanical, photocopying, recording or otherwise, without the prior written permission of the publisher.

Printed in Latvia, www.unimaps.eu

FSC
www.fsc.org
FSC® C216080

Foreword

Chris Brain

I've been paddling in the Lake District for many years. It's been the location for some memorable experiences on and off the water, always providing an incredible atmosphere in very grand surroundings. I feel very connected to the water here and, whether I travel by open canoe, kayak or paddleboard, it feels fresh and enjoyable every time. With so much to explore and so many places to see, I've always felt like there is a lifetime of adventures waiting for paddlers.

Over the years I've returned, over and over again, for the wonderful expanses of open water, with their spectacular scenery and surrounding landscapes. There is always such a warm and welcoming feeling to the paddling, an incredible combination of wonderful locations and lovely people. Whether you would like the gentle bustle of the more popular locations or would appreciate somewhere quieter, there is always something to see and do. I enjoy watching from the water as the clouds hover around the summit of the Old Man of Coniston, as much as I enjoy waving to the people on the ferry as we pass one other on the water.

There really is something magic that draws me back time and time again, with every single paddle giving a unique experience. If you paddle here, you will have the pleasure of experiencing stunning sunsets; there really is nothing like returning to Glencoyne Bay as the sun is heading in. You will also experience epic downpours and probably some breezy conditions too. The weather is an integral part of every adventure on the water and it should be embraced with a smile on your face. After a full day on the water, I can't help but feel revitalised and energised: it always seems to have a wonderful calming effect on my mind and my body. To top it all off there is a fine selection of cakes and coffee available locally; there is no better way to end a day on the water.

After much time spent in canoes and kayaks, paddleboards offered new challenges. On my 'Big Day Out', I paddleboarded the lengths of Derwent Water, Bassenthwaite Lake, Windermere, Coniston Water and Ullswater in a single, exhausting day!

For me, there are still many adventures left to be had in the Lake District and I'm looking forward to spending the rest of my time seeking them out and continuing my ever-growing love for the area.

I hope you enjoy paddling here; I certainly do.

Chris Brain, paddlesport coach and enthusiast
www.chrisbraincoaching.com

Yewbarrow, Kirk Fell, Great Gable and Lingmell, Wast Water

About the Author
Mark Rainsley

Mark has spent four decades using paddlesport as a means of avoiding adulthood and responsibility. He has descended white-water rivers on six continents, kayaked solo around the UK and is dedicated to exploring every nook and cranny of the UK's lakes and rivers by paddlecraft.

The author lives and works in the Lake District. As well as exploring the lakes, he has canoed and kayaked the white-water rivers, summitted all 214 Wainwright fells, completed the gruelling Lakeland 200 mountain bike circuit, and, most importantly, critically assessed the scone and cake quality in countless tea rooms.

Mark is a prolific contributor to paddlesport magazines and other media. He has authored numerous Pesda Press guidebooks including **Paddle the Severn**, **Paddle Shakespeare's Avon**, *Paddle the Thames*, **Paddle the Wye** and **South West Sea Kayaking**.

Acknowledgements

Pete and Sue were, hands down, my favourite aunt and uncle … and I had a lot of them. My dad and his numerous siblings all settled in Coventry and worked in the factories, except for his youngest brother, Pete. Pete broke the mould, by heading north. In 1974, he married Sue in a flower-power-themed wedding in Borrowdale, and they lived on Helvellyn, running the youth hostel at Greenside Mine. Dad would drive us north along the brand-new M6 to stay with them in Bell Cottage, their tiny home alongside Glenridding Beck. It was immensely cool to have an aunt and uncle who lived on an actual mountain. My Midlands and Lake District lives even collided, when my primary school's deputy headteacher gave an assembly talk about being rescued by Pete, who was part of Patterdale Mountain Rescue Team. Five decades later, my family and I followed Pete and Sue north, and we now live not far from the pair. I have them to thank for my life-long love of Lakeland and they are still, hands down, my favourite aunt and uncle.

A big thanks to those friends and family who joined me in researching the English Lakes. I loved paddling with my girls: my wonderful wife Heather, and my gorgeous daughter Ellen. I especially enjoyed the company of hyper-motivated Leigh Van Der Byl, who, despite living in Hertfordshire, seems to spend more time paddling the lakes than I do.

I'm hugely grateful to those who helped create this book. Chris Brain was kind enough to supply the foreword. Dr Lizzie Garnett and my wife Heather ran their expert red pens over, respectively, my geology and ecology efforts. Franco Ferrero at Pesda Press edited the whole thing, Sarah Warburton and Andrew Whiting proofread my childish scrawls, Franco did a grand job of the design work and Don Williams of Bute Cartographic produced the stunning maps.

Important notice – disclaimer

Paddlesports, whether in a river, lake or sea environment, have their inherent risks, as do all adventurous activities. This guidebook highlights some considerations to take into account when planning your own paddlesport journey.

While we have included a range of factors to consider, you will need to plan your own journey and within that ensure there is scope to be adaptable to local conditions, for example, the ever-changing weather. This requires knowing your own abilities, then applying your own risk assessment to the conditions that you may encounter. The varying environmental conditions encountered on the English Lakes mean that good judgement is required to decide whether to paddle or not.

The information within this book has been well researched. However, neither the author nor Pesda Press can be held responsible for any decision of whether to paddle or not and any consequences arising from that decision.

Cat Bells, Derwent Water

Contents

Foreword 3
About the Author 5
Acknowledgements 6
Introduction 11
Lake District Highlights 13
The Lake District 17
Planning to Paddle 25
Access to the Lakes 36
Launching on the Lakes 39

THE NORTHERN LAKES 45

Bassenthwaite Lake 47
Derwent Water 57
Thirlmere 71
Ullswater 81
    Ullswater – northern 85
    Ullswater – southern 93
Other lakes 101
    Brothers Water 101
    Haweswater 101

THE SOUTHERN LAKES 103

Windermere 105
    Windermere – southern 111
    Windermere – central 119
    Windermere – northern 127
Grasmere 139

◉ *Ullswater from Hallin Fell*

Coniston Water	147
Coniston Water – southern	151
Coniston Water – northern	157
Other Lakes	165
Rydal Water	165
Elter Water	165
Esthwaite Water	166

THE WESTERN LAKES — 169

- Wast Water — 171
- Ennerdale Water — 181
- Crummock Water — 189
- Loweswater — 197
- Buttermere — 201

CULTURE AND LANDSCAPE — 211

- Geology — 213
- History — 221

WILDLIFE AND ENVIRONMENT — 235

- Habitats — 237
- Wildlife — 243
- Environmental Issues — 251

APPENDICES — 255

- Camping — 255
- Further Reading — 263
- Index of Placenames — 265

Peel Island, Coniston Water

Introduction

"They were quite different places now that you came to them by water ... It was like exploring a place that you have seen in a dream, where everything is just where you expect it and yet everything is a surprise."
Arthur Ransome, *Swallows and Amazons*, 1930

At primary school, the author devoured all twelve of Arthur Ransome's *Swallows and Amazons* books. The stories were pretty unrelatable to the author, living in the industrial Midlands; they conjured up a mythical inter-war era when upper-middle-class kids would, apparently, be set free for the summer by indulgent parents, unsupervised and buoyancy aid-less, to explore an unnamed and uncharted lake.

And yet ... it turned out that the places in the books were real, more or less, and that the adventures were there to be had, for all.

The Lake District National Park is among the finest places you can paddle your canoe, kayak or paddleboard (but do please wear a buoyancy aid; it's not the 1930s any more). Dipping a paddle into any of the dozen of the 'English Lakes' which are available to paddlers, gives you access to unique, stunning landscapes, backdropped by wonderful and iconic mountains. With a total shoreline length of over 220km, adventures on offer range from exploring secluded beaches and rocky shores, to picnicking on uninhabited islands, to using your paddlecraft to access England's highest summits! The lakes are far from uniform, offering startling variety; each possesses its own individual character and quirks, influenced by its underlying geology, its flora and fauna, and, especially, its human history.

In the Lake District, paddling a lake is never just paddling a lake. *Swallows and Amazons* is just a 'gateway drug' and paddlers will find themselves going down the rabbit hole to learn more about the eclectic and eccentric folk who created 'the Lake District': the early, enraptured visitors; the 'Lake Poets', such as the Wordsworths and Coleridge; Beatrix Potter and her tales for children; Hardwicke Rawnsley and the creation of the National Trust; Donald Campbell's doomed speed record attempts.

This book sets out to supply paddlers with the information that they need to access, understand and enjoy paddling in this most special of places. I hope that it helps you to experience many fine Lake District adventures.

Mark Rainsley

Scafell Pike and Scafell, Wast Water

Lake District Highlights

"We thought we had got into fairy-land."
Charles Lamb, letter, 1802

We hope that this book will inspire you to explore and enjoy as much of the wonderful English Lakes as possible. However, here are just a few suggested highlights to get you started …

SHORELINE SECRETS

Beaches, becks and bays where you will want to linger and, if permitted, land to explore.

- Lodore Falls (Derwent Water)
- Helvellyn Gill (Thirlmere)
- Silver Bay (Ullswater – southern)
- River Brathay (Windermere – northern)
- The Screes (Wast Water)
- Wild Ennerdale (Ennerdale Water)
- Scale Force (Crummock Water)
- Holme Wood (Loweswater)

FELLS AND CRAGS

Enjoy these mountains from the water, or ascend them for a grand perspective.

- Cat Bells (Derwent Water)
- Raven Crag (Thirlmere)
- Hallin Fell (Ullswater – northern)
- Gummer's How (Windermere – southern)
- Loughrigg (Grasmere)
- Scafell Pike (Wast Water)
- Mellbreak (Crummock Water)
- Fleetwith Pike and Hay Stacks (Buttermere)

SECLUDED ISLES

Diverse, intriguing islands to circumnavigate or, if permitted, explore on foot.

- St Herbert's Island (Derwent Water)
- Haws How Island (Thirlmere)
- Norfolk Island (Ullswater – southern)
- Belle Isle (Windermere – central)
- Thompson's Holme (Windermere – central)
- The Island (Grasmere)
- Peel Island (Coniston Water – southern)
- Woodhouse and Holme Islands (Crummock Water)

📷 *Wythburn Church, Thirlmere*

HISTORY AND HERITAGE

Engaging historical sites which can be appreciated from the water or via forays ashore.

- St Bega's Church (Bassenthwaite Lake)
- Wythburn Church (Thirlmere)
- Storrs Temple (Windermere – southern)
- Claife Viewing Station (Windermere – central)
- Wray Castle (Windermere – northern)
- Galava Roman Fort (Windermere – northern)
- Steam Yacht *Gondola* (Coniston Water)
- St Olaf's Church (Wast Water)

MUSEUMS AND MEMORIALS

Places which commemorate the English Lakes' personalities and past.

- Ruskin Monument (Derwent Water)
- Hundred Year Stone (Derwent Water)
- Brantwood (Coniston Water – northern)
- Clarkson Memorial (Ullswater – northern)
- Donald Campbell Memorial (Ullswater – southern)
- Windermere Jetty Museum (Windermere – northern)
- Dove Cottage (Grasmere)
- Ruskin Museum and *Bluebird K7* (Coniston – northern)

Windermere Jetty Museum

Wray Castle and the Langdale Pikes, Windermere

The Lake District

"Oh, the Lake District's lovely. Let's go there. We can eat scones. They do great scones in 1927."
Doctor Who, *The Rings of Akhaten*, 2013

An overview of the Lake District

The English Lake District, also known as 'Lakeland' or simply 'The Lakes', is a small mountainous area, located in the county of Cumbria, in North West England. The mountains, known locally as fells, are relatively small in stature, with only six summits topping 900m, and another hundred and twenty (ish) higher than 600m. The fells are divided up by deep valleys, spanning out radially from the centre, *"like spokes from the nave of a wheel"* (William Wordsworth, *Guide to the Lakes*, 1835). Within these valleys, seventeen lakes give the region its name; these are commonly referred to as 'the English Lakes'.

The Lake District was awarded National Park status in 1951. The National Park originally encompassed 2,292km², but was expanded to 2,362km² in 2016. In 2017, the Lake District was designated as a UNESCO World Heritage Site.

So far, so Wikipedia. What these dry facts and figures fail to convey is what an astonishingly, breathtakingly beautiful place the Lake District is. There are fells, and there are lakes. Each is, individually, attractive and engaging. However, put them all together, and then – and this is crucial – factor in the various, complex and interconnected layers of human interaction: poets, travellers, miners, artists, naturalists, adventurers, writers. The Lake District emerges as far, far greater than the sum of its parts. There is nowhere on earth remotely like this breathtaking, ethereal landscape.

"The whole territory … is scarcely more than thirty miles square; yet within this limit, comparatively narrow, are comprised all possible beauties of land and water that the most passionate worshipper of natural loveliness could desire."
William Winter, *Gray Days and Gold in England and Scotland*, 1909

Lake District placenames

The oldest Lake District placenames are British / Celtic ('Cumbria' comes from *cymru* or *combrogi*, 'country-men' / 'compatriots'). The Romans brought Latin (*mare*, meaning lake or sea, is the origin of 'mere' in the lake names). Most placenames are either Old English (e.g. *nab*: promontory) or Old Norse, the language of the Vikings (e.g. *holme*: island, *wyke*: creek).

"Beck, *brook*; Combe, *hollow*; Dodd, *a spur of a mountain*; Force *(Icelandic, 'Fors'; Norwegian 'Foss'), a waterfall*; Gill, *a gorge*; Hause, *the top of a pass, French 'Col'*; Holme, *an island*; How, *a mound-like hill*; Nab *(A.S. Nebbe, nose), a projecting rock*; Pike, *a peak*; Raise, *the top of a ridge*; Scar, *a wall of rock*; Scree, *steep slope of loose stones*; Thwaite, *a clearing*."

Baedecker's Great Britain, 1887

Ullswater from Hallin Fell

The lakes

The classic Lake District 'Dad joke' is, *"How many lakes are there in the Lake District?"*. Answer: *"Only one: Bassenthwaite Lake"*. Of the seventeen bodies of water, Bassenthwaite is the only one with 'lake' in the name. The others are all called '-mere' or '-water'.

All are 'ribbon' lakes, meaning that they are deep, narrow and finger-shaped, occupying valleys gouged by glaciers. Despite their common Ice Age origins, the English Lakes each have distinctive character, due to local geology and human influence:

"The Scotch Lakes are so alike one another, from their great size, that in a picture you are obliged to read their names; but the English lakes … once seen, no one ever requires to be told what it is when drawn."

Samuel Taylor Coleridge, **Table Talk**, 1835

THE NORTHERN LAKES

Many regard either Derwent Water or Ullswater as the most scenic of all the lakes, because of the amphitheatres of diverse mountains encompassing them; both span differing geological regions (Skiddaw Group and Borrowdale Volcanics). Derwent Water's beauty more or less kickstarted Lake District tourism and, later, inspired Beatrix Potter. Bassenthwaite Lake offers more subdued charms, with the finest birdlife of all the lakes. Thirlmere (like Haweswater, where paddling is not permitted) is an artificial reservoir which has drowned a natural lake.

THE SOUTHERN LAKES

Windermere and Coniston Water are surrounded by low fells (geologically, the Windermere Supergroup), swathed by the Furness forests. Both lakes have become synonymous with leisure and boating and were fictionalised in Arthur Ransome's **Swallows and Amazons** adventure stories. Coniston Water acquired international fame via Malcolm and Donald Campbell's water

📷 *Windermere from above Troutbeck*

	Page No.	Length (km)	Maximum width (km)	Maximum depth (m)	Surface area (km²)	Catchment area (km²)	Height above sea level (m)
Bassenthwaite Lake	47	6.2	1.1	19	5.24	359.77	68
Brothers Water	101	0.7	0.4	16	0.19	13.26	157
Buttermere	201	2	0.59	28.6	0.91	18.68	103
Coniston Water	147	8.7	0.79	56.1	2.78	42.47	46
Crummock Water	189	4.1	0.9	43.9	2.5	62.69	96
Derwent Water	57	4.6	1.93	22	5.29	85.40	76
Elter Water	165	0.9	0.33	7	0.18	51.30	53
Ennerdale Water	181	3.8	1.2	42	3.01	43.46	113
Esthwaite Water	166	2.5	0.59	15.5	0.96	17.01	65
Grasmere	139	1.5	0.65	21.5	0.61	28.73	61
Haweswater	101	6.5	0.89	57	3.79	32.25	246
Loweswater	197	1.7	0.56	16	0.6	8.19	125
Rydal Water	165	1.2	0.36	18	0.3	32.38	53
Thirlmere	71	6	0.74	46	3.13	30.21	178
Ullswater	81	11.7	1.2	63	8.68	146.80	144
Wast Water	171	4.8	0.78	79	2.78	42.47	64
Windermere	105	16.8	1.5	64	14.36	248.77	37

Woodhouse Islands, Crummock Water

speed record attempts. Grasmere and nearby Rydal Water (no paddling) are small lakes nestled among imposing fells, immortalised by the Wordsworth siblings and their 'Lake Poets' friends, who based themselves here.

THE WESTERN LAKES

West is best! Well, the author would say this, being based there himself. The western lakes are relatively small but located among varied and complex geology (Skiddaw Group, Borrowdale Volcanics and Ennerdale Granites), giving rise to spectacular mountainous surrounds, including England's highest summit. This being some distance from the M6, these are the least frequented lakes, with no tourist ferries or powerboats. The western lakes are probably the best for combining paddling and fellwalking adventures.

ISLANDS

> "On the lake they had seen the island. All four of them had been filled at once with the same idea. It was not just an island. It was the island, waiting for them."
>
> Arthur Ransome, *Swallows and Amazons*, 1930

There is something wonderful about paddling to islands. The English Lakes host at least forty-six named islands and many more unnamed islets and rocky reefs. Windermere hogs fifteen of the named islands and has at least ten more. Derwent Water comes in second, with four sizeable islands and many more islets.

It should be noted that most islands are used by nesting birds (especially geese) during the spring months; when approaching, keep a careful lookout for nests and avoid causing disturbance.

The islands fall into four categories:

- Rocky islands in mid-lake are *roches moutonnées*. These are humps of rock which forced the valley's glacier to flow over them. They form the divide between ice-scoured basins; the classic example is the archipelago mid way along Windermere.

- Rocky islands close to shore, such as Coniston Water's Peel Island, mark the fringes of glacial troughs; the ice squeezed past them.
- Oval-shaped islands, rounded in profile, are likely to be drumlins; these are elongated heaps of glacial till, likely deposited beneath glaciers. Derwent Water's larger islands fall into this category.
- The shallow, splayed gravel spits formed by river deltas are often colonised by trees and plants, forming small islets such as those at the head of Ennerdale Water; these islands are relatively ephemeral and are regularly flooded over.

Tarns

This book is not intended to cover the Lake District's small upland bodies of water, known as tarns (Old Norse *tjorn*), not least because there are so many. Over 170 have the name 'tarn', but the definition is flexible and in the 1950s Grasmere residents Timothy Tyson and Colin Dodgson bathed in 463 of them. Tarns fall into three categories: long ribbon lakes like the larger lakes; cirques, deeply scoured into circular form and backed by cliffs; and those dammed either by moraines or by human industry.

The tarns should be mentioned because many (notably Burnmoor Tarn, Devoke Water and Seathwaite Tarn) are larger than the smallest of the seventeen lakes and, more crucially, because they have intriguing paddling potential, often being located in stunning mountainous locations. Of course, tarn paddling is only for those committed (or deranged) enough to lug their paddlecraft and gear high into the fells. Packrafts are the obvious vessel of choice here.

Two tarns are mentioned here as worthy objectives for record-tickers. Blea Water, below High Street, is the deepest, at an amazing 63m; only Wast Water and Windermere are deeper. The highest, at 718 metres / 2356 feet, is Red Tarn, below Helvellyn. In pre-packraft days, the author's university canoe club lugged a Perception Dancer* all the way up here.

Ask any paddler with grey hair.

Climate and weather

"No other rain anywhere, or at least in the British Isles (which have a prerogative of many sorts of rain), falls with so determined a fanatical obstinacy as does this rain."
Hugh Walpole, *Rogue Herries*, 1930

Many of the photos in this book depict bluebird skies and unruffled, mirrorlike lake surfaces. These photos are a **lie**, cynically Photoshopped to generate book sales! The truth is that the rain is always falling and a gale is always blowing …

… well, it can often seem like that.

Lakeland rain is orographic: caused and enhanced by mountainous topography. Average annual rainfall is in excess of 2,000mm, but this varies wildly, with Seathwaite in Borrowdale (England's wettest village) averaging 3,400mm, Windermere receiving 1,500mm and Penrith, in the drier east, averaging 929mm. The wettest months are October to January, the driest are March to June. Around 9% of annual rainfall falls in August, as the author can attest from a lifetime of camping holiday washouts! Climatologists believe that, long-term, climate change is causing summer rainfall to reduce, and winter rainfall to increase.

In terms of the wind, the fell summits are subjected to gale force winds on around a hundred days annually. However, the picture is much better down at lake level, where gales occur about five times a year.

Cumbria has a maritime climate, being close to the Irish Sea and influenced by the North Atlantic Drift. This means that seasonal temperature variations are not huge. Summer temperatures are lower than those in the south of England, but temperatures in winter are actually similar.

Exceptional, 'Hoth-like', conditions can cause the lakes to freeze over. In *The Prelude*, Wordsworth described a day off school spent skating on Windermere, and Arthur Ransome's *Winter Holiday* was inspired by his schoolboy experience of the 1895 Great Freeze. On the latter occasion, ice yachts criss-crossed Windermere and two thousand skaters amassed at Bowness Bay. Climate change is making these rare events even rarer: England's largest lake has since only frozen in 1929, 1946 and 1963. On the latter occasion, the ice was firm enough for people to drive on it! Windermere last partially froze in 2021.

Extremes of rainfall have become more common; in November 2009 and December 2015, Cumbria experienced its worst flooding in 550 years. In the latter instance, Storm Desmond broke the UK's rainfall records, with 341.4mm recorded in 24 hours at Honister Pass and 405mm in 38 hours at Thirlmere. Bassenthwaite Lake and Derwent Water were temporarily reunited.

What to do, when faced with crappy weather? Dress up warm and dry, get out there, and (cautiously, carefully, safely) embrace it as part of the Lakeland experience.

Lake District rivers

The lakes are, of course, connected to the mountains and sea by a radiating pattern of engaging and attractive rivers. These rivers offer many great adventure possibilities; however, most involve a degree (or more) of white water, with appropriate skills and expertise necessary. For more information, two detailed sources of information are recommended:

Canoe & Kayak Guide to North West England, Stuart Miller, Rivers Publishing UK 2013, ISBN 9780955061455

The UK Rivers Guidebook website – www.ukriversguidebook.co.uk

Scale Force, near Crummock Water

📷 *Mid-lake, Bassenthwaite Lake*

Planning to Paddle

This section outlines the factors involved in paddling on the English Lakes, whether you intend to splash about for simple fun, or whether you have grand exploratory plans.

Who?

The lakes are suitable for and accessible to all ages, genders and abilities. Complete beginners or novices will find a perfect environment for learning and progressing quickly, provided they plan appropriately and take due care, of the weather in particular. Experienced / expert paddlers can seek out more challenging, breezier conditions if they so desire, but the lakes are predominantly a calm and friendly environment: they do not flow and there are no tides.

When?

The lakes offer fantastic paddling, year-round. Naturally, summer offers warmer and more settled weather (in theory) and winter is more prone to rain and strong winds. The summer months can see the lake levels drop low, with wide beaches and occasional shallows; but, don't worry: they aren't going to dry out! The winter months offer bare shoreline trees and cold water, but also snowclad mountain backdrops. More pertinently, in winter, the tourists retreat to go fleece shopping in Keswick, Ambleside or Bowness-on-Windermere, a ceasefire is held in the eternal battle for lakeside parking, and the lakes themselves are wonderfully empty.

Which paddlecraft?

Canoes are open-topped craft within which one or more paddlers sit or kneel, propelling themselves with single-bladed paddles. They are also known as 'open canoes' or 'Canadian canoes'.

Kayaks can have closed decks or open decks (known as 'sit on tops' or SOTs) but the key difference is that the paddlers sit, propelling themselves with a two-bladed paddle. Some kayaks have seats for more than one paddler. Just to complicate and confuse things, in Britain it is normal to use the word 'canoe' to refer to both canoes and kayaks.

Stand up paddleboards (or SUPs) are ubiquitous, outnumbering canoes and kayaks. Their huge popularity (with a notable bias towards female participation) is partly explained by their accessibility (stand up, paddle) but also by the pure pleasure of travelling in this simple way, with an elevated viewpoint and the whole body's musculature actively involved, despite minimal connection to the craft.

Packrafts are becoming increasingly popular: a lightweight, portable (and expensive) type of inflatable kayak. Packrafts are slow, sluggish and susceptible to the wind. Hence, they are generally suited to paddling short distances, but come into their own when you combine paddling with hiking, or even biking, adventures.

Which is best for the English Lakes? All are great. Canoes carry far more food and equipment, and are quicker to learn how to handle than kayaks. Kayaks are more manoeuvrable and less affected by wind, while paddleboards are extremely quick to learn but hard work in wind, tricky to handle in waves and limited in gear-carrying capacity.

📷 *Packraft on Windermere*

The following books are recommended if you want to learn more about selecting and handling paddlecraft:

The Practical Handbook of Kayaking & Canoeing, Bill Mattos, Southwater 2015, ISBN 9781780193496

Sit-on-top Kayak, Derek Hairon, Pesda Press 2007, ISBN 9781906095024

Canoeing, Ray Goodwin, Pesda Press 2016, ISBN 9781906095543

Stand Up Paddleboarding: A Beginner's Guide, Simon Bassett, Fernhurst 2019, ISBN 9781912177974

Packrafting – a UK Manual, Jason Taylor, Pesda Press 2023, ISBN 9781906095918

Getting to the lakes

For those travelling to the lake by car, one item of equipment is strongly recommended: a trolley, to transport your paddlecraft to the water's edge. Many launch spots are some distance from the parking spot. A sturdy trolley, which can be dis-assembled and packed away while paddling, will save you a great deal of sweat and tears.

Those with portable paddlecraft can reduce their carbon footprint and make use of the Lake District's cheap and reliable bus services. These access the following lakes:

- Northern lakes: Bassenthwaite Lake, Derwent Water, Thirlmere, Ullswater
- Southern lakes: Windermere, Grasmere, Coniston Water
- Western lakes: Crummock Water, Buttermere

Dressed for winter on Loweswater – Cagoules, dry trousers and drysuits

Safety

"BETTER DROWNED THAN DUFFERS IF NOT DUFFERS WON'T DROWN"

Arthur Ransome, *Swallows and Amazons*, 1930

Confused? The above quote is the cryptic telegram sent by 'Daddy' to the 'Swallows' children, warning them of the lake's dangers, while simultaneously inviting them to trust their common sense and get afloat.

This section is about *safety*: planning, selecting appropriate equipment and understanding hazards encountered on the lakes, to avoid getting into difficulty.

In normal summer conditions, the English Lakes are a forgiving and safe environment which is entirely suited to novices and the inexperienced, if common sense is applied.

CLOTHING AND EQUIPMENT

Flotation

Canoes or kayaks must have some form of fixed buoyancy to prevent them from sinking when waterlogged. This is usually achieved through inflatable air bags, solid foam or sealed chambers in the boat.

Buoyancy aids

A well-fitted buoyancy aid is absolutely essential and will make a swim far less dangerous. This message has not yet filtered through to the paddleboard community; the overwhelming majority of paddleboarders currently encountered on the lakes do not wear one*. Disturbingly, this trend is exacerbated by social media 'influencers', who post images of themselves wearing only designer swimwear, even in exposed and committing locations. Wear a buoyancy aid!

Note, some of the photos in this book: it was sometimes impractical to get the needed shot without featuring buoyancy aid-less paddleboarders.

Clothing

Your clothing needs to protect you from becoming hypothermic by remaining warm when wet and by providing a shield from the wind. Even in the warmest months, swimwear is not adequate protection from the elements (talking to you, social media influencers). Wetsuits are a good solution but may be over-warm and restrictive in summer. A decent compromise is wearing polypropylene or fleece thermals with a cagoule on top. Legs need similar protection, and don't forget a warm hat for your head. Helmets also retain heat well and may be a good idea for young or inexperienced paddlers. Footwear should offer adequate protection when scrambling ashore on rocky beaches. You should also carry spare dry clothing.

Sun protection

Waterproof suncream and a brimmed hat will protect your skin and save you from the prospect of having to paddle with painful, chafing sunburn on the following day.

Phones

A mobile phone (packed in a waterproof case) is very useful to carry, for summoning assistance in an emergency. Mapping apps can also help you to monitor your progress. Note that phone reception is limited in some areas, especially around the western lakes.

LAKE HAZARDS

Wind

> *"This great water seemes to flow and wane about with ye wind but it does not Ebb and flow Like the sea with the tyde."*
>
> Celia Fiennes, Through England On a Side Saddle, 1698

Fiennes witnessed storm winds blowing on Windermere. Wind is the overriding factor in determining the safety of your planned paddle. Strong winds, or gusts, make all paddlecraft difficult to control. Managing a paddleboard is especially demanding in these conditions.

Wind also whips up the lake surface, forming waves. Waves are usually short and steep but can build along a lake's length (known as 'fetch') to form a notable rolling swell; in late 2024, Storm Bert's northerly winds, blowing along Windermere, generated waves large enough to overtop and damage Fell Foot Country Park's quayside.

Study the weather forecast before paddling. Note the predicted wind speed, but also the predicted *gust* speed. In land area forecasts, the terminology 'calm / light / moderate / fresh / strong / gales' is used. These aren't just vague terms; they have very specific meanings (see opposite).

With any forecast of wind, or gusts, above 'Light', then you will need to carefully re-evaluate your plans. A number of the routes described in this book involve paddling *across* the respective lake; in such conditions, these exposed, open water crossings will be challenging and possibly dangerous.

'Moderate' winds will likely be manageable by experienced and skilled paddlers. 'Strong' winds (or stronger) might be manageable by experts, but this will be the overriding element of the day's paddling and will strongly influence the direction of travel.

The wind direction given in a weather forecast will not take Lake District topography into account. Wind tends to be funnelled along a lake's length following the direction of its valley, but it can also blow strongly from side valleys or over fell-tops. There is no such thing as a 'sheltered' lake: regardless of the prevailing wind direction, if it is windy, then the wind will find you.

📷 *Storm force winds on Bassenthwaite Lake*

Wind Description	Wind Speed	Lake state	Beaufort scale equivalent
Calm	0-2kph 0-1mph 0-0.5m/s	Like a mirror	0
Light	2-19kph 1-12mph 0.5-5m/s	Ripples and wavelets	1-3
Moderate	20-30kph 13-18mph 6-8m/s	Small waves	4
Fresh	31-39kph 19-24mph 8-11m/s	Moderate waves, with white horses	5
Strong	40-61kph 25-38mph 11-17m/s	Crested waves, some spray lifted	6-7
Gales	63-74kph 39-46mph 17-21m/s	High waves, streaks, spray lifted	8

Be aware of the notable hazard of offshore winds. With the wind blowing away from the shore, the water can deceive paddlers by appearing smooth and calm. However, as soon as you launch, the wind pushes you offshore, where the water becomes progressively rougher, with decreasing shelter, making it increasingly difficult to turn back: an extremely dangerous trap!

Katabatic winds are sometimes encountered on the lakes, especially in the winter months. These are sudden, powerful gusts which occur when colder, higher-density air slides off a fell-top

📷 *Mist on Coniston Water, from Coniston Old Man*

and rushes downhill under gravity's force. Experiencing a katabatic wind is an intense experience, especially if the wind blows directly from above, exerting downward pressure on the lake surface (and yourself). Your paddles will vibrate, whistle and sing …

Water temperature

In the summer months, the lakes are, while not exactly bath-warm, comfortable for brief immersion. In the winter, all of the lakes cool to low-single-digit temperatures and any immersion (or even just repeated splashing) could quickly lead to hypothermia. As a guide, Windermere averages 14.6°C in summer, and 4.9°C in winter. Windermere is the lowest of the lakes in altitude; of course, the higher lakes become even chillier.

Incidentally, the above only describes the lakes' surfaces, or at least the upper 'layer' of five to ten metres of water. Through a process known as 'thermal stratification', the deeper layer is significantly colder, separated by a distinct thermocline, markedly so in the summer before autumn gales mix the two layers.

Visibility

"Vapours exhaling from the lakes and meadows after sunrise in a hot season, or in moist weather brooding upon the heights, or descending towards the valleys with inaudible motion, give a visionary character to everything around them."

William Wordsworth, ***Guide to the Lakes***, 1835

Mists and fog are common on the lake surfaces, especially in the early morning before the sun warms the air. These can make for a wonderfully atmospheric experience, both figuratively and literally. However, of course they bring a risk of collision with other lake traffic. The simplest solution is to stay close inshore. On Windermere, paddlers are required to always carry a whistle, to advertise your presence; this seems a wise strategy to adopt for all of the lakes.

📷 *Miss Lakeland I on Windermere*

Land area weather forecasts refer to 'mist' and 'fog'. These terms have precise definitions:

Visibility definition	Visibility
Mist	2000m-1000m
Fog	<1000m
Dense fog	<50m

If paddling before dawn or after sunset, common sense suggests that you display a light to make you safely visible to others. On Windermere, this is compulsory.

Other water users

Derwent Water, Ullswater, Windermere and Coniston Water are the only lakes on which powered leisure craft are normally permitted, including large, passenger-carrying launches and 'steamers'. Give all a wide berth and pass them astern (i.e. behind them). Most powered craft adhere to the local speed limit and are mindful of paddlecraft. Some do not fit this description*: remain situationally aware and alert to what any approaching vessels may do.

Rowing crews train on Derwent Water and Windermere. These travel dauntingly fast, have their backs to you, and their sleek craft are pointy at the ends. To avoid being kebabbed, keep well clear of their path. If there is a risk of collision, shout out a warning or blow a whistle.

Anglers are occasionally encountered along the lake shores, although never in the dense numbers found lining rivers and canals. Avoid entanglement by keeping a careful eye out ahead (unhelpfully, they insist upon wearing camouflage!). Steer a course wide around their lines, and pass quietly and considerately.

*The author has encountered nocturnal waterskiing on Ullswater, and 40+mph powerboating on Windermere: both illegal.

River outflows

Several of the lakes are drained by sizeable rivers, with significant flow year-round. Following heavy rain or snowmelt, all of the lakes* can have surprisingly strong currents at their outlets. This can extend for up to a week, as the lakes are natural cisterns and only gradually release flood waters. Avoid the 'tractor beam' effect (the risk of being pulled into more dangerous moving water) by crossing lake outflows at a safe distance.

Some of the lakes have small weirs at their outlet: don't stray close to the event horizon! Likewise, avoid any sluices, or water extraction facilities, as if they carry bubonic plague.

Except Thirlmere, which is dammed.

Blue-green algae

Blue-green algae can be encountered on any lakes where urban or agricultural effluent enters the water. It appears most commonly, indeed increasingly commonly, on Windermere. It is actually cyanobacteria, not algae. In warm conditions, unsightly blooms appear on the surface, a glossy layer of green slime. Not all forms are poisonous; nevertheless, paddlers will need no encouragement to avoid skin contact or (heaven forbid) drinking the afflicted water.

Seeking help

If you find yourself in serious difficulty and in need of assistance, do not hesitate to call the UK emergency phone number: 999. Give details of your group, your difficulty and perhaps most importantly your location. The operator will summon the Police, Ambulance, Fire Service or Mountain Rescue as appropriate.

Lake levels

Many people are surprised to learn that the lakes rise and fall. They are natural cisterns, holding back the water after rainfall. Variations in level of several metres are possible. Derwent Water is susceptible to especially dramatic changes in level, possibly because of its basin-like profile.

In summer or drought, the beaches extend further and further and, in some places, extra reefs or islets appear. When lake levels are high, beaches disappear and the water laps tree roots, while lakeheads extend up-valley. In extreme but far from rare instances, roads are flooded and properties endangered.

The levels of most lakes are monitored by the Environment Agency: Google 'check for flooding', along with the name of the lake.

Maps

"Give me a map to look at, and I am content."
Alfred Wainwright, *A Pennine Journey*, 1938

The maps in this book are more than adequate for finding your way around the English Lakes. Ordnance Survey (OS) maps and Harvey maps offer additional detail for those venturing into the surrounding fells. OS maps can be bought in waterproof format ('Active Maps'), Harvey maps are waterproof as standard. If you were to buy just one map for the Lake District, Harvey's 1:40000 scale British Mountain Map is excellent, and recommended on Mountain Leader courses. It doesn't quite cover all of the lakes, however. The table below lists which maps cover each lake. The letters in brackets indicate which part of the lake is covered.

Lake	Ordnance Survey 1:50000 Landranger Map	Ordnance Survey 1:25000 Explorer Map	Harvey 1:25000 Superwalker/ 1:40000 Ultramap	Harvey 1:40000 British Mountain Map
Bassenthwaite Lake	89, 90	OL4	Lake District North	Lake District (S)
Derwent Water	89, 90	OL4	Lake District North	Lake District
Thirlmere	90	OL4 (W), OL5	Lake District East, Lake District North (N), Lake District West (S)	Lake District
Ullswater	90	OL5	Lake District East, Lake District North (W)	Lake District
Windermere	90 (N), 96 (S), 97 (S)	OL7	Lake District East (N), Lake District South East	Lake District (N)
Grasmere	90	OL7	Lake District East, Lake District South East (S), Lake District West (W)	Lake District
Coniston Water	96, 97	OL6 (W), OL7 (E)	Lake District East (N), Lake District South East, Lake District West	Lake District (N)
Wast Water	89, 90 (E)	OL6	Lake District West	Lake District
Ennerdale Water	89	303, OL4	Lake District North, Lake District West (E)	Lake District

Biosecurity

It's essential to avoid introducing invasive non-native species to a lake, or spreading these between lakes. These can hitchhike on equipment, clothing and boats; for example, only a 2cm piece of New Zealand pygmyweed is needed to colonise and contaminate a new lake. The National Park offers the following advice:

> **Every time you leave any water such as a river, tarn or lake:**
>
> ### Check – Clean – Dry
>
> - Check equipment / clothing for living organisms.
> - Pay attention to damp, hard to inspect areas.
> - Clean and wash all equipment, footwear and clothes thoroughly.
> - If you find organisms, leave them at the water body on a hard surface to die out.
> - Dry all equipment and clothing.
> - Some species can live for many days in damp conditions.

Get into the habit of performing these actions and checks at the water's edge, before leaving a lake. Further information and advice can be found from the GB Non-native Species Secretariat www.nonnativespecies.org.

Paddling and walking

All of the lakes adjoin footpaths, bridleways, byways or Access Land. Combining a paddle on a lake with a walk can make for a fantastic adventure. The lake route descriptions include suggestions for walking excursions and side-tours, as well as hints for fell ascents directly accessible from the lake shore. Needless to say, the latter will require a bit of prior thinking and planning. While exploring the lakes, why not make a start on ticking off the 214 Wainwright summits?

Walking the Wainwrights, Graham Uney, Pesda Press 2021, ISBN 1906095787

The Screes, Wast Water

Access to the Lakes

"We can only learn liberty by the use of liberty; and until we get this free access to the open country back again into our city life, we shall be still unsatisfied."

H. H. Symonds, *Walking in the Lake District*, 1933

Where can you paddle?

Paddlers enjoy access to twelve of the seventeen lakes. With several of these lakes, mostly owned by the National Trust, permits are required; the author's impression is that the main purpose of these seems to be regulating and monitoring paddler numbers.

Many of the lakes have restricted or 'no boating' areas, based on environmental considerations; these are detailed in the individual lake information later in this book.

Paddleboarders get a rough deal on Thirlmere and Ennerdale Water: while other paddlecraft are permitted, United Utilities has banned paddleboards from these reservoirs, pretty much arbitrarily. Those who wish to use a sail on their canoe or kayak should be aware that some lakes have restrictions on sailing. Canoeists or kayakers using small outboard motors (is it *really* then still a canoe or a kayak?*) should note that powered craft are heavily restricted. In 2025, the 1971 by-law banning boats *"propelled by an internal combustion engine"* was updated to outlaw vessels using *"any mechanical or electrical device"*. Electric motors are now only allowed on Derwent Water, Ullswater, Windermere and Coniston Water.

Paddlers are not generally permitted on five of the lakes; these are each discussed in their respective regional chapter.

* No. It is not.

Responsibilities

It should go without saying that your basic right to enjoy the English Lakes comes with responsibilities: most importantly, to respect and preserve the lake and shore environments, both for their own sake and for others to enjoy. The passage of paddlecraft by definition has minimal impact upon the environment, but employ common sense to ensure that this always and absolutely remains the case. Be prepared to pick up and remove other people's waste, when you encounter it.

Sensible advice can be found in Paddle UK's *Paddler's Code*, downloadable as a leaflet from their website.

	Page no.	Canoes and kayaks permitted?	Paddle-boards permitted?	Powered craft permitted?	Permit / licence required?	Notes
Bassenthwaite Lake	47	Y	Y	N	Y	Two 'no boating zones'. Restrictions on sailing.
Brothers Water	101	N	N	N	-	No paddling.
Buttermere	201	Y	Y	N	Y	Limits on group sizes. Seasonal landing restrictions.
Coniston Water	147	Y	Y	Y	N	Several 'wildfowl areas' to be avoided.
Crummock Water	189	Y	Y	N	Y	Limits on group sizes. Seasonal restrictions on the islands.
Derwent Water	57	Y	Y	Y	N	Several 'wildlife areas' to be avoided.
Elter Water	165	N	N	N	-	No paddling.
Ennerdale Water	181	Y	N	N	Y	Permits only needed for larger groups. No sailing.
Esthwaite Water	166	N	N	N	-	No paddling.
Grasmere	139	Y	Y	N	N	No landing on The Island.
Haweswater	101	N	N	N	-	No paddling.
Loweswater	197	Y	Y	N	Y	Limits on numbers. No sailing.
Rydal Water	165	N	N	N	-	No paddling.
Thirlmere	71	Y	N	N	N	No landing on the islands.
Ullswater	81	Y	Y	Y	N	One 'wildlife area' to avoid. Seasonal restrictions on Norfolk Island.
Wast Water	171	Y	Y	N	N	No sailing. Limits on group sizes.
Windermere	105	Y	Y	Y	N	One 'wildlife area' to avoid. No landing on Belle Isle.

Launch point on Crummock Water

Launching on the Lakes

The English Lakes all have some points from which you can access the water and launch your paddlecraft. The suggested routes in this book are designed to start and finish at launch points where accessing the water is reasonably simple … or is the least awkward of the various options.

One of the biggest challenges is finding parking space; understandably, paddlers need to be able to transport their paddlecraft to the lakes, while minimising local impact and disruption. Pretty much all of the parking spots outlined in this book are regularly full-up, especially so in the summer. There is only one real solution to this, although it may not be a popular one: simply get out of bed earlier. Much, much earlier.

Wherever you park, *don't be an idiot*. Anyone spending time in the Lake District will come to recognise these folk soon enough, but as a primer, idiots can be recognised by their being parked in any of the following ways: in Passing Places, on grass verges and fellsides*, blocking driveways or farm gates, sticking out of lay-bys because the lay-by was already full, etc, etc, etc.

The list below is by no means exhaustive, but it offers a wide enough range of possibilities to give access to all lake sections. Unless a launch point is indicated as being appropriate for larger groups, assume that there is only space, or it is only appropriate, for a handful of paddlers and a very small number of vehicles. Exercise discretion, act respectfully and ideally don't linger while changing or getting organised at these places: not because you aren't allowed to be there, but because you want to be welcomed back there.

Some marinas and campsites have been included because they allow launching of private paddlecraft. Check ahead that they are open. Not all of the launch points listed are on public land; check details in the individual lake description later in this book.

The postcode given refers to the parking spot, while the grid reference and what3words locations are the actual launch point.

As the author writes, Cumbria Police had issued sixty-four parking tickets in a single day along the shores of Wast Water, for cars left blocking the road or driven on to the land, which is designated as a Site of Special Scientific Interest.

Launch points

THE NORTHERN LAKES

Launch point	Grid reference	what3words	Postcode	Larger groups?
Bassenthwaite Lake				
Peel Wyke car park	NY 203 308	region.column.curve	CA13 9YE	Y
Banks Point	NY 201 319	critic.march.distilled	CA13 9YD	Y
Scarness Bay	NY 218 303	venue.trophy.tidying	CA12 4QZ	N
Blackstock Point	NY 222 273	readers.barstool.skipped	CA12 5SQ	Y
Woodend Brow car park	NY 219 276	neatly.dart.else	CA12 5SL	N
Beck Wythop	NY 214 286	squashes.digitally.defends	CA12 5SL	N

Launch point	Grid reference	what3words	Postcode	Larger groups?
Beck Wythop	NY 215 282	serious.listening.shredding	CA12 5SL	N
Derwent Water				
Crow Park, Keswick	NY 263 228	dogs.attic.copies	CA12 5DG	Y
Calfclose Bay	NY 269 213	pockets.picnic.mindset	CA12 5UP	Y
Barrow Bay	NY 268 204	little.worth.storming	CA12 5UR	Y
Kettlewell car park	NY 266 195	walked.pedicure.lifelong	CA12 5UU	Y
Brandelhow Bay	NY 251 197	brain.tolerable.built	CA12 5UQ	N
Thirlmere				
Armboth car park	NY 305 171	extremely.skin.curtail	CA12 4TW	Y
Dam Triangle car park	NY 306 189	spine.match.apprehend	CA12 4TW	Y
Station Coppice car park	NY 313 168	culling.radically.wriggle	CA12 4TP	Y
Steel End car park	NY 320 132	providing.zooms.bulges	CA12 4TW	Y
Dob Gill car park	NY 317 141	groups.animator.blazers	CA12 4TP	Y
Ullswater				
Gowbarrow Park to Gowbarrow Bay lay-bys	NY 422 206	snow.maps.storeroom	CA10 2NF	Y
Pooley Bridge (Dunmallard car park)	NY 470 245	crispier.backfired.developed	CA10 2NP	Y
Pooley Bridge (Eusemere car park)	NY 470 244	bland.shapes.gambles	CA10 2NE	Y
Park Foot Holiday Park	NY 467 238	galleries.bubble.rebounded	CA10 2NA	Y
Waterside House Campsite	NY 463 232	steady.washing.heavy	CA10 2NA	Y
Howtown Wyke	NY 443 198	jeep.imprinted.irrigate	CA10 2ND	N
Side Farm Campsite	NY 395 168	abandons.fairly.submit	CA11 0NL	Y
Glenridding	NY 389 168	jotting.tradition.supreme	CA11 0US	Y
Glenridding Sailing Centre	NY 389 170	donor.venturing.alongside	CA11 0PE	Y
Stybarrow Crag lay-bys	NY 387 178	beats.community.future	CA11 0NG	N

Launch point	Grid reference	what3words	Postcode	Larger groups?
Glencoyne Bridge car park	NY 386 188	test.packet.anchorman	CA11 0NQ	Y
Glencoyne Park lay-bys	NY 389 191	rainfall.sank.cosmic	CA11 0JS	N
Aira Force and Gowbarrow Park car park	NY 399 197	reefs.carpets.ranches	CA11 0JS	Y

THE SOUTHERN LAKES

Windermere				
Fell Foot Country Park	SD 379 869	proofread.accordion.intention	LA12 8NN	Y
Ash Landing car park	SD 387 953	noise.diverting.solves	LA22 0LP	Y
Harrowslack car park	SD 388 959	books.fidgeting.responded	LA22 0LR	Y
Red Nab car park	SD 385 994	beaten.parade.glad	LA22 0JH	Y
Wray Castle	NY 376 012	teaching.notched.wasps	LA22 0JA	Y
Ambleside RUFC	NY 371 033	basically.marked.herbs	LA22 0EN	Y
Waterhead car park	NY 376 032	blinking.clef.kicked	LA22 0ES	Y
Low Wood Bay Watersports Centre	NY 385 019	steamed.princely.goggle	LA23 1LP	Y
Millerground Landing	SD 402 988	replace.impressed.deck	LA23 1EY	N
Rayrigg Meadow	SD 402 984	improves.punctual.acute	LA23 1BP	Y
Cockshott Point	SD 395 964	most.pollution.emeralds	LA23 3HE	Y
Ferry Nab	SD 397 959	backfired.destined.persuade	LA23 3JH	Y
Beech Hill car park	SD 388 921	bonds.sake.tradition	LA23 3LR	Y
Grasmere				
Penny Rock Wood	NY 342 060	panic.bloomers.sweated	LA22 9SE	N
Penny Rock Beach	NY 343 059	alongside.assist.branch	LA22 9SE	Y
Faeryland Grasmere	NY 333 071	dreading.triathlon.factoring	LA22 9PX	N
A592 lay-by	NY 342 064	intensely.celebrate.pipeline	LA22 9SE	N

Launch point	Grid reference	what3words	Postcode	Larger groups?
Coniston Water				
Brown Howe car park	SD 291 910	education.dishes.calculate	LA12 8DW	Y
Thrang Crag Wood lay-bys	SD 290 913	pixies.crumb.washroom	LA12 8EZ	N
Sunny Bank jetty	SD 292 928	tarnished.lace.blasted	LA21 8BJ	Y
Coniston Boating Centre	SD 308 970	whiplash.ritual.awoken	LA21 8AN	Y
Monk Coniston car park	SD 316 978	mouths.layers.slot	LA21 8AA	Y
Machell Coppice	SD 309 952	fussed.village.comforted	LA21 8AD	Y
Bailiff Wood car park	SD 302 935	upgrading.relishes.survive	LA21 8AX	Y
Dodgson Wood car park	SD 299 927	youth.comforted.spices	LA21 8AX	Y
Dales Wood lay-by	SD 298 923	jumbo.frozen.credit	LA12 8DW	N
Low Peel Near lay-by	SD 296 914	egging.improvise.invent	LA12 8DW	N
Lake Bank jetty	SD 288 900	initial.common.haystack	LA12 8EZ	Y
Boon Beck	SD 288 903	shops.saddens.decreased	LA12 8EZ	N

THE WESTERN LAKES

Launch point	Grid reference	what3words	Postcode	Larger groups?
Wast Water				
Countess Beck	NY 151 054	famines.plantings.frozen	CA20 1EU	N
Overbeck car park	NY 168 068	task.informal.clerk	CA20 1ET	Y
Lake Head car park	NY 181 075	tango.responds.library	CA20 1EX	Y
Ennerdale Water				
Bleach Green	NY 089 152	painters.armrest.glassware	CA23 3AS	Y
Bowness Knott	NY 112 150	adopts.insulated.canal	CA23 3AU	Y
Crummock Water				
Rannerdale Knotts	NY 162 183	plantings.fixtures.soccer	CA13 9UZ	Y

Launch point	Grid reference	what3words	Postcode	Larger groups?
Hause Point	NY 162 182	glassware.condense.powerful	CA13 9UZ	N
Woodhouse Islands	NY 167 177	escapades.repeating.nightlife	CA13 9UZ	N
Wood House	NY 168 173	ribcage.looms.rattled	CA13 9UZ	Y
Lanthwaite Wood	NY 151 208	tanked.sharpens.novelist	CA13 0RT	Y
Cinderdale Common	NY 161 194	prompting.commended.sketches	CA13 9UZ	Y
Loweswater				
Loweswater–Lamplugh road lay-by	NY 128 217	garden.influence.yelled	CA13 0SU	N
Loweswater–Lamplugh road lay-by	NY 126 219	exotic.penned.savers	CA13 0SU	N
Loweswater–Lamplugh road lay-by	NY 123 221	plod.generated.nervy	CA13 0SU	N
Watergate Farm	NY 126 211	wasps.bottled.meant	CA13 0SU	Y
Buttermere				
Buttermere's north-west beach	NY 174 164	grid.vitamins.elders	CA13 9UZ	Y
Hassness Crag Wood	NY 186 157	protected.clearcut.picturing	CA13 9XA	N
Lower Gatesgarth	NY 191 153	liberty.costumed.masters	CA13 9XA	Y
Buttermere south shore	NY 186 150	comforted.learns.freshest	CA13 9XA	Y

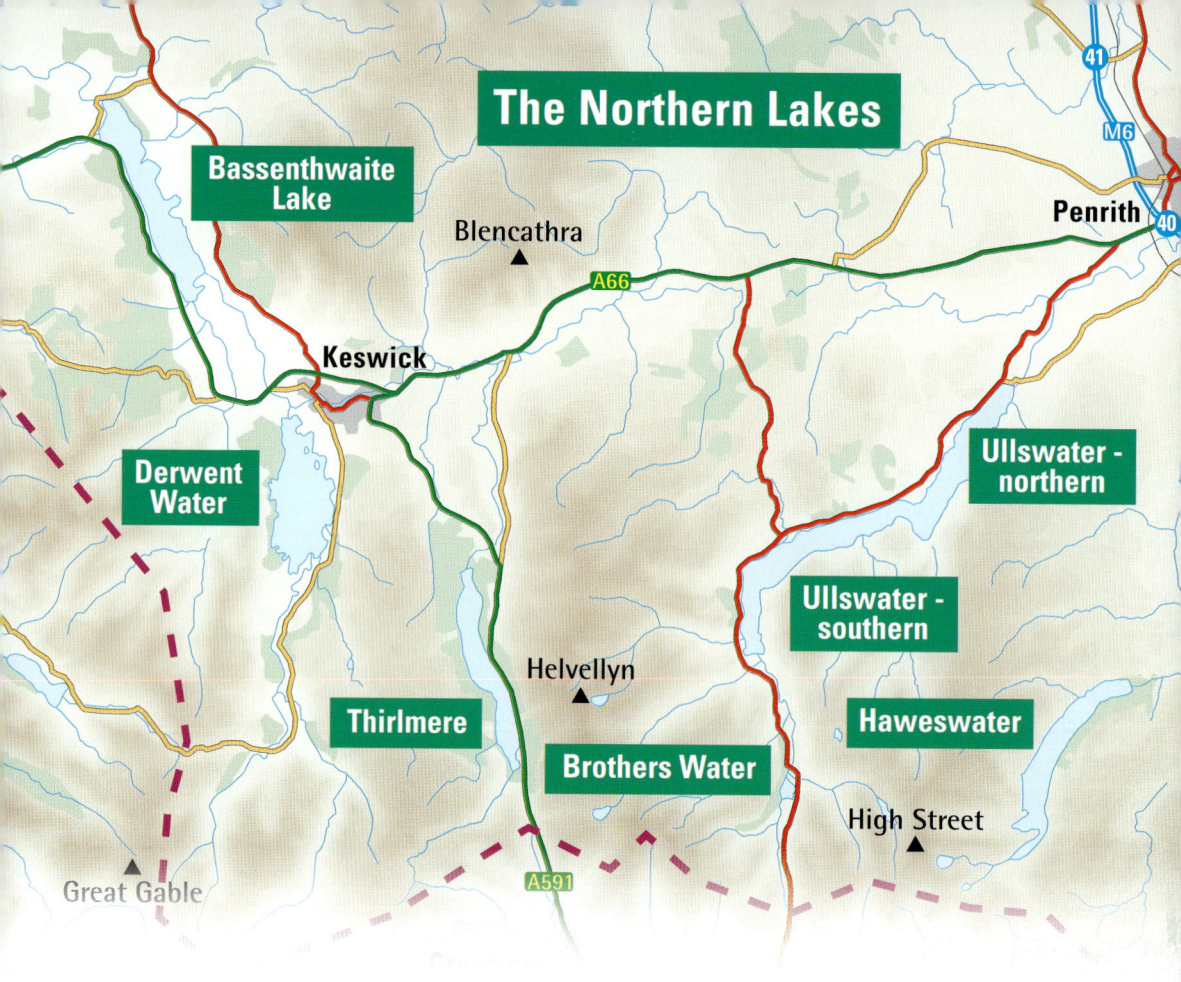

Key to symbols used

- Marina
- Boathouse
- Sailing club
- Campsite
- Caravan park
- Motorhomes only
- Bunkhouse, camping barn or bothy
- Youth hostel
- Holiday park
- Car park
- Café or pub
- Rock/reef
- Iron Age hillfort
- Historical features
- Named church
- Railway stations
- Monument/place of tourist interest
- Area with restrictions
- Restricted wildlife area
- Vulnerable lake shore
- Start/finish launch point
- Alternative launch point

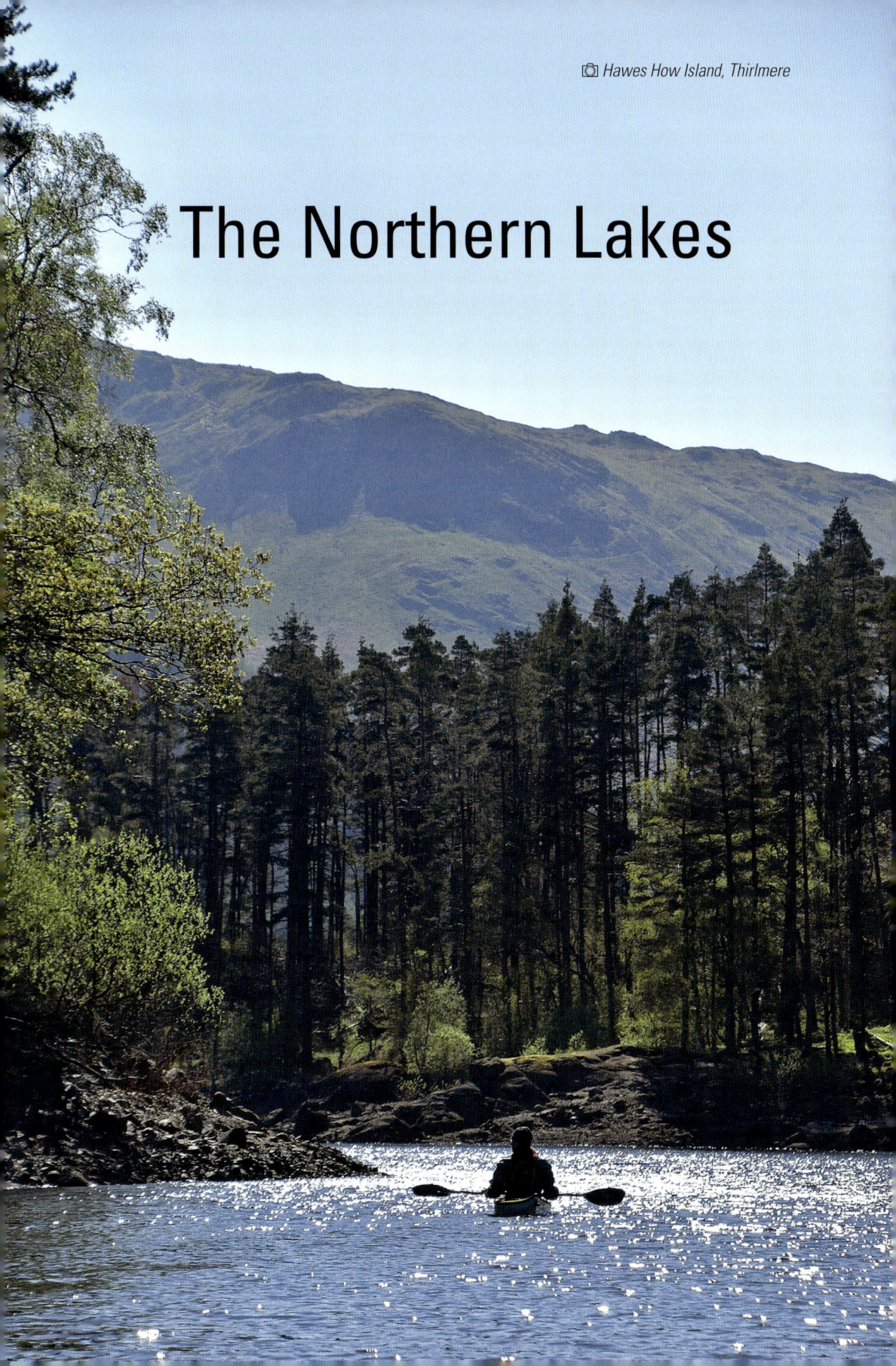

Hawes How Island, Thirlmere

The Northern Lakes

Blackstock Point

◎ *Ouse Bridge*

Bassenthwaite Lake

Length (km)	Maximum width (km)	Maximum depth (m)	Surface area (km²)	Catchment area (km²)	Height above sea level (m)
6.2	1.1	19	5.24	359.77	68

Trip Distance	12km / 7.6 miles
Start / Finish	Peel Wyke car park NY 203 308 / region.column.curve / CA13 9YE

Introduction

"Not one tourist in a hundred knows anything of the real beauty of Bassenthwaite"

Eliza Lynn Linton, *The Lake Country*, 1864

Bassenthwaite Lake attracts just a fraction of the visitors and attention that nearby Derwent Water does. Yet, it has its own individual charms, not least its undisturbed flora and fauna, including ospreys! This happened to be the author's most local lake when he first moved to the Lake District, and he has loved paddling it in every mood and season.

Bassenthwaite's form is strangely asymmetric, with the east shore indented with bays and headlands and the west shore almost straight. This undeviating profile encouraged the routing of Bassenthwaite's notable negative: the noisy and noxious A66, built in the 1970s along the former course of the Cockermouth, Keswick and Penrith Railway.

This is the Lake District's only lake! None of the others are called 'lake'. That said, Bassenthwaite Lake goes by various names; Wordsworth called it Broadwater and Alfred Wainwright noted, *"Bassenthwaite, Bassenthet and Bass: all are acceptable"* (*Wainwright in the Valleys of Lakeland*, 1992). Bassenthwaite means 'Bastun's clearing' (Old Norse *þveit:* clearing).

Access

Paddling is allowed, as are sailing and rowing. A permit must be bought online from the National Park before paddling, costing £7 per day in 2025; Google 'Bassenthwaite permits'. You are supposed to carry an email copy of the permit while paddling (printed, or on your phone), in case you are challenged by a Lake Warden or Ranger.

Two areas of the lake are designated as 'no boating zones', to protect breeding and overwintering birds: Bowness Bay on the eastern shore, and the southern end of the lake, past Blackstock Point. These areas are marked by white-topped posts on the shoreline.

North of Scar Ness, use of a sail is reserved for Bassenthwaite Sailing Club only.

Wildlife and environment

Bassenthwaite is home to Atlantic salmon, brook lamprey, perch, pike and trout. The vendace is a rare whitefish found naturally only here and in Derwent Water. Bassenthwaite has extensive undeveloped natural lakeshore ecosystems, including wetlands where thread rush and water sedge thrive and shallow bays covered with floating water plantain. Birdwatchers regard Bassenthwaite as the best of the lakes; over 70 species of bird and wildfowl breed here, with over 2,000 ducks overwintering. The celebrity avian is of course the magnificent osprey.

The Bassenthwaite ospreys

When ospreys are nesting at Bassenthwaite, paddlers are in for a treat. They hunt at dawn and dusk, swooping to the lake surface to pluck fish from the water.

When an osprey pair first nested here in 2001, they were the first to do so in England since the 1830s. There was understandable rejoicing by the Forestry Commission and RSPB, who had encouraged their return by building artificial nest platforms in Dodd Wood. They have continued to return to Bassenthwaite, now nesting at a less publicised spot; a pair of chicks hatched during the writing of this book.

Ospreys have since nested across the Lake District (page 246) and indeed England.

Bassenthwaite has the largest catchment area of any of the lakes. Vast quantities of sedimentary alluvium have accumulated at the southern end, with pollution and silting caused by urban effluent, run-off from farming, mining practices, and fell erosion. This has damaged the ecological health of the lake, including fish spawning and populations. The good news is that long-term projects to mitigate these problems have begun to restore Bassenthwaite. In 1993, it became the first British lake to be designated as a National Nature Reserve and it is additionally protected within the Bassenthwaite Lake Site of Special Scientific Interest (SSSI) and the River Derwent and Bassenthwaite Lake Special Area of Conservation.

📷 *Bowness Wood*

Invasive New Zealand pygmyweed has blighted the lake; follow the biosecurity practices outlined on page 34.

Launch points

Peel Wyke car park NY 203 308 / region.column.curve / CA13 9YE – a free National Park car park and slipway / quay, beneath the A66. Turn off the A66 following signs for the Pheasant Inn. Follow this lane to its end, where there is a gate accessing the car park.

Banks Point NY 201 319 / critic.march.distilled / CA13 9YD – two adjacent (free) car parks alongside the B5291. Steep steps access small beaches.

Scarness Bay NY 218 303 / venue.trophy.tidying / CA12 4QZ – a lay-by at the end of the lane accessing Bassenthwaite Lakeside Lodges holiday park. A narrow footpath leads 260m to Scarness Bay.

Blackstock Point NY 222 273 / readers.barstool.skipped / CA12 5SQ – a large lay-by alongside the A66 southbound (towards Keswick). Pass through a gate and follow the path for 120m to a beach.

Woodend Brow car park NY 219 276 / neatly.dart.else / CA12 5SL – a free National Park car park just off the A66. Take the turn-off signed 'Thornthwaite'. A path leads from the back of the car park to the A66. Cross this and pass through a gate to a beach beside Hursthole Point. Crossing the A66: not fun.

Beck Wythop NY 214 286 / squashes.digitally.defends / CA12 5SL – a small, narrow lay-by alongside the A66 southbound. A path leads 70m to a beach. Not a great place to leave a vehicle.

Beck Wythop NY 215 282 / serious.listening.shredding / CA12 5SL – a free car park just off the A66. Take the turn-off signed 'Beck Wythop'. Cross the A66 from the car park to a gap in the wall, accessing steps down to a gate and small beach. Crossing the A66: again, not fun.

📷 *Banks Point*

Description

Peel Wyke, sheltered beneath the rumbling A66, makes for one of the stranger Lake District launch points. There are few clues as to the lake's character until you paddle from the inlet and Bassenthwaite's bulbous northern end is revealed. Incidentally, a path leads from the car park on to Castle How Fort, a small Iron Age hillfort overlooking the lake, now obscured by trees.

It's a short paddle west to Bassenthwaite Sailing Club, where the water is often busy with sailing races underway, looping around the yellow buoys punctuating the lake's northern third. The reeds around the club obscure Dubwath Beck, which flows into Bassenthwaite but was likely once the lake's outflow. Out of view across the A66, Dubwath Silver Meadows (the Lake District's first wetland nature reserve) is home to a population of roe deer, sometimes spotted at the lake shore.

At Banks Point, a series of small beaches among the trees, accessed down steps, are popular with wild swimmers and paddlers. These beaches, like all around Bassenthwaite, are regularly submerged, after the lake level has risen. There is a fine view along the lake's length:

> "… the sublimer mountains, pile upon pile, lift up their heads, and, from the western sun, cast long shadows on the lake, whose distant shores catch the surpassing beams, and glow with additional beauty from the contrasting shades."

William Hutchinson, *The History of the County of Cumberland*, 1794

From 1779, John Spedding of Mirehouse laid on festivals at Banks Point. Horses would be floated offshore on barges which were then sunk, with bets laid on which unfortunate equine would swim back to shore first.

The River Derwent is the largest river draining any of the lakes; in the week following rainfall, the flow towards Bassenthwaite's exit can be surprisingly strong. Ouse Bridge's two sandstone arches have spanned the river since the early nineteenth century. The bridge survived being *over-topped* by the lake during 2015's Storm Desmond.

📷 *Armathwaite Hall*

Across the River Derwent, the shore is guarded by reeds. The wooded slope behind is a terminal moraine: an earth and rubble bank, deposited at the foot of a glacier, which once dammed Bassenthwaite. Above is Armathwaite Hall (visible from mid-lake), originally a Tudor mansion but rebuilt in 1882 and since 1930 a rather grand-looking, castellated hotel.

Paddling to Scar Ness, it's easy to imagine that you are somewhere much wilder. Unfrequented bays and small beaches indent the shoreline, backed by tangled carr (wet woodland, see page 236): Cottage, Lakeside and Orchard Woods. The beaches reveal more glacial traces: 'erratics', out of place Borrowdale Volcanics boulders which hitched a ride, on ice, from central Lakeland. These have been left exposed and isolated where waves have eroded back softer clays. Glaciers also flowed from the opposite direction: some erratics are granite, transported from Scotland's Southern Uplands!

Halls Beck enters the lake through a shallow, jutting bird's foot delta (the geographical term describes its splayed shape, seen from above) and then the slender headland of Scar Ness arcs even further into the lake. Scar Ness is the tip of another moraine bank. Its boulders continue far into the lake, beneath the surface; as evidence of this, the author can attest to a broken surf ski rudder and an embarrassing swim!

Scarness Bay is a sharp contrast, revealing a sizeable pier and the wooden chalets of Bassenthwaite Lakeside Lodges holiday park. The fields south of the pier are a Scout campsite.

The remainder of Bassenthwaite's eastern shore is gently sloping farm pastures, with woodland interludes. Broadness and Bowness are two successive headlands, the former a drumlin (a rounded hill of glacial till) rimmed by a wooden walkway and the latter an intrusion of igneous diorite, lurking beneath Bowness Wood. Between the headlands, Broadness Farm overlooks Bowness Bay's reedbeds, designated a no boating zone to protect breeding and overwintering birds.

Church Bay's name is explained by St Bega's Church, Bassenthwaite's finest secret. Just 150m from the water's edge, in theory access is via a footpath behind the church, from the A591.

📷 *St Bega's Church*

St Bega's

"… in complete isolation stands the humble church of St Bega, shy and rather forlorn but immensely proud of its long history and spiritual influence."

Alfred Wainwright, *Wainwright in the Valleys of Lakeland*, 1992

This lonely little church was renovated in 1874 but dates from c. AD 950, or older; large stones in its walls may be Roman. Inside, note the Norman chancel arch and fourteenth-century font. Above a doorway, George II's coat of arms is dated to 1745, the year of Bonnie Prince Charlie's rebellion: a reminder to locals to stay loyal! The then-dilapidated church influenced Tennyson's *Morte d'Arthur*: "*a chapel nigh the field, / A broken chancel with a broken cross, / That stood on a dark strait of barren land*".

By legend, St Bega was a ninth(?)-century Irish princess who fled marriage to a Viking by crossing the Irish Sea to St Bees, wearing an arm-ring gifted by an angel. Local author Melvyn Bragg based his novel *Credo* upon her life.

The shores around Castocks Wood are overlooked by Mirehouse, a Georgian mansion. Built in 1666 as the Earl of Derby's hunting lodge, since 1802 it has been home to the Speddings, who have made various rebuilds. Mirehouse can be visited in summer; public access is from the A591 behind.

The boathouse and jetty in Castocks Wood are used by the Calvert Trust, a charity founded in 1976 by John Fryer-Spedding to enable people with disabilities to benefit from outdoor activities. They are based at Little Crosthwaite, the complex of buildings overlooking Derwent Foot, where the River Derwent enters the lake, six kilometres downstream of Derwent Water. The whole lakehead is a no boating zone, protecting the avian fauna, admittedly a shame as the

📷 *Skiddaw and Ullock Pike*

extensive wetlands around Bridges Hole, Redness Point and Newlands Beck would make for engaging exploration.

> ### King Arthur at Bassenthwaite
>
> Alfred Tennyson made long stays at Mirehouse in 1835, and for his honeymoon in 1850. 1850 was the year that William Wordsworth died and Queen Victoria appointed Tennyson as Poet Laureate. Bassenthwaite inspired his epic retellings of Arthurian legend: *Morte d'Arthur* (1842) and *Idylls of the King* (1870). King Arthur's death in *Morte d'Arthur* was written while sitting beside, *"the shining levels of the lake"*. The dying Arthur instructs Sir Bedivere to cast the sword Excalibur into the water. Bedivere vacillates for numerous stanzas, *"I heard the ripple washing in the reeds, / And the wild water lapping on the crag"*, before finally flinging it into the lake.
>
> The Tennyson Society erected the shoreline memorial stone, depicting Excalibur grasped by the Lady of the Lake.

Winter floods submerge Braithwaite Bog, extending the lake up-valley for kilometres. Like nearby Buttermere and Crummock Water, Bassenthwaite and Derwent Water were once joined (the height difference is only eight metres), yet have always had separate glacially scoured troughs; in this case, separated by a rock band buried beneath twenty metres of alluvium.

It's time to address the elephant in the valley, which is Skiddaw.

"the inhabitants here … pronounce the name of Skiddaw-fell with a sort of terror & aversion."

Thomas Gray, *Journal of A Visit to the Lake District*, 1775

📷 *The Bishop, Barf*

England's fourth-highest mountain (931m) looms over the eastern shore, utterly dominating the view from every corner of the lake. Seen from Derwent Water, Skiddaw presents an imposing, yet uniform, front; paddling along Bassenthwaite, it becomes three-dimensional, revealing its true complexity. Wainwright noted, *"three great steps of Skiddaw rising from the head of Bassenthwaite Lake"* (***The Northern Fells***, 1962). These successive steps have impressive symmetry: Dodd, Ullock Pike, and Skiddaw itself. Dodd is smothered by Dodd Wood, with only the summit exposed. Through the 1860s, Dodd was home to George Smith, the 'Skiddaw Hermit', who lived in a teepee and painted portraits for Bassenthwaite's residents. *"He seems to assume the appearance of a religious fanatic, and wanders about the hills preaching to the sheep"* (***Westmorland Gazette***, 1866). This unfortunate man later converted after listening to a Gospel preacher alongside Windermere, and returned home to Banff, where he died in an asylum. Ullock Pike is a slender ridge best appreciated from Bassenthwaite's northern end, while Skiddaw's summit plateau is a broad bulk of shattered slate, regularly wreathed in cloud.

Skiddaw has a modest yet still-impressive rival, facing it from the western shore: Barf. Barf's unrelenting, exposed crags and uninviting scree rear steeply behind Blackstock Point.

The Bishop of Barf

By legend, the bishop stayed beside Bassenthwaite in 1783 before sailing to Ireland. He wagered, fuelled by drink, that he could ride his pony up Barf's slopes to the summit.

It ended in tears, with both rider and steed plunging to their deaths. The spot where they supposedly fell is marked by the large rock prominently painted white: The Bishop. On the water, this is only visible from the no boating zone. The rocks were regularly repainted by staff of Thornthwaite's Swan Hotel; since this closed in 2006, Mountain Rescue members have kept the paint fresh.

◎ *Blackstock Point and Skiddaw*

Blackstock Point, the no boating zone's northern limit, is a promontory of boulder clay, eroded back to reveal erratics on the beaches: geologically incongruous rocks, transported by glacier. This spot is popular with picnicking tourists.

The paddle back to Peel Wyke is somewhat anticlimactic: the western shoreline becomes almost die-straight, often buttressed to support the dual-carriageway A66, and the traffic noise is unrelenting. It's best enjoyed early morning: before the sun rises behind Skiddaw, when the traffic is low, the water smooth and Wythop Wood's conifers are swathed in mist. So the author has heard, anyway.

◎ *Castle Crag and the Jaws of Borrowdale*

Derwent Water

Length (km)	Maximum width (km)	Maximum depth (m)	Surface area (km²)	Catchment area (km²)	Height above sea level (m)
4.6	1.93	22	5.29	85.40	76

Trip Distance	10.8km / 6.7 miles (11.9km / 7.4 miles)
Start / Finish	Crow Park, Keswick NY 263 228 / dogs.attic.copies / CA12 5DG

Introduction

"It was perfectly calm & the Mountains, Rocks & Trees etc. were reflected so perfectly on the Water … it was difficult to say which was the Shadow and which the reality."

William Wilberforce, *Journey to the Lake District*, 1779

Derwent Water, you absolute beauty! First visiting Keswick landing stages as a teenage Scout, the author was staggered by the view: the wooden rowboats on the beach, Derwent Isle in the foreground, wooded Castle Crag jutting upwards within the 'Jaws of Borrowdale' beyond the lakehead and, above all, the perfect symmetry of Cat Bells and Causey Pike behind the western shore – mountain ridges descending towards one another, mirrored horizontally in profile and vertically in the water. The author's life-long love for Derwent Water was cemented when it appeared, unmistakeably, in a *Star Wars* movie; fellow geeks will know which one.

The Victorians dubbed Derwent Water 'Queen of the Lakes'. Exploring paddlers are treated to a constantly varying array of scenery, landforms, historical sites and islands; a low boredom threshold will not be a problem here. The route described can be varied almost infinitely; the main choice is whether to include the two accessible, but offshore, islands in your itinerary. Note that the lake's width coupled with winds funnelled down Borrowdale can make offshore conditions pretty rough.

Derwent Water has seen its share of visitors. It heavily influenced the earliest tourists (page 229) and poets Samuel Taylor Coleridge (who named a son 'Derwent'), Percy Shelley and Robert Southey all resided at Keswick.

Derwent Water's unique oval shape is caused by its position on the Derwent Water Fault. The glacier which poured down Borrowdale was bottlenecked and compressed by the resistant Borrowdale Volcanics rocks at the Jaws of Borrowdale, then, boosted by Watendlath's glacier, it crossed the Fault into weaker Skiddaw Group slates and decompressed outwards. The four large islands (there are at least a dozen others) are probably drumlins, formed from heaps of glacial till deposited beneath the ice.

Derwent Water is also commonly called Derwentwater. It takes its name from the River Derwent which flows through, meaning, 'river where oaks grow' (Celtic *derw*: oaks and *nant*: valley / stream). An older name for the lake was Keswick Water.

Access

Paddling is allowed, as are sailing and rowing. Powered craft are allowed, with a speed limit of 10mph.

The National Park asks paddlers to avoid several designated 'wildlife areas': Strandshag Bay, the passage between Lord's Island and the lake shore; Lord's Island's shoreline; Great Bay at the lake's southern extremity; and Otterbield Bay and Derwent Bay on the western side. Paddlers are also asked to avoid launching and landing at reeds and wetlands.

Landing is permitted on Rampsholme Island and St Herbert's Island. Lord's Island is Access Land; however, the shoreline is a wildlife area (above). Derwent Isle is private.

Be mindful of the Keswick Launches, which loop around at a fair clip, and avoid their jetties. Lakeland Rowing Club trains on the lake.

Wildlife and environment

A two-metre rise in level is common after very heavy rainfall. This is a consequence of the lake having England's rainiest spot in its catchment and also its basin-like profile. Whenever a mayor of Keswick dies, a slate plaque is placed below Friar's Crag recording the water level; the plaques extend some distance above and below the water.

Derwent Water has perch, pike, roach, trout and verdace. The latter is a rare whitefish found only here and in Bassenthwaite Water. The shores and islands are lined with larch, oak, Scots pine and silver birch. On the water, wildfowl reside year-round, including goosander, mute swans, pochard and tufted duck. Barnacle, Canadian and greylag geese are well fed at Keswick landing stages.

Derwent Water is protected within the River Derwent and Bassenthwaite Lake Special Area of Conservation.

📷 *Hundred Year Stone, Calfclose Bay*

Invasive New Zealand pygmyweed has blighted the lake; follow the biosecurity practices outlined on page 34.

Launch points

Crow Park, Keswick NY 263 228 / dogs.attic.copies / CA12 5DG – a wide beach in a public park. From Lakeside car park, cross Lake Road and pass through a gate, reaching the beach after 150m. Launching is discouraged beside the jetties at Lake Road's end. Cheaper, park at Keswick Rugby Club at CA12 5EG on Crow Park Road, or on the road itself. A gate accesses Crow Park. It's a 600m walk.

Calfclose Bay NY 269 213 / pockets.picnic.mindset / CA12 5UP – a wide beach accessed from the National Trust's Great Wood car park. Cross the B5289 and follow paths 250m to the lake shore.

Barrow Bay NY 268 204 / little.worth.storming / CA12 5UR – the beach alongside Ashness Gate jetty. Turn off the B5289 on to the lane signposted for 'Ashness Br. / Watendlath' to reach a small National Trust car park, uphill and 100m from the water. Accessing the beach involves crossing the B5289 to a gap in the wall and descending steps.

Kettlewell car park NY 266 195 / walked.pedicure.lifelong / CA12 5UU – a lakeside National Trust car park, with direct lake access. This was the best place to launch on Derwent Water; however, the National Trust installed a stupid height barrier, set ludicrously low, making it impractical for vehicles carrying paddlecraft. Unloading outside, beside the B5289, is possible but dangerous.

Brandelhow Bay NY 251 197 / brain.tolerable.built / CA12 5UQ – the beach alongside High Brandelhow jetty. Turn off the B5289 to cross the bridge at Grange village. Park at the lay-by 2.2km from the bridge and directly after Brackenburn Lodge, a prominent house on the left. A rough path leads 550m, descending 44m, to the pier: light paddlecraft only!

📷 *Keswick landing stages*

Alternatively, park in the small quarry 460m further on, or in the lay-by another 350m further on, and descend following the paths signposted from there; both options are even higher above the water.

Description

Crow Park belongs to the National Trust. This broad, grass-covered mound is a drumlin; much of Keswick is built on these heaps of glacial till. A curved plaque, unveiled by Prince (now King) Charles, commemorates the National Park's 2017 inception as a World Heritage Site. Keswick Mountain Festival is held in the park over an early summer weekend, at which time it will be smothered with marquees and stalls.

The iconic Keswick landing stages are mobbed by tourists and well-fed geese. Note the boathouse, with bell, alongside. Behind is the Theatre by the Lake, a splendid cultural venue. From 1975 to 1999, the trailer-mounted Century Theatre occupied the spot. Keswick's centre is, of course, a short walk away following Lake Road. The town grew from mining. Borrowdale was the first known source of graphite, used of course in pencils. This valuable resource was the origin of the phrase 'black market'. The mines were eventually exhausted, and Keswick transitioned into the first Lake District resort: *"For two thirds of the year we are in complete retirement – the other third is alive & swarms with Tourists of all shapes & sizes, & characters"* (Coleridge, 1800). Now, of course, the fleece-shopping hordes are a year-round fixture.

Opposite the landing stages is Derwent Isle, which spans three hectares and curves eleven metres above the water. The National Trust leases it to private residents, and only infrequently* permits small groups to land and visit. However, a paddle around provides great views of the boathouse and house.

None at all in 2024 and 2025.

📷 *Derwent Isle and Blencathra*

Pocklington's Island

Derwent Isle has gone by various names: Hest Holm (Old Norse: horse isle), Vicar's Island, Paradise Island and Pocklington's Island. Fountains Abbey owned it until 1539. In 1569 it was bought to safely* house German engineers of the newly formed 'Company of Mines Royal', shipped in to mine Borrowdale and the Newlands valley. They settled long-term (many Keswickians can trace descent) and built a brewery, bakery, windmill, pigsty and orchard.

Joseph Pocklington bought the island for £300 in 1778 and styled himself 'Island Governor and Commander-in-Chief'. He seems to have been, in medical parlance, batshit crazy. He built the house, as well as an array of eccentric edifices: a mock-Gothic wooden church, a boathouse with a belfry styled to resemble a non-conformist chapel, grottoes, cannon batteries modestly named 'Fort Joseph' and a 'druid's' stone circle.

Pocklington appointed Peter Crosthwaite, retired from the East India Company, as his 'Admiral'. From 1781 to 1790, they staged the 'Keswick Regattas', with cannon-fire and mock naval battles drawing the crowds. Crosthwaite also surveyed the lakes and produced the first accurate maps.

Only the boathouse-chapel survives of Pocklington's *"puerilities"* (Wordsworth). After Henry Marshall bought the island in 1844, architect Anthony Salvin expanded the house with two Italianate wings. David Marshall bequeathed the island to the National Trust in 1951.

One of them had been murdered by a Keswick mob.

Friar's Crag is a tree-covered intrusion of resistant diorite, jutting into the lake. Possibly named for medieval pilgrims embarking for St Herbert's Island, it has quite a heritage. John Ruskin (page 160) described the spot as *"One of the three most beautiful scenes in Europe"* and the crag is topped by The Ruskin Monument (1900), a Borrowdale slate monolith, designed by the Victorian polymath's friend W.G. Collingwood:

'THE FIRST THING WHICH I REMEMBER AS AN EVENT IN LIFE WAS BEING TAKEN BY MY NURSE TO THE BROW OF FRIAR'S CRAG ON DERWENT WATER'.

The National Trust acquired Friar's Crag (along with Lord's Island and Great Wood) in 1922, in memory of founder Hardwicke Rawnsley. Friar's Crag also made an appearance in *Swallows and Amazons* as 'Darien', where the children camped:

"At last he came out of the trees on a small open space of bare rock and heather. This was the Peak of Darien. There were trees all round it, but through them could be seen the bright glimmer of the lake."

Arthur Ransome, *Swallows and Amazons*, 1930

Lord's Island, which has also gone by the names Lady Island and Crow Island, is seven metres high and heavily wooded. It lies less than 100m offshore from Strandshag Bay and The Ings, an area of woodland carr where Brockle Beck percolates into the lake. Pass Lord's Island by the offshore side, avoiding the wildlife area, where geese nest. A pair of shallow reefs lie just west of the island, unlikely to trouble paddlecraft.

The Lord's Island Jacobites

Lord's Island gets its name from its former residents, the Earls of Derwentwater. The overgrown outline of their manor house, built c. 1460, is still discernible; this was connected to the mainland by a bridge. The house was ruinous by the mid-1600s, the stones used to construct Keswick's Moot Hall (the current building dates from 1813).

James Radclyffe, 3rd Earl of Derwentwater, joined the 1715 Jacobite uprising in support of James Stuart, the Catholic 'Old Pretender'. For his troubles, he was beheaded and in 1735 the Derwentwater estates, including the island, were awarded to Greenwich Hospital. James's brother Charles, the 5th Earl, regarded the Jacobite cause as unfinished business and joined 'Bonnie' Prince Charlie's 1745 uprising. For supporting the 'Young Pretender', he also was beheaded.

Derwent Water's eastern shoreline, subject to the prevailing wind and waves with a long 'fetch', is scoured and eroded, with wide stony beaches and exposed tree roots. Broomhill Point is a cliff-fronted drumlin, protected by a beach extending into Calfclose Bay. On the beach, The Hundred Year Stone is a three-metre glacial boulder of Borrowdale andesite (lava). To commemorate the National Trust's centenary in 1995, Peter Randall-Page sliced this boulder into neat halves, carving the face of each with ten connected wedges representing the century. It's sometimes possible to paddle around, or over, this artwork.

Rampsholme Island is a possible diversion, 300m offshore. It's tree-covered, 75m long and 3m high. A shallow stony spit extends from its north-west corner, created by wind action and shifting sediment. A foray ashore will allow you to assess whether it deserves its name, which means 'garlic

◎ *Cat Bells and Causey Pike*

island' (Old Norse). Rampsholme's shores are littered with 'clinker', dark slag waste: it was the site of a medieval 'bloomery' ironworks. The tiny array of rocks located 250m south of Rampsholme, usually bedecked with cormorants, are the Scarf Stones (Old Norse *skarfr*: cormorant).

A series of imposing cliffs rear behind the eastern shore, commencing with conifer-strewn Walla Crag. The prominent cleft, high above Calfclose Bay, is Lady's Rake, named for Lady Derwentwater, wife of the 3rd Earl who was arrested for treason. A tattered cloth hanging in the ravine would be pointed out to tourists, allegedly dropped by the fleeing noblewoman.

Falcon Crag rises behind Ashness Gate jetty. Barrow Bay and Barrow Point are backed, across the B5289, by Barrow House. Barrow Point is Barrow Beck's bouldery, arcuate (curved) delta. Until 2024, this mansion was an independent youth hostel. It was built, in 1787, for Joseph Pocklington, idiosyncratic owner of Derwent Isle. Pocklington also engineered Barrow Beck to create waterfalls behind the house and advertised for a hermit to occupy a cell alongside, the seven-year contract stipulating that said recluse could never leave, speak or wash. There were no takers.

Kettlewell car park is hidden in Lowcrag Wood, alongside Cat Gill. Watendlath Beck joins shortly after. The Mary Mount Hotel which sits beside it has been known, when pre-warned, to admit dripping paddlers.

The Environment Agency monitors the lake height beside Lodore jetty. A cannon here entertained early tourists with reverberated blasts: *"English echoes appear to be the most expensive luxuries in which a traveller can indulge"* (Robert Southey, **Letters from England**, 1807).

Describing an 1886 tragedy in her **Journal**, Beatrix Potter revealed her worldview: *"Five Keswick men and one from Penrith went to Lodore Hotel to drink, and coming back at 8 o'clock, dusk, began fighting, upset the boat, and they were drowned ... They belonged to the lowest set in the town, and will not be missed."*

The Floating Island

On rare occasions, Derwent Water acquires an extra island. The near-mythical 'Floating Island' supposedly surfaces every few years within the south-east corner … its most recent appearances being in 2003 and 2005. Harriet Martineau observed how it, *"… rises when distended with gases, and sinks again when it has parted with them at the surface"* (*A Complete Guide to the English Lakes*, 1855).

The Floating Island appears in hot weather, seemingly when the water level is also high. It can range from barely discernible to a reported 7,500km^2 in size and has lasted from several days to an entire summer. In 1930, Keswick Girl Guides planted a Union flag on it.

Lodore Falls, spectacular after rainfall, is one of the author's favourite spots. The falls can be glimpsed from the water when the trees are bare, nestled in the ravine between Gowder Crag and Shepherds Crag (beloved of climbers). However, the Lodore Falls Hotel & Spa's extensions partially obscure the falls; this expensive retreat has been permitted to sprawl and proliferate, while any development which may attract the 'masses' is invariably refused permission. Anyway, rants aside, a shore patrol to visit the falls is highly recommended.

The River Derwent unloads into the lake it gave its name to. It has formed half a dozen alder-clad islets: a bird's foot delta straight from a geography textbook. It's usually possible to paddle 900m up this winding channel to 'Chinese Bridge' above Cannon Dub, a popular swim spot. After heavy rainfall, the channel, islets, and entire lakehead submerge, up to a kilometre up-valley.

The Cataract of Lodore

Lodore Falls are an 800m walk from Kettlewell car park: cross the B5289 to a footpath and follow this south, veering uphill when the hotel boundary wall is reached.

Poet Laureate Robert Southey, living at Keswick, described the falls in verses of doggerel, written for his young son:

"Collecting, projecting, / Receding and speeding, / And shocking and rocking, / And darting and parting, / And threading and spreading, / And whizzing and hissing, / And dripping and skipping …"

Robert Southey, *The Cataract of Lodore*, 1823

It's worth looking up the whole poem: Southey goes on like this for about a hundred lines!

The falls are at their best after rain (not unheard of hereabouts), so heed the warning of **Baedecker's Great Britain**, in 1887: *"There is usually more rock than water, Southey's jingling verses are responsible for a good deal of disappointment."*

Crossing the mouth of Great Bay (a wildlife area), soak up the Jaws of Borrowdale: the narrowing of the valley around towering Castle Crag. Borrowdale derives its name from the Old Norse *borgar*, meaning 'fortified place': the Viking settlers were referring to Castle Crag's Iron

Lodore Falls

Age hillfort. A friend of the author's summed up this vista, *"Bloody hell, we're in The Lord of the Rings"*. It also freaked out early visitors:

> *"… a composition of all that is horrible. An immense chasm opens up in the midst, whose entrance is divided by a rude conic hill, once topt by a castle, beyond a chain of craggs …"*

William Camden, *Britannia*, 1586

Derwent Water's heavily wooded south-west is its most peaceful quadrant. Yet, Myrtle Bay, Abbot's Bay and Brandelhow Bay were once a hive of activity. At Manesty, eighteenth-century visitors flocked to drink saltwater from a well, as a spa treatment. Mines were opened up at Manesty Park and Brandelhow Park by Derwent Isle's Germans. In its 1840s heyday, the Brandelhow Point mine produced 300 tons of galena (containing lead and silver) annually, as well as cobalt, gold and zinc. It closed in 1891, after pumping out water became uneconomic. The exposed shoreline spoil tips hint at the industrial wasteland this area once was.

Abbot's Bay House, the enviable villa atop Brandelhow Point, overlooking diminutive Otter Island, was built in 1902 for poet Percy Withers. Some while back, the author wrote to the owners with what he felt was a fair offer for the place; oddly enough, they have yet to reply. Above the woods behind, Brackenburn House was, from 1923, the home of novelist Hugh Walpole.

Scots pines line Derwent Water's western shores. Along the water's edge around Withesike Bay, note mudstone slabs striated by glacial scouring and the boulder erratics dumped by the ice. Overlooking Victoria Bay, 'Entrust', a (now dilapidated) pair of giant wooden hands, sculpted by local artist John Merrill in 2002, commemorates the National Trust's first Lake District land acquisition: Brandelhow Park. Queen Victoria's daughter, HRH Princess Louise, dedicated the park in 1902, accompanied by the Trust's founders: Octavia Hill, Sir Robert Hunter and Hardwicke Rawnsley. Hill recorded the role played by the Lakeland weather: *"I never saw light more beautiful, it was not what people would call fine, but it was very beautiful and did not rain. The wind was high and tore the tent to ribbons …"* Manesty Park was acquired five years later, in the nick of time: it had already been divided into villa plots.

St Herbert's Island

Otterbield Bay and Derwent Bay are small inlets designated as wildlife areas; in-between, Kitchen Bay is served by Hawes End jetty. Hawse End, an outdoor activities centre in the trees behind, is the first of a succession of mansions and villas lining Derwent Water's north-western shores. The paddle across to crag-fronted Copperheap Hill passes Otterbield Island (also called Trippet Holme), a single-tree islet where gulls nest.

A popular alternative is to deviate 600m offshore, to St Herbert's Island. The longest (300m) and tallest (14m) Derwent Water island spans about two hectares and is covered by beech and hazel. Landing is simple, with a beach spanning the southern end and a long spit at the northern tip, formed by sediment drift towards the lake's outlet. Camping on St Herbert's Island has always been popular. However, it is not officially permitted and the National Trust (which acquired it in 1951) has had to deal with some cretinous behaviour, including groups who in 2023, incredibly, felled trees by chainsaw. Be mindful (as if anyone should need reminding) to show care for this SSSI and archaeological site.

St Herbert and his island

"There was a priest of praiseworthy life named Herbert, who had for a long time enjoyed a spiritual friendship with St Cuthbert. He lived the life of a hermit on an island in a great lake which is the source of the river Derwent."

Bede, *History of the English Church*, c. AD 731

The closeness of St Herbert's friendship with St Cuthbert (of Lindisfarne fame) extended to them both dying on the same AD 687 day, or so Bede claims. It's not clear where Herbert's cell was located; the foundations near the island's centre are traces of a pilgrim chapel, built c. 1387, and the circular ruins near the northern tip were a 'pleasure house', built c. 1750 for then-owner Sir Wilfred Lawson.

Cat Bells

Derwent Water

During the English Civil War, royalist Sir Wilfred Lawson stored gunpowder on the island. Parliamentarian Robin 'The Devil' Philipson (page 125) rode non-stop from the siege of Carlisle to capture these supplies, but the guards had been tipped off; all the boats were on the island, and Philipson was laughed away.

William and Dorothy Wordsworth visited in 1794, the time of their reunion (page 145):

"Wilt thou behold this shapeless heap of stones,

The desolate ruins of St. Herbert's Cell".

William Wordsworth, *For the Spot where the Hermitage stood*, 1800

Pilgrims hold a sermon on the island every April 13th, the purported date of Herbert's and Cuthbert's deaths.

Cat Bells! No one forgets their first sight of this shapely mini-mountain (451m), soaring skywards above Derwent Water's southern half.

"The lofty and steep slope of Catbells, decked in all those hues with which October invests the hills, rich brown and lemon colour, mingled with green, and streaked here and there like a dove's neck from the effect of slate and metallic ore, was illuminated by a brilliant morning sun; and the whole hill side was reflected from the mirror of Derwentwater without a wrinkle."

Sir Edward Baines, *A Companion to the Lakes*, 1834

The name (Cat Bells and Catbells are both used) possibly references a wildcat's bield (Gaelic: shelter) on the bracken and gorse slopes, or it may come from the Old Norse *belja*: bell, describing Cat Bell's bell-curve profile.

◎ *Lingholm Boathouse*

Copperheap Bay takes its name from a mound of Newlands valley copper ore, marking where it was loaded; supposedly, an Elizabethan ore boat sank in the bay.

Paddling northwards, Skiddaw's rounded slate bulk (931m) spans the horizon, with Blencathra's sharply defined ridges (868m) laying on a sideshow, further east.

Potter at Derwent Water

Beatrix Potter took inspiration from summers with her family at Lingholm (ten from 1885 to 1907) and Fawe Park (1903). Lingholm's kitchen gardens were written and painted as Mr McGregor's vegetable garden in *The Tale of Peter Rabbit* (1902) and Fawe Park's gardens formed the backdrop for *The Tale of Benjamin Bunny* (1904). The titular hedgehog of *The Tale of Mrs. Tiggy-Winkle* (1905) lived behind a little door on *"a hill that goes up—up—into the clouds as though it had no top!"* (Cat Bells) and in *The Tale of Squirrel Nutkin* (1903), said anthropomorphic rodent voyages offshore to Owl Island (clearly St Herbert's Island), utilising his tail as a sail: *"In the middle of the lake there is an island covered with trees and nut bushes …"*

In 1903, Potter cannily made Peter Rabbit the first ever licensed and merchandised character; the wealth that she eventually used to buy, and conserve, hefty chunks of the Lake District (15 farms and 1600 hectares) came primarily from stuffed toys.

A landing stage serves Lingholm, an 1870s mansion and walled gardens, shrouded by conifers. The Lingholm Islands are rather grandly named, an archipelago of four islets with a few trees clinging, extending from the shore; the gaps between are shallow. Past Lingholm's stylish boathouse and across Galemire Bay, Fawe Park is another hidden Victorian mansion (1850s), fronted

Skiddaw, Derwent Isle and Crow Park

by a stone boathouse with a crumbling harbour. In 1887, Fawe Park was the scene of an early 'Right of Way' showdown, between the owner and hundreds of 'trespassers' from the Keswick Footpath Preservation Society, egged on by Hardwicke Rawnsley.

Two marinas are tucked into Derwent Water's north-west corner, both hiring out paddlecraft: Nichol End Marine was the site of a shrine to St Nicholas, a stop-off for pilgrims heading to St Herbert's Island, and Derwentwater Marina is home to West Cumbria Canoe Club. Alongside Derwentwater Marina, the River Derwent escapes, the outflow obscured by reedbeds and tangled carr.

The northernmost point, often shallow, is occupied by a campsite. It's run by the Camping and Caravan Club, so it is strictly for those who relish regimentation and rules. The promontory around to Crow Park is Town Cass, almost an island as a wetland stream seeps across it. Isthmus Bay, at the tip, was once a bathing station for Keswick's tourists.

Let's give the last word to ***Baedecker's Great Britain***, published 1887: *"Perhaps the loveliest of the English lakes"*. What do you think: did these Germans know what they were talking about?

📷 *Thirlmere from Raven Crag*

Thirlmere

Length (km)	Maximum width (km)	Maximum depth (m)	Surface area (km²)	Catchment area (km²)	Height above sea level (m)
6	0.74	46	3.13	30.21	178

Trip Distance	13.6km / 8.5 miles
Start / Finish	Armboth car park NY 305 171 / extremely.skin.curtail / CA12 4TW

Introduction

"O Thirlmere!—let me some how or other celebrate the world in thy mirror.—Conceive all possible varieties of Form, Fields, & Trees, and naked or ferny Crags— ravines, behaired with Birches …"

Samuel Taylor Coleridge, *Notebooks*, 1803

The Thirlmere which the opium-addled poet raved about is gone. In the late nineteenth century, it was controversially dammed and enlarged into the present reservoir, then surrounded by stifling conifer plantations. Yet … time and increasingly sensitive tree planting practices have been kind to Thirlmere. Even Alfred Wainwright, a savage critic of plantations, conceded in old age, *"The area has matured into an impressive beauty"* (***Wainwright in the Valleys of Lakeland***, 1992). Provided the lake level is not low – at which times, the water is rimmed by an unsightly bleached scar – Thirlmere offers a beautiful, and always uncrowded, day of paddling. It has a Scandinavian appearance, filling out its valley within sheer sides which include the Helvellyn fells. This is due

partly to the damming and partly to the deep-scouring glacier which followed the underlying geology of the north–south aligned Coniston Fault.

Thirlmere was one of various names given to the lake prior to damming. It likely derives from the Old English *thirl*, meaning 'hole' or 'aperture'. W.G. Collingwood, who proposed that the reservoir be named Thirlmere, suggested that it was Old Norse: 'Thorolf's Mere'.

Access

Thirlmere is a reservoir owned by United Utilities, supplying about 11% of the North West's water. It was built to serve Manchester, but, since 2022, a pipeline also serves Keswick and West Cumbria. United Utilities owns 4,700 hectares around the lake.

Canoes and kayaks have been allowed since 1983. Sailing craft are allowed, but no powered vessels. Arbitrarily, paddleboards are not allowed. United Utilities has cited *"preventing deaths"* as the reason for this, the same rationale given for the blanket swimming ban at their sites.

Landing is not permitted on Thirlmere's islands.

United Utilities can be contacted at accessnorthcatchment@uuplc.co.uk.

Wildlife and environment

Thirlmere's waters contain brown trout, char, perch and pike. In 2005, Thirlmere became the UK's first national reserve for red squirrels and they are often spotted. Red deer roam the forests and fells.

The lake is completely surrounded by 810 hectares of coniferous plantations: larch, spruce and Douglas fir. Indigenous alder, ash, birch and oak have been added over recent decades. The larch provides welcome lighter patches and in autumn turns golden yellow.

Launch points

Armboth car park NY 305 171 / extremely.skin.curtail / CA12 4TW – a National Park car park with direct lake access. Unhelpfully, the machine is coin-only, like all around the lake.

Dam Triangle car park NY 306 189 / spine.match.apprehend / CA12 4TW – a small parking area beside the lane leading to Thirlmere dam from the west. Popular with walkers ascending Raven Crag. Across the lane, a path leads 30m downhill to a beach.

Station Coppice car park NY 313 168 / culling.radically.wriggle / CA12 4TP – a small National Park car park beside the northbound A591. A permissive path leads 300m, steeply descending 45m, to the lake shore, alongside Helvellyn Gill.

Steel End car park NY 320 132 / providing.zooms.bulges / CA12 4TW – a National Park car park with a permissive path leading 300m to the lake's southern tip. Not useful when the reservoir level is low.

Dob Gill car park NY 317 141 / groups.animator.blazers / CA12 4TP – a National Park car park with a permissive path across the road, leading 170m downhill to the lake shore.

📷 *Deergarth How Island*

Description

Armboth car park occupies the site of Armboth House, a mansion demolished and flooded in 1894, which overlooked the undammed lake's narrowing. The only hint of the house is a monkey puzzle tree, looking discombobulated among the conifers. Unloading your paddlecraft, be mindful for supernatural phenomena …

> *"Lights are seen there at night, people say, and the bells ring; and just as the bells set off ringing, a large dog is seen swimming across the lake … the preparation for the ghostly wedding feast of a murdered bride, who comes up from her watery bed."*

Harriet Martineau, *A Complete Guide to the English Lakes*, 1855

The black dog is apparently a harbinger of ill fate: if seen, consider changing your plans.

Armboth directly faces the Helvellyn fells. This towering rampart rises without interruption along the whole eastern lake shore to the rounded summits, often obscured by clouds, of Watson's Dodd, Stybarrow Dodd, Raise and Helvellyn. On 29th August 1800, Samuel Taylor Coleridge completed his epic poem ***Christabel*** in Keswick, and then, by moonlight, he trekked thirty kilometres to Grasmere, traversing this entire skyline, to read it to the Wordsworth siblings.

Helvellyn's 949m summit, the third-highest of the Lake District's four 3,000-foot mountains, is identified by following Helvellyn Gill's waterfalls above the treeline, to the ridge of Browncove Crags.

Most first paddle south towards the islands, so we'll describe an anti-clockwise route. Along this western shore, a complex myriad of crags rears through the ubiquitous conifers. Fisher Crag overlooks 150m-long Deergarth How Island (Old Norse: Deer enclosure hill), located 50m offshore. The island rises 12m from the water, boosted further by the trees.

Hawes How Island (Old Norse: mountain pass hill) is 600m south and 150m offshore, past the bubbling outflow of Launchy Gill. This larger island is 19m high and crossed by a wall which

📷 *Island south-east of Hawes How Island*

pre-dates the flooding. It briefly appeared, as the planet Takodana, in the 2015 movie *Star Wars: The Force Awakens*, with X-wing fighters zooming past!

Both islands are shrouded in Scots pines, with fly agaric mushrooms abundant. When Thirlmere is low, both become promontories. Both are criss-crossed with paths and bear plenty of traces of visits.

Just south-east of Hawes How Island is a third island, a tiny, bare reef.

Thirlmere is narrowed by Rough Crag and then Hause Point jutting into the lake. Rough Crag is an exposed cliff looming above the west shore road, which was opened in 1894. Several inlets and promontories, with the occasional beach or small meadow, provide a bit of interest and variation within the treescape. Dob Gill trickles in at the head of the first inlet; here, you are paddling above The City, once the valley's largest settlement.

An elegantly inverted curve frames the lakehead, dipping between Steel Fell and Dollywaggon Pike: this is Dunmail Raise, the pass leading to the southern Lake District. A cairn at the high point of the pass (unglamorously hemmed in by the A591's carriageways) is supposedly Dunmail's burial place. This legendary last King of Cumbria was supposedly killed by English invaders, around AD 945.

The lakehead area is still named Wythburn (Old Norse: valley of willows), despite the village of that name being drowned. Wyth Burn and Raise Beck merge into Thirlmere via a single long creek, where the water laps willow and alder roots. This Lakeland mangrove (known as carr) is being recreated by felling conifers to create space for the deciduous trees and by dismantling flood barriers on the rivers; hence, sediment settles on the river bends and clear water flows into Thirlmere.

Turning north from the lakehead, Thirlmere's eastern shore is quite straight and uniform, with the A591's noise sometimes a distraction. That said, there are points of interest.

📷 *The Straining Well and the slopes of Helvellyn*

A wooded and overgrown delta marks Whelpside Gill and Comb Gill's inflow. Landing can be awkward, but hidden ashore are the ruins of the Nag's Head Inn, where Matthew Arnold and John Keats stayed (*"many fleas were in the beds"*). Further inland, across the A591, Wythburn Church stands, sole survivor of Wythburn village.

Wythburn's modest house of prayer

Visiting Wythburn Church is recommended but crossing the A591 has its challenges: consider visiting after paddling, parking at Wythburn car park. The chapel originated in 1554, but the current building, with its quirkily rounded apse, mostly dates from 1740. It featured in William Wordsworth's 1806 poem *The Waggoner* (*"Wythburn's modest house of prayer / as lowly as the lowliest dwelling"*) and Hartley Coleridge's 1854 *Wytheburn Chapel and Hostel*. The latter poem was written from the perspective of a drinker at the Nag's Head; a life-long alcoholic, Hartley had expertise in this area.

The church and car park are the start of a popular route to Helvellyn's summit. Wordsworth, Walter Scott and Humphry Davy once completed this path, together!

You won't fail to notice the Straining Well, an eccentric sandstone *"sham castle"* (W. G. Collingwood) at the water's edge. This was built by Manchester Corporation Waterworks in 1894, complete with turrets and castellations. What you can't see is that the whole thing stands above a 20m-deep pit, daylight-lit by a glass dome roof. Its purpose was to extract and 'strain' water entering a tunnel beneath Dunmail Raise then flowing onwards to Manchester via aqueduct, a 27-hour journey of 163km, descending at a rate of 20.4cm a kilometre. The impressive engineering doesn't alter the fact that the Straining Well was seen as an ugly and triumphal ego

Helvellyn Gill

project; a plaque lists the dignitaries who pushed through Thirlmere's damming. Has it improved with age? You judge. Incidentally, this now Grade II-listed building is redundant: there is a water treatment works at the tunnel's far end.

A 'syphon pipe' floats on the water surface, extending from the Straining Well for 100m or more towards Hause Point on the far shore. You will need to deviate around the pipe, which doesn't seem to serve any current purpose.

Just north is Clark's Loup, a rock where a woman supposedly harassed her husband into killing himself, by jumping off:

"The story goes that his widow only remarked "he had often threatened it, but she never thought the fool had the courage.""

W.G. Collingwood, *The Lake Counties*, 1902

Perhaps the main interest of this eastern shore is that the hinterland of sprawling, boggy fells topping the opposite shore's cliffs is revealed: Bleaberry Fell, High Seat, Armboth Fell and Wythburn Fells. However, don't miss Helvellyn Gill's inflow. A secret tree-covered ravine leads to where the beck's white water tumbles into the lake. It's a wonderful spot, only slightly diminished by the realisation that the gorge is partially engineered: several of Helvellyn's becks were captured from flowing north into St John's Beck and diverted here, by leat stream.

Dale Head Hall was a sixteenth-century fortified tower converted into a mansion by the Leathes family. It survived the dam project and is now a hotel.

Great How is the wooded hill overshadowing the dam. It was climbed in 1881 by Pre-Raphaelite artist Dante Gabriel Rossetti, apparently in an attempt to cure his chloral hydrate addiction. This wasn't a success: he died the following year.

It is perfectly safe to paddle alongside the high, dark wall of Thirlmere's dam. It extends 261m and is 17.7m high, 15m thick at the base and 5.6m thick on top. The foundations were dug, by hand, 17.7m deep to the bedrock below. It is faced with Lancashire millstone grit on the lakeside

The battles for Thirlmere

Thirlmere's fortunes and fate have been at the heart of the issues of conservation and public access in the Lake District and indeed nationally.

During the nineteenth century, Manchester expanded rapidly into 'Cottonopolis', the world's foremost industrial centre. When the city council sought new water supplies for their booming population, the scene was set for a very public showdown. The opposing sides were labelled 'vandals' and 'sentimentalists'.

The Bishop of Manchester provided the 'vandal' perspective on Thirlmere: *"If it had been made by the Almighty expressly to supply the densely populated district of Manchester with pure water, it could not have been more exquisitely designed."*

The Bishop of Carlisle represented the 'sentimentalist' view: *"May Cottonopolis be sent nearer home for its water supply and not interfere with the public pleasure in things on which it has itself never set any value."*

The Thirlmere Defence Association was formed in 1877, supported by a pantheon of Victorian public figures including Matthew Arnold, Thomas Carlyle, Octavia Hill, William Morris, Canon Hardwicke Rawnsley and John Ruskin. The latter declared: *"Manchester should be put to the bottom of Thirlmere"*. Despite their campaigning, the 'Thirlmere scheme' received royal assent in 1879 and Manchester bought Thirlmere's entire 4,453-hectare catchment. Their new dam was filled in stages, only reaching 9,000-million-gallon capacity after the First World War. The lake level had been raised by 16.3m and 324 hectares flooded.

At Thirlmere's Grand Opening in 1894, the first water was piped to Manchester. In a surprising *volte-face*, Rawnsley gave his blessing in gushing speeches: *"Let this river of God flow through the far-off city to cleanse and purify; to help and heal"*. Nevertheless, it's no coincidence that he and Octavia Hill were founders of the National Trust (page 232), the following year.

The conifer plantations appeared from 1907, and public access was restricted by barbed wire and warning signs. In 1985, author Susan Johnson defeated North West Water Authority (NWWA) in court, noting that the 1879 *Thirlmere Act* required it to show *"reasonable regard to the beauty of the scenery in general"*. It was forced to soften the plantation lines and begin the planting of native hardwood trees, which continues today. Public access was only granted to Thirlmere's shores in 1989; this was after NWWA was forced to build a water treatment facility, as a condition of being able to extract water from Windermere.

In 2018, plans for eight zipwires criss-crossing the valley encountered vociferous opposition and were finally withdrawn after the RAF expressed concerns about low-flying jets.

◎ *The Dam and Blencathra*

and Dumfries sandstone on the outer. Atop are the remains of machine gun posts; during the Second World War, the Keswick Home Guard was concerned that the Nazis might invade using flying boats. This was the first masonry gravity dam and is one of two arch dams in England, although the author happily admits to having no clue what either of those things are. At the western end, an arched pier juts into the lake above an overflow outlet; although this is usually dry, give it a wide berth nonetheless.

Raven Crag rears from the western shore. Those who slog to the top of this truly impressive cliff face (you can trek direct from the lake shore, if really keen) are rewarded with a fabulous view along Thirlmere's length, provided you can find a spot among selfie-seeking Instagram-ers, with whom it is a hit.

"… the awful form

Of Raven-crag--black as a storm--

Glimmering through the twilight pale"

William Wordsworth, *The Waggoner*, 1805

Armboth car park is just over a kilometre south.

Thirlmere Lake, by Cornelius Pearson 1856 - note the bridge between the two lakes

Thirlmere as it was

Prior to damming, the valley contained a 5km-long lake, just 1.34km² in expanse, with a narrow waist crossed by the 'Celtic bridge', a ramshackle string of stone piers and three bridges. It went by various names: Laythes Water, Leathes Water, Thirle Water, Thirlmere and Wythburn-Water. There were several hamlets, with three inns; the hamlets are now gone, with only Wythburn Church surviving.

> "Thirlmere ... once was the richest in story and scenery of all the Lakes. The old charm of its shores has quite vanished, and the sites of its old legends are hopelessly altered."

W.G. Collingwood, *The Lake Counties*, 1902

📷 *Ullswater from Glencoyne*

Ullswater

Length (km)	Maximum width (km)	Maximum depth (m)	Surface area (km²)	Catchment area (km²)	Height above sea level (m)
11.7	1.2	63	8.68	146.80	144

Introduction

"… the winding of a majestic River, a little below Placefell a large Slice of calm silver—above this a bright ruffledness, or atomic sportiveness—motes in the sun?—Vortices of flies?—how shall I express the Banks waters all fused Silver …"

Samuel Taylor Coleridge, *Notebooks*, 1799

Coleridge's unfiltered stream of consciousness* splendidly attempted to articulate Ullswater's magnificent scenery and ever-changing moods and weather. Paddlers are privileged to explore and experience this ineffable winding waterway more intimately than most visitors, just so long as they arrive early enough to park.

Could Ullswater be the most beautiful of the English Lakes? The Lake District's second largest lake has plenty of fans, not the least of them William Wordsworth: *"the happiest combination of beauty and grandeur, which any of the Lakes affords"* (***Guide to the Lakes***, 1835). A less obvious admirer was Germany's Kaiser Wilhelm II, who, as the guest of the Earl of Lonsdale, cruised on the lake in 1895, 1902 and 1912.

Ullswater wows through the impressive diversity of stunning scenery along its unique, serpentine course. The two routes described here explore two distinct halves. For paddlers newly arrived from Penrith and the M6, the northern half offers a gradual, almost gentle, introduction to the Lake District, with low, inhabited shores backed by rounded fells. The southern half plunges deep into the National Park; the shores grow wilder and the fells steeper and loftier, as Ullswater narrows towards its dramatic, island-sprinkled lakehead.

A paddle around the whole lake would be around 29km / 18 miles in length. An end-to-end trip between Pooley Bridge and Glenridding, perhaps shuttling utilising the 508 bus service, would be at least 12km / 7.5 miles.

Ullswater's shape – it has corners! – is explained by the geology. The northern tip touches Devonian sandstone, explaining the soft, rounded shape of Dunmallard Hill at the lake outlet. Skiddaw Group rocks underly the gentle slopes found along the lower half and most of the northern shores. The up-valley half and southern shores venture into Borrowdale Volcanics, with steep fells formed from lavas and tuffs. It was once thought that the glacier gouging Ullswater altered course whenever it encountered these resistant volcanic rocks; actually, the ice exploited a SW–NE upfold between the rock types, which had been scrambled out of alignment by shifting fault lines. Complicated!

The lake's three segments sit atop three distinct glacial basins, with the middle being deepest. The islands are *roches moutonnées*, which withstood the glacier's immense pressure.

Ullswater means 'Ulf's lake'. Ulf could have been a Viking settler, or the name could derive from *ulfr*, Old Norse for 'wolf'. Just possibly, it might be honouring Ullr, Norse god of skiing!

* *Lord Byron on Coleridge's prose: "Explaining metaphysics to the nation— / I wish he would explain his Explanation."*

Access

Paddlecraft are allowed on Ullswater, as are rowing and sailing boats. Powered craft are restricted by a 10mph speed limit, imposed since 1983.

The red buoys dotted around the lake mark shallow rocks or reefs, which should not pose a problem for paddlecraft.

The bay to the east of Goldrill Beck's inflow, at the lake's southern extremity, is designated as a wildlife area, which paddlers are asked to avoid. Also, don't land on Norfolk Island from 1st March to 1st July, because of nesting wildfowl.

Keep clear of the Ullswater steamers and their landing piers and be mindful that they are less manoeuvrable than you.

Ullswater is owned by the National Park, the National Trust, and the Dalemain Estates.

Wildlife and environment

In 1961, Manchester Corporation Waterworks proposed raising the level by 0.9m. After this dam scheme was struck down by the House of Lords, the Corporation re-submitted plans and since 1967, water has been extracted and piped underground to supplement the reservoir at Haweswater, without altering the lake's level. The pumping station, now operated by United Utilities, is at Park Foot Holiday Park, largely hidden underground.

📷 *Ullswater campsites*

Fish in the lake include char, perch and trout. The stand-out species is the schelly, the 'freshwater herring'. This endangered whitefish is a relic of the Ice Ages, only surviving here and in nearby Haweswater, Brothers Water and Red Tarn.

Ullswater's shores, reedbeds and islands are host to an impressive array of birdlife, including Canada geese, coots, cormorants, greylag geese, herons, little grebes, moorhens, mute swans, oystercatchers, whooper swans and a wide range of duck species. In winter, barnacle geese and oystercatchers visit, alongside roosting gulls.

The shores are lined with birch, hazel and native oak. Red deer come to the water's edge in winter, especially below Place Fell. They are part of the 300-year-old Martindale Deer Forest herd.

Launch points

Gowbarrow Park to Gowbarrow Bay lay-bys NY 422 206 / snow.maps.storeroom / CA10 2NF – there are ten lakeside lay-bys between Aira Force car park and Gowbarrow Bay, where the A592 departs the lake shore. The biggest are the seventh and eighth encountered coming from Glenridding (third and fourth from Pooley Bridge), run by Gowbarrow Hall Farm and charging a donation to the local primary school. Access from the sixth lay-by is barred by a lakeside wall. The last lay-by does not give access. All fill up rapidly in summer.

Pooley Bridge (Dunmallard car park) NY 470 245 / crispier.backfired.developed / CA10 2NP – a National Park car park beside the River Eamont, directly downstream of Pooley Bridge's bridge. Paddle 300m upstream to the lake, avoiding shallow areas where fish may spawn. This may be difficult if the river level is high, or impractical if the level is very low. In theory, you are supposed to contact the Dalemain Estates (01768 486450) before launching on to 'their' river.

Pooley Bridge (Eusemere car park) NY 470 244 / bland.shapes.gambles / CA10 2NE – a National Park car park located across the bridge from Dunmallard car park. Follow the footpath track 290m from the car park, passing Lakeland Boat Hire and a broken stone jetty, to a beach.

Park Foot Holiday Park NY 467 238 / galleries.bubble.rebounded / CA10 2NA – a large lakeside campsite that offers parking and launching, from a day to a year. Book online beforehand.

Waterside House Campsite NY 463 232 / steady.washing.heavy / CA10 2NA – a lakeside campsite offering day parking and launching. Book online beforehand or pay on arrival via QR code.

Howtown Wyke NY 443 198 / jeep.imprinted.irrigate / CA10 2ND – this roadside slipway is the only public launch point along Ullswater's southern shore. There is no parking, so it can only be used for rapid drop-offs. The nearest parking is in Pooley Bridge, or 1.25km further along the lane, at the top of the pass into Martindale (a demanding drive). The lakeside lay-bys between Pooley Bridge and Howtown Wyke are all reserved for permit-holders only.

Side Farm Campsite NY 395 168 / abandons.fairly.submit / CA11 0NL – a lakeside campsite offering day parking and launching. Call ahead to check availability, 017684 82337.

Glenridding NY 389 168 / jotting.tradition.supreme / CA11 0US – launch from the wide beach south of the Ullswater Steamer pier. Park at Ullswater Steamers car park beside the pier, or Jenkins Field Community car park (summer only), further back along the access lane.

Glenridding Sailing Centre NY 389 170 / donor.venturing.alongside / CA11 0PE – a lakeside outdoor activity centre that offers parking and launching, from a day to a month.

Stybarrow Crag lay-bys NY 387 178 / beats.community.future / CA11 0NG – six lay-bys give access to the lakeside between Glenridding and Glencoyne Bridge car park, the last being the least convenient. The first is best, just past where the A592 passes below Stybarrow Crag. All fill up rapidly in summer.

Glencoyne Bridge car park NY 386 188 / test.packet.anchorman / CA11 0NQ – a National Trust car park directly across the A592 from a beach.

Glencoyne Park lay-bys NY 389 191 / rainfall.sank.cosmic / CA11 0JS – there are two lay-bys between Glencoyne Bridge and Aira Force car parks; the first encountered is tiny, so the second one is best. They fill up rapidly in summer.

Aira Force and Gowbarrow Park car park NY 399 197 / reefs.carpets.ranches / CA11 0JS – a large National Trust car park. From the car park entrance, follow the path alongside the A592 past the café, cross the road and pass through a gate to a path leading to a beach beside the steamer jetty, 300m in total.

📷 *Howtown Wyke*

Ullswater – northern

Trip Distance	14.3km / 8.9 miles
Start / Finish	Gowbarrow Park to Gowbarrow Bay lay-bys NY 422 206 / snow.maps.storeroom / CA10 2NF

Description

"Majestic in its calmness, clear & smooth as a blew mirror with winding shores & low points of land cover'd with green inclosures, white farm-houses looking out among the trees, & cattle feeding. the water is almost everywhere border'd with cultivated lands gently sloping upwards till they reach the feet of the mountains."

Thomas Gray, *Journal of A Visit to the Lake District*, 1775

The two Gowbarrow Hall Farm lay-bys access the lake shore below Swinburn's Park. Here, as with most of Ullswater's northern half, the beaches, shores and slopes behind are a mix of glacial deposits: boulders, clays and gravels, dumped as moraines by retreating ice. Eleven millennia later, this bequeaths us a lush landscape of green pastures and parkland, descending, rarely steeply, to the wooded water's edge. Bays and headlands have eroded into smoothly rounded forms.

Wherever you manage to launch (competition for Ullswater parking is savage), the first landmark is Gowbarrow Bay and Skelly Neb. Skelly Neb (Old English *Neb*: headland) is named for the schelly and overlooks 'The Narrows', a 400m-wide constriction which was, historically, netted across to catch them. The cream-coloured mansion perched behind the bay is Hallsteads, better known as Outward Bound Ullswater. It was built in 1813 for Leeds mill owner John Marshall,

Dunmallard Hill

who later bought up much of Patterdale and Glenridding (his brother Henry acquired Derwent Water's Derwent Isle).

The paddle towards Pooley Bridge passes a succession of houses, farms and hotels, fronted by fields extending to the lake shore, with a boathouse usually present. Scoping out the boathouses is a pastime in itself; they are engagingly diverse, ranging from ramshackle rustic relics, through ramparted redoubts, to richly refurbished rentals. For a vicarious thrill, search up the price of a sleepover at Far Boathouse, in Oldchurch Bay. Further affluence-envy is offered by Leeming House Hotel, formerly a Georgian mansion. You almost certainly can't afford to stay; perhaps compromise by booking 'champagne afternoon tea'.

The buoys offshore from Beauthorn mark out Peely Slapehold, a cluster of shallow rocks. Pencilmill Beck trickles in at Castlehows Point, with another to-die-for boathouse. Rounding the point, you are confronted by a busy scene: the numerous jetties of Fairfield Marine and Ullswater Marine, adjacent private marinas. The sprawling country house hotel which follows is Another Place, The Lake and then a boathouse cluster marks Ramps Beck's inflow, named for wild garlic (ramsons).

The A592 comes alongside for the final approach to the lakefoot, as do two successive wooded hills: Salmond's Plantation and rounded Dunmallard Hill. Between the two, the Duke of Portland boathouse is Ullswater's most photographed scene. At the more modest end of the boathouse spectrum, this unadorned eighteenth-century building belonged to the 3rd Duke, who was Prime Minister twice (24 years apart). After disputes with the Earl of Lowther, the Duke was forced to sell the boathouse (and surrounding estates) to cover his legal bills.

Dunmallard Hill is topped by an Iron Age hillfort. Its name is corrupted from the Gaelic *dun mallach*: 'fort of curses'. Off-putting! Trees cover the summit, but many have made the mild ascent.

Ullswater Steamers' pier guards the approach to the River Eamont. Their most prestigious vessels are the M.Y. *Raven* (1889) and M.Y. *Lady of the Lake* (1877), both built on the Clyde and transported to the lake in sections, by rail. The latter may be the world's oldest working passenger

Pooley Bridge

ferry. It served as Ullswater's mail boat and has sunk more than once, something the website selling tickets oddly fails to mention. These steamers are now diesel-powered. The viewing platform beside the Pier House is a disused United Utilities pumping station. A large plaque, by Cumbrian lettercarver Pip Hall, commemorates Lord Birkett (page 91).

Ullswater is confined at the lake outlet between sandstone Dunmallard Hill and limestone Heughscar Hill. The eastern bank of the River Eamont (Old English *ea-gemot*: meeting of streams) is low-lying clay, with no moraine dam, and geologists are unsure whether a buried bedrock reef hems the lake in.

Give the outflow to the River Eamont a wide berth in high flows, because of the risk of being pulled into more dangerous moving water. Pooley Bridge's bridge is visible 300m downstream. This was opened in 2020, the UK's first of stainless steel. The previous bridge survived from 1764 until December 2015, when Storm Desmond's astonishing floods destroyed it; the river level exiting Ullswater peaked at 3.76m.

Pooley Bridge

The village located at Ullswater's foot was originally Pool How, from the Old English *pollr*: pool and Old Norse *haughr*: hill. In 1216, King John granted the village a charter to hold a fish market. The Fish Monument outside the Crown Hotel was erected in 2000 to commemorate this, recalling an ancient market cross removed in 1859, to make way for traffic. The village only acquired a bridge, built across a fish trap, in the sixteenth century.

Pooley Bridge is usually overrun in summer, but it has plenty of eateries and a notably fine bookshop.

Boathouse in Sharrow Bay

To visit the village, cross the river and land on the beach south of Lakeland Boat Hire's slipways and a long, broken, stone jetty. Check out James Reynolds's 2017 Clarkson Memorial, a modest plaque set into a wall end. Thomas Clarkson oversaw the 1795 construction of Eusemere House, the mansion behind, then lived there for ten years.

Am I not a man and a brother?

The Clarkson Memorial depicts a kneeling, chained, black man and the words, '*AM I NOT A MAN AND A BROTHER?*'. Henry Webber designed this motif in 1787, for potter Josiah Wedgwood. It became the seal of the Society for the Abolition of the Slave Trade, founded by Thomas Clarkson. Clarkson's wife Catherine became close friends with Dorothy Wordsworth. Upon the abolition of the Slave Trade in 1807, William Wordsworth celebrated Clarkson's contribution with a sonnet: *"Clarkson! it was an obstinate Hill to climb …"*

Ullswater's southern shore begins much like the northern shore you've just negotiated, but the fells gradually encroach and the scenery builds to something of a wild crescendo.

Lakeside campsites crowd the shores. At Gale Bay, water is discreetly extracted into the Tarn Moor tunnel, which leads to Heltondale, from where an aqueduct supplies Manchester. Within a week of Lord Birkett's 1962 victory and death (page 91), a Mancunian councillor declared, *"They can stop gloating down at Ullswater, for we need that water and intend to get it"*. The city renewed its assault, utilising a Statutory Order. Its plans were approved at a Public Inquiry, albeit with no Pooley Bridge dam, no raising of the lake level, and minimal visual impact.

Lord Birkett memorial plaque, Pooley Bridge

Hodgson Hill was the site of an enclosed medieval farmstead, preserved and stabilised by lakeside fencing and planting; archaeologists discovered fourteenth-century pottery and waste pits. Far more ancient archaeology looks down from Askham Fell; High Street Roman road bypasses Ullswater along its summit ridge, passing through over forty Bronze Age burials and two stone circles.

The tracks sloping into the water at Waterside House Campsite are for hauling Ullswater's steamers ashore; they undergo maintenance here. Thwaitehill Bay is usually crammed with moored sailing boats, being alongside Ullswater Yacht Club's jetty and slipway. The club operates a fleet of international 10 square metre sailing canoes; no paddling is involved: these 'canoes' are slim, lightweight affairs upon which the sailor perches on a sliding plank.

Wooded Thwaitehill Neb marks a transition; the shores become less frequented and lake traffic noticeably quieter. The fells encroach closer, as the geology transitions to craggy Borrowdale Volcanics. Early tourists on the lake were entertained by cannons fired from this headland:

"The report is reverberated from rock to rock, promontory, cavern, and hill, with every variety of sound; now dying away upon the ear, and again returning like peals of thunder ..."

Thomas West, *A Guide to the Lakes*, 1778

When opened in 1948, the Sharrow Bay Hotel, looming alongside the lake shore, was the first modern 'country house' hotel. More pertinently, sticky toffee pudding was invented here. Chef Francis Coulson's 1970s creation was first billed as, *'icky sticky toffee pudding'*. There should be a blue plaque, or something. The hotel reopened in 2025 after refurbishment.

When Swarthbeck Gill enters, trace its course up Swarth Fell, to Bonscale Tower at the top. Actually, two cairn 'towers' look down upon the lake.

Howtown Wyke is a deep embayment, wonderfully hemmed in by enticing hills; the public slipway alongside Ullswater Steamers' pier is a great stopping off point for a hillwalking interlude.

Howtown consists of simply an Outward Bound centre and the Howtown Hotel, not so much of a 'town'. Divers search here for the undiscovered wreck of the *Enterprise*, Ullswater's original steamer, which sank in 1859. There are also rumours of three mini-submarines, somewhere down there: these were tested on Ullswater during the Second World War.

The distinctive rounded mini-mountain overshadowing Ullswater's central dogleg / zigzag is Hallin Fell; the enormous cairn tower at its summit (a fabulous viewpoint for the lake) is visible from afar. Hallin Fell's flanks plunge to the water's edge, literally so at Geordie's Crag and Kailpot Crag. The latter is named for a pothole scoured at its base and is a popular jumping spot for the brave / foolish; if you really must, be sure to clear the rocks below! The memorial plaque set into this four-metre crag commemorates Lord Birkett.

Ullswater's saviour

On 8th February 1962, Lord Birkett made a speech to the House of Lords, opposing a bill to convert Ullswater into a reservoir. He referenced Haweswater and Thirlmere, *"lovely lakes which have been murdered"*, before a rousing conclusion:

> *"Thus far and no farther. Go away. Come again another day, if you will. But … you have no right whatever to invade the sanctity of a National Park."*

Birkett's speech, praised by the Leader of the House as *"deeply felt and highly eloquent"*, carried the day: the Lords voted 70 to 36 against the bill, and Ullswater was saved. Birkett, however, collapsed following his speech and died two days later.

Birkett, a native of Ulverston (south of Coniston Water), had a distinguished career, including representing Britain in the Nuremberg War Trials. His final achievement was honoured by the naming of Birkett Fell, above Glencoyne. Two lakeside plaques commemorate Birkett: at Kailpot Crag (*'HE LOVED ULLSWATER. HE STROVE TO MAINTAIN ITS BEAUTY FOR ALL TO ENJOY'*) and beside the Pooley Bridge steamer pier (*'SI MONUMENTUM REQUIRIS CIRCUMSPICE**'). In early July, 230 yachts race from Ullswater Yacht Club, around Norfolk Island, for the Lord Birkett Memorial Trophy.

* *'If you seek his monument, look around you': from Christopher Wren's tomb in St Paul's Cathedral.*

Beautiful, untamed Hallinhag Wood clings to Hallin Fell's scraggy north-west flank. The native broadleaf trees, home to woodpeckers and flycatchers, are protected as an SSSI and part of the Ullswater Oakwoods Special Area of Conservation. Kailpot Bay and Tablerock Bay are potential rocky landings; however, the Access Land ends *before* the woods at Kailpot Crag. Consider a lunch stop here, maybe following the footpath into the woods to search out the Kathleen Raine Poetry Stones. These three rocks, near Sandwick Bay, are inscribed by Pip Hall with poems by Raine, a resident of Martindale through the 1940s:

◉ Hallin Fell

"… Deserted by the silver lake
Lies the wide world, overturned.
Cities rise where mountains fell,
The furnace where the phoenix burned.
The lake is in my dream …"

Kathleen Raine, *Night in Martindale*, 1943

Hallinhag Wood ends at Sandwick Bay. Sandwick Beck's arcuate delta marks the point at which, weather allowing, you need to paddle across to your start point.

📷 *Ullswater southern end from Gowbarrow*

Ullswater – southern

Trip Distance	12.8km / 8 miles
Start / Finish	Glencoyne Bridge car park – NY 386 188 / test.packet.anchorman / CA11 0NQ

Description

The National Trust's popular Glencoyne Bridge car park sits atop Glencoyne Beck's broad arcuate delta. Those arriving early will encounter Andy Butcher, who at the time of writing has been feeding the geese and swans from his paddleboard, daily, for five years. The shore here is similar to that of Ullswater's northern half: beaches of glacial clays and boulders, backed by verdant estate parkland. One mystery is the straight rows of shoreline boulders; these alignments may have been made by people, but geologists suspect that sheet ice shoved them up the beach. Unlike Ullswater's northern half, the shoreline clays overlay Borrowdale Volcanics: craggy bedrock which reveals itself behind as a backdrop of lofty summits, including Helvellyn:

> *"These hills having their summits sharp and pointed resemble more the Alpine forms than any which are to be found in this country."*
>
> William Cookson, *Views of the Lakes*, 1789

Ullswater's deepest point is located hereabouts, gouged by a glacier plunging from Glencoyne Beck's hanging valley and exerting downward pressure on the main river of ice.

📷 *Wild daffodils, Glencoyne Bay*

A mere 600m from the car park, a barely discernible headland has been dubbed 'Wordsworth Point'; hereabouts within Glencoyne Bay, the famous siblings were inspired …

The Wordsworths' daffodils

I wandered lonely as a cloud

That floats on high o'er vales and hills,

When all at once I saw a crowd,

A host, of golden daffodils;

Beside the lake, beneath the trees,

Fluttering and dancing in the breeze.

William Wordsworth, *I Wandered Lonely as a Cloud*, 1804

One of the most famous and beloved poems in the English language, often simply titled *Daffodils*, was inspired by a windy lakeshore walk on 15th April 1802. William and Dorothy were walking home to Grasmere, from a visit to the Clarksons at Eusemere House. Dorothy recorded:

"… *we saw a few daffodils close to the waterside. We fancied that the lake had floated the seeds ashore and that the little colony had sprung up. But as we went along there were more and yet more … seemed as if they verily danced with the wind, that blew them over the lake*".

Grasmere Journals, 1800–1803

When William wrote his poem, he noted, "*The two best lines in it are by Mary*" (his wife), but he failed to acknowledge his sister's obvious influence.

> The daffodils which enchanted the Wordsworths were not the bright garden varieties commonly seen nowadays but *narcissus pseudonarcissus*, the wild daffodil. This now-rare flower is recognisable by its two-tone look; pale petals surround the bright central 'trumpet'.

Aira Point (Old Norse *eyrr*: gravel spit), is another arcuate delta, marked by Ullswater Steamers' pier, with a picnic spot alongside. Aira Force car park and café are a short walk away, across the A592. The Dorothy Gate, outside the café, is worth a quick look: this reconstructed traditional gate has five ash poles, which slide out horizontally to open it. Lakeland woodworker James Mitchell has carved the poles with quotations from Dorothy Wordsworth's *Grasmere Journals*.

Aira Force

A popular tourist attraction and possibly Lakeland's finest waterfall, Aira Force is located a kilometre's walk up Aira Beck.

> *"… a considerable stream of water falls near 40 yards perpendicular, with a most tremendous noise, over a rough craggy rock; and by the violence of its fall raises a vapour or mist that reflects the suns rays into the most vivid prismatic colours".*

James Clarke, *A Survey of the Lakes*, 1787

The stone bridges above and below the chasm commemorate Sir Cecil Spring-Rice, who grew up alongside Ullswater. As Ambassador to the United States, Spring-Rice engineered America's entry into the First World War. He also composed the hymn *I Vow to Thee My Country*.

The tree-covered fellside past Aira Point is Gowbarrow Park. Borrowdale Volcanics (igneous andesite) descend from Hind Crag and Yew Crag to the shore. Red deer still visit this former hunting park, which the National Trust acquired (including Aira Force) in 1906, to ward off inevitable shoreline villa development.

Lyulph's Tower is less than a hundred metres from the lake, but often obscured by trees; it is most easily seen from the far shore. This sprawling white pseudo-castle, built in 1780, was a hunting lodge for the Duke of Norfolk. Its garish Gothic styling was mocked by Eliza Lynn Linton as *"a mere modern make-believe"* (*The Lake Country*, 1864). It did, however, inspire Walter Scott's *The Bridal of Triermain*, 1813, and Wordsworth's *The Somnabulist*, 1833, which relates why the tower is (possibly) haunted by a sleep-walking, shrieking, noblewoman.

When the shores become less steep following Gowbarrow Park, this is the signal for the 500m crossing to the southern shore, weather and conditions allowing. Aim for the valley and arcuate delta of Sandwick Beck, joining Ullswater between Hallin Fell and Place Fell.

You're in for a treat! Ullswater's shores to the lakehead at Patterdale are roadless. The sprawling mass of 657m Place Fell reigns over this untamed cragscape, which tumbles down to the lake, beneath a covering of tangled birch. Red deer descend to drink among shoreline scree, while buzzards hunt overhead. Wainwright described this wild tract as, *"The most beautiful and rewarding*

◉ *Silver Bay*

walk in Lakeland." Exploring by paddlecraft is (author's humble opinion) even finer than walking it; I'll bet the house that had curmudgeonly Wainwright discovered paddlesport, his Lakeland guidebooks would have turned out very differently indeed.

Paddling up-valley from Sandwick, the first landmark is Scalehow Force, glimpsed cascading off Place Fell's northern flank, above Scalehow Wood. This waterfall is partially engineered, as the Marshalls of Hallsteads had it redirected, using dynamite, so that it was visible from their dining table!

Samuel Taylor Coleridge described a transcendental experience (everything he did seems to have been one) when he visited Scalehow Wood with Wordsworth on a 1799 winter's morning:

> *"Went down the lake by the opposite shore – the hoar-frost on the ground, the lake calm & would have been mirrorlike but that it had been breathed on by the mist – & that shapely white Cloud, the Day-moon, hung over the snowy mountain opposite to us ... What a scene!"*

Samuel Taylor Coleridge, *Notebooks*, 1799

Birk Fell's steep screes plunge to the lake beneath gnarled birch and the National Park's largest area of juniper scrub: spiky and horrible to pass through, *"never get out of the boat"*.

Silver Bay is a wonderfully remote beach, a great rest spot. Legend has it that Silver Point's name comes from monks who, confronted by robbers, flung their coins into the lake rather than surrender them. Rounding the point, consider a side-tour, offshore, to Norfolk Island. Ullswater's largest island, barely 40m across, was named after the Duke of Norfolk, but is also known as House Holm. This 6m-high lump of ice-scoured volcanic andesite resisted the glacier's erosive forces, clinging on between the upper two of Ullswater's three basins. A collection of wind-stunted trees adorns it: ash, beech, holly, oak and willow. Don't land from March to June, when cormorants, greylag geese, oystercatchers and red-breasted mergansers variously nest. In the seventeenth century, John Mounsey, the 'King of Patterdale', was shipwrecked here during a gale for two days.

📷 *Goldrill Beck*

Lingy Holm (Old Norse *lyng holmr*: heather island) is the next 'island' encountered, no more than two inshore rocks clung to by heather, willow scrub and a rowan.

The Devil's Chimney is a fissure in a cliff plunging sheer into the lake, a popular cliff-jump. The name comes from vapour venting through the cleft as it rises from the lake on cold mornings; the hyper-imaginative perceived this as emerging from the depths of Hell.

Purse Point is a lovely wooded headland, enclosing a secretive inlet. It points towards Wall Holm, where two Corsican pines rear above a glacially striated and rounded *roche moutonnée*. Dorothy Wordsworth described an 1805 boating trip in Blowick Bay in her Grasmere Journal: *"Place Fell steady and bold as a lion; the whole lake driving onwards like a great river, waves dancing around the small islands"*. From 1805 to 1820, Blowick House was home to artist John Glover. Glover, unkindly noted for his club feet and obesity, is now little known in the UK but is considered the father of Australian landscape painting, having emigrated to Van Diemen's Land (Tasmania) in 1830.

Opposite the village of Glenridding, Ullswater pinchpoints to just 250m, with tiny, metre-high Cherry Holm, offshore of a pair of rocks, offering a halfway stepping stone.

Cross direct from Side Farm Campsite to Goldrill Beck, avoiding the south-eastern bay's wetland wildlife area. Alder carr islets guard the beck's inflow; discreetly exploring upriver towards Patterdale is a magical experience, not unlike passing through the back of the wardrobe.

St Patrick's Church is glimpsed from the south-western bay. The tower marks the location of Patterdale, so-named as it was, by legend*, visited by the Irish saint. Patterdale's modern claim to fame is that the village store (closed 2021) was, in 1955, the first place to stock Alfred Wainwright's newfangled guidebooks. The A592 comes alongside at the bay's western edge, and sticks close to Ullswater for the rest of this trip. Some pleasant boathouses are followed by St Patrick's Boat Landing, worth visiting for the café. Just across the road is Patterdale's War Memorial and also St Patrick's Well, restored. Here, legend** has it, the saint baptised locals.

◉ *Donald Campbell memorial and Glenridding Pier*

Folk converge on Glenridding, en masse, to ascend Helvellyn. You won't get an unobstructed view of the fell and its spectacular ridges from the water, as it is hidden five kilometres up-valley. Glenridding is fronted by parkland and hotel grounds atop Glenridding Beck's delta. This is an arcuate 'fan' delta; however, it has a tacked-on 'bird's foot', jutting into the lake. This extension (now the site of Glenridding Sailing Centre) was formed by silt from Greenside Mine, up-valley, where lead ore and silver were dug out until 1962. The bird's foot extended 1.4m annually from 1859, and it was then hugely augmented by the Keppel Cove Disaster.

* *So, probably not.*

** *Again, probably never happened.*

Glenridding floods

On 29th October 1927, the moraine dam containing Keppel Cove's cirque tarn, modified to supply Greenside Mine, failed. Glenridding was devastated by the ensuing flood … and again in 1931, when a new concrete dam also breached. Incredibly, there were no deaths on either occasion. Glenridding was also hit by severe flooding on three successive occasions through December 2015.

Beside Ullswater Steamers' Glenridding Pier, check out the slate Donald Campbell Memorial, unveiled in 1997 by his daughter Gina. In 1955 on Ullswater, he achieved a water speed record of 202.32 mph, in his newly launched *Bluebird K7*. Campbell was later to lose his life on Coniston Water (page 164).

The paddle back to Glencoyne Bridge passes beneath the crags of 442m Glenridding Dodd: a superb viewpoint of Ullswater, should you head up there. The prominent lakeside cliff is Stybarrow

Ullswater – southern

Glencoyne Bay

Crag, also known as 'Hanging Rock'. Before the A592 was blasted around its base in the 1920s, this was quite the pivotal spot. John Mounsey made a stand here in 1648, against Scottish raiders en route to support King Charles I at Preston. Mounsey and his descendants subsequently styled themselves, 'King of Patterdale'. Teenage William Wordsworth stole a rowboat from Patterdale one moonlit night, and scared himself by unexpectedly encountering the crag. This formative experience was described in his autobiographical *The Prelude*:

"… *a huge cliff*

As if with voluntary power instinct

Uprear'd its head. I struck and struck again,

And, still growing in stature, the huge Cliff

Rose up between me and the stars …"

Finally, pre-A592, Stybarrow Crag marked the limit of road access from the Penrith direction. Glenridding was served by road from Ambleside, over the 455m Kirkstone Pass, and mail arrived by steamer. Given that Ullswater was also the Cumberland–Westmorland boundary until 1974, it must have all been rather vexing.

The craggy shores around Mossdale Bay and a boathouse (splendidly hidden from the road) lead you to Glencoyne Beck's shallow outflow; the car park is on the far side.

Other lakes

Brothers Water

"I was delighted with what I saw. The water under the boughs of the bare old trees, the simplicity of the mountains, and the exquisite beauty of the path."

Dorothy Wordsworth, *Grasmere Journals*, 1800–1803

Brothers Water is a small, attractive lake, alongside the A592, up-valley from Ullswater. It is surrounded by steep fells, with some of Lakeland's oldest oak woodlands covering the scree descending to the western shore. The name references two brothers who fell through the ice and drowned, in 1785.

Paddling is not allowed, supposedly because the lake is an SSSI; however, pretty much all of the lakes are SSSIs, in whole or part. The author is aware of various paddlers who have, discreetly, either launched into Brothers Water or passed through from Kirkstone Beck, as part of expedition journeys continuing down-valley into Ullswater and beyond. Anyone doing this would need to be extremely sensitive to their surrounds, especially the southern shore's wetlands of carr, reeds and lily pads.

Haweswater

"We've gone on holiday by mistake."

Withnail and I, 1987 (filmed at Haweswater)

Haweswater is the highest of the lakes, and the largest where paddling is not permitted. It's a reservoir owned by United Utilities, dammed between 1929 and 1941 to supply water to Manchester. Like Thirlmere, Mardale previously had two small lakes (High Water and Low Water) joined by a narrowing, The Straits. The water level was raised by over thirty metres, drowning the villages of Measand and Mardale Green and extending the lake almost three kilometres up-valley. The southern end is now directly overshadowed by spectacular cliffs and corries, with a ridge descending from the 828m summit of High Street down into the water at The Rigg, a wooded promontory overlooking Wood Howe island. Poet Norman Nicholson: *"what we see is not a dale with a lake in it, but a group of fells plunged up to the waist in cold water."* Haweswater is an RSPB reserve, until 2015 the home of England's last golden eagle.

The apparent reason for paddlers being denied access is to protect drinking water. It has to be hoped that eventually, as happened at Thirlmere, United Utilities will install a filtering system and lift the ban.

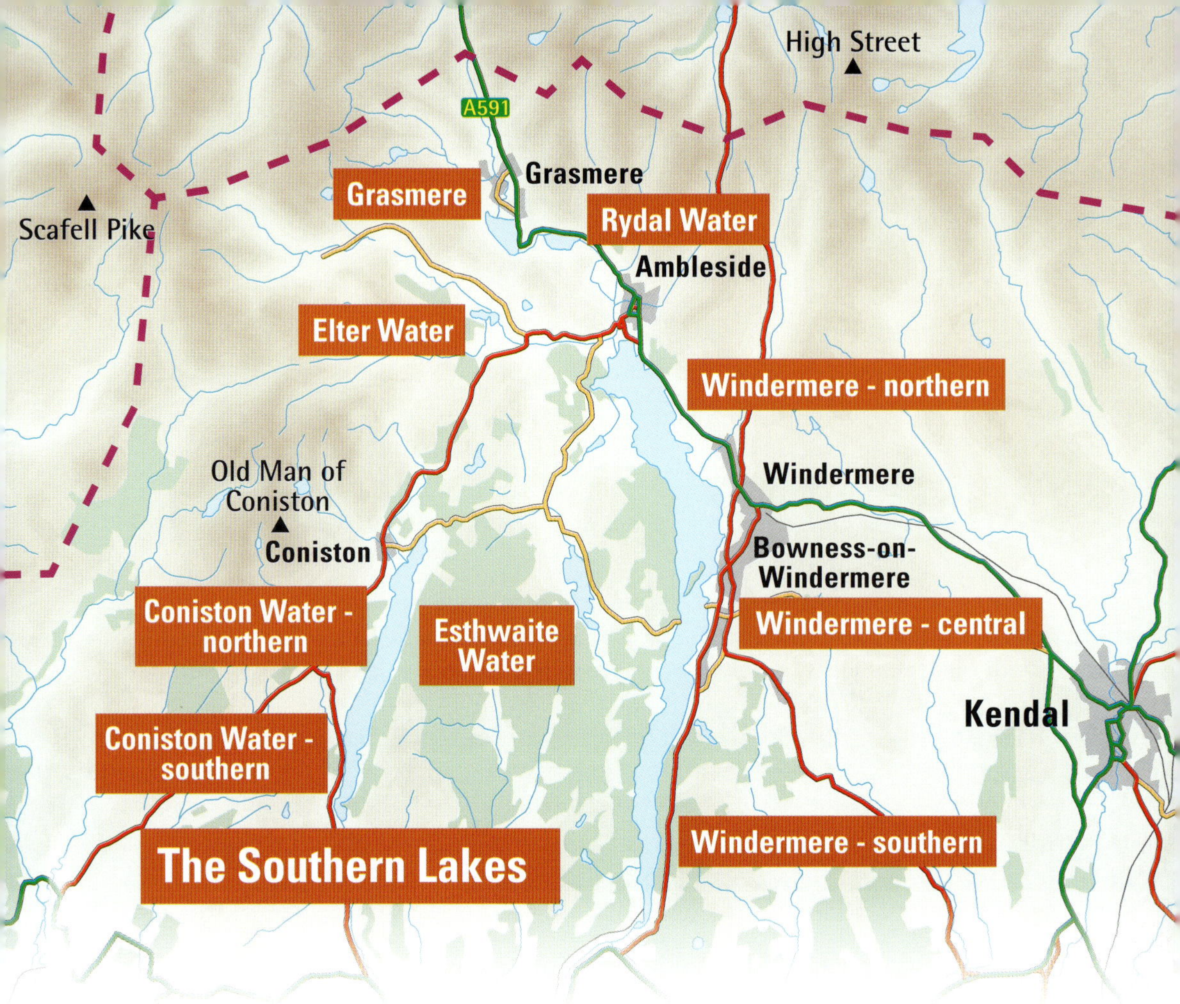

The Southern Lakes

▲ High Street

▲ Scafell Pike

Grasmere

Grasmere

Rydal Water

Ambleside

Elter Water

Windermere - northern

Old Man of Coniston ▲

Coniston

Windermere

Bowness-on-Windermere

Coniston Water - northern

Esthwaite Water

Windermere - central

Kendal

Coniston Water - southern

Windermere - southern

Key to symbols used

Symbol	Meaning	Symbol	Meaning
⚓	Marina		Rock/reef
	Boathouse		Iron Age hillfort
▲	Sailing club	✱■✚	Historical features
24 ▲	Campsite	✚	Named church
	Caravan park	●	Railway stations
	Motorhomes only	■✚	Monument/place of tourist interest
	Bunkhouse, camping barn or bothy		Area with restrictions
	Youth hostel		Restricted wildlife area
	Holiday park		Vulnerable lake shore
P	Car park	△	Start/finish launch point
	Café or pub	○	Alternative launch point

The Southern Lakes

River Crake, Coniston Water

Silver Holme - reading 'Swallows and Amazons'!

📷 *Storrs Temple*

Windermere

Length (km)	Maximum width (km)	Maximum depth (m)	Surface area (km²)	Catchment area (km²)	Height above sea level (m)
16.8	1.5	64	14.36	248.77	37

Introduction

"I overlooked the bed of Windermere,
Like a vast river, stretching in the sun.
With exultation, at my feet I saw
Lake, islands, promontories, gleaming bays,
A universe of Nature's fairest forms
Proudly revealed with instantaneous burst,
Magnificent, and beautiful, and gay."
William Wordsworth, *The Prelude*, 1850

Windermere, England's longest and largest lake! Along its length, there is a wonderful array of attractive landscapes, with something for every paddler; exploration of Windermere's nabs (Old English: promontories), wykes and holmes (Old Norse: creeks and islands) reveals plenty of engaging geology, nature and history.

📷 *Fell Foot Country Park*

There is a clear distinction between Windermere's two shores. The western shore is largely undeveloped and abuts the forests of Furness, which extend all the way to Coniston Water. The eastern shores are much more developed; the eighteenth- and nineteenth-century tourist boom created the resorts of Ambleside and Bowness-on-Windermere. Wealthy industrialists bought up the land around to build lavish villa-mansions and create a kind of rural Arcadia, away from their factories and workers; many of these are now hotels.

The route outlined around the southern half (page 111) is the quietest option here, including the eastern shore's least developed parts, where Windermere's steepest shores ascend to Gummer's How. In these lower reaches, Windermere occupies a narrow and almost-straight glacial basin, 42m deep.

Despite the central route (page 119) being adjacent to Bowness, it's perfectly possible to seek out quiet space. This route explores the archipelago of islands which almost sever Windermere into two separate lakes. Among them is Belle Isle, the Lake District's biggest island. The islands are low-lying *roches moutonnées*, where Windermere's glacier extended across resistant bedrock. Among the islands, the water is around ten metres deep.

The route around the northern half (page 127) is the most varied, with castles and mansions, as well as hidden bays and wooded crags, backed by a fabulous fell backdrop. This is Windermere's deeper (64m) and wider end, containing 60% of its 314 million cubic metres volume; the main glaciers converging from the Rothay and Brathay valleys at the lakehead were boosted by side-valley glaciers to scour a basin extending far below sea level.

A paddle around the entire lake would be at least 37km / 23 miles in length. An appealing option is the end-to-end trip between Waterhead and Fell Foot, shuttling back to the start utilising the X6 and 555 or 599 buses, changing at Bowness or Windermere. This would be a paddle of at least 17km / 10.5 miles.

Windermere is thought to mean 'Vinander / Winander's Lake', referring to a Viking incomer.

Tern at Waterhead

Access

Paddlecraft are allowed on Windermere, as are rowing and sailing boats.

Most of the lakeshore is privately owned. Belle Isle is also privately owned and landing is not permitted.

Paddlers are asked to 'please avoid' a number of 'wildlife areas': on the eastern shore, from south of White Cross Bay past Trout Beck, Rayrigg Wyke, and the southern tip of the lake at Fell Foot; on the western shore, Silverholme to past Rawlinson Nab, Eply Point to Watbarrow Point, Bee Holme and Pull Wyke. Most of these areas are private land, in any case. Additionally, powered craft are not permitted in Pull Wyke bay from March to July.

Windermere has exponentially more traffic than any of the other lakes: around 4,000 powered craft are registered for use. These vessels come in all shapes and sizes: the huge Windermere 'steamers' carrying tourists, the Windermere ferry connecting Bowness and Hawkshead, yachts from various sailing clubs, privately-owned cruisers, and hired powerboats. Paddleboarders will need to be confident of handling the criss-crossing wakes of these craft. Most of this traffic is focused around Windermere's central part, which can become something of a zoo; however, boat numbers dip off dramatically outside summer, and the author has enjoyed winter trips during which he has paddled for hours without encountering another craft.

There are a dizzying array of rules and by-laws for leisure craft. Those concerning paddlers are:

- Carry a whistle at all times, for use in fog or restricted visibility.
- Sunset to sunrise, carry a torch, or similar, with a white light. Keep it to hand, ready to be, *'exhibited in sufficient time to prevent collision'*.
- Approaching paddlers, *'the vessel which is not under oars shall keep out of the way of the other'*. Don't count on it.
- Pass astern of the Windermere ferry, no closer than two ferry lengths (60m). Don't go within 90m of the ferry landings when the ferry is present.

Lake Wardens patrol the lake and operate a rescue service: try not to require this! Their office (01539 442753) is alongside the Ferry Nab launch point.

Powered craft are restricted by a 10-knot speed limit, reduced to 6 knots in the northern part past Green Tuft Island and Holme Crag, in White Cross Bay, in the central part between Rough Holme and the ferry, and also south of Ringing Crag. The speed limits were imposed by the National Park in 2005, after a prolonged and polarised Public Inquiry; this concluded that high-speed powerboats could not co-exist with paddlecraft and sailing boats, on safety grounds. However, 'sustainable' powerboat races have since been permitted on several days annually, based from Windermere Motor Boat Racing Club.

Wildlife and environment

Windermere's fish include perch, pike and trout, but the most famous species is the char, an Ice Age survivor which has been fished for centuries and was regarded as a delicacy (see page 243).

Otters and crayfish are present in the lake and surrounding streams. Perhaps surprisingly, otters are regularly spotted at Waterhead, Ambleside's busy beach, and visit the flooded hangar at Windermere Jetty Museum.

Windermere hosts more aquatic birds than any of the other lakes: around 1,000 in summer, 2,500 in winter. Summer residents include coots, cormorants, Canada and greylag geese, mallards, mute swans, and mergansers. In winter, they are joined by goldeneyes (300+), gulls (in often huge roosts), great-crested grebes, pochards and tufted ducks.

Tizzie-Whizie and Bownessie

According to cryptozoologists*, Windermere is inhabited by not one, but two cryptids: creatures whose existence is disputed. The first is the Tizzie-Whizie, which has a hedgehog body, a squirrel tail, bee wings and butterfly antennas. A Tizzie-Whizie was captured by a Bowness boatman around 1908, who, thankfully for scientific posterity, was able to take a wholly convincing photo before it flew out of the window. Asked why Tizzie-Whizie wasn't commonly spotted flying above the lake, he replied, *"it was a very good underwater swimmer"*. Since 2006, there have also been sightings of Bownessie, a *"Loch Ness-type monster"*. Sadly, none of Bownessie's witnesses appear to have owned camera phones.

* Cryptozoology: the pseudoscience of studying disputed or legendary creatures. Basically, these people are nutters.

England's largest lake is struggling. The biggest concern is huge volumes of untreated sewage: there were an incredible 8,787 hours of spills in 2023, more than there are hours in the year! Sewage spikes phosphorus levels, which leads to blooms of blue-green algae (page 32). These unsightly and potentially toxic slicks are a commonplace sight on Windermere, no longer confined to the summer months; the author most recently paddled through them in January.

📷 *The Lake Warden*

Save Windermere versus United Utilities

Half of the phosphorus entering Windermere comes from United Utilities' sewage treatment facilities. In 2025, United Utilities lost a court dispute over refusing Freedom of Information requests about phosphorus levels. The 'Save Windermere' group has placed United Utilities firmly in its sights, with a campaign bringing Windermere's health to the attention of the national media and even Prime Minister Sir Keir Starmer: *"I was furious and sickened to hear that millions of litres of raw sewage have been illegally pumped into Lake Windermere"*. Save Windermere demands the complete cessation of sewage discharges into the lake, citing how Switzerland's Lake Annecy was restored. United Utilities claims that such a scheme would cost £6.4 billion and has instead announced £200 million to repair and upgrade the current sewage treatment works and storm outflows. Save Windermere points out that from 2015 to 2020, United Utilities returned £1.6 billion to its shareholders.

Don't be put off enjoying Windermere: it is still an attractive lake with much healthy flora and fauna.

"Despite overmuch exploitation for leisure pursuits and by commercial interests … It is the most graceful of the lakes and grace is a virtue that survives and is never lost."

Alfred Wainwright, *Wainwright in the Valleys of Lakeland*, 1992

Launch points

Fell Foot Country Park SD 379 869 / proofread.accordion.intention / LA12 8NN – a large National Trust estate with several public slipways, at the lake's southern tip. The southern of the two car parks is lower and closer to the water, 150m along a track.

Ash Landing car park SD 387 953 / noise.diverting.solves / LA22 0LP – a small National Trust car park, beside the B5285, just before the Bowness-on-Windermere ferry. Walk 60m south along the road and descend steps to a beach beside a jetty.

Harrowslack car park SD 388 959 / books.fidgeting.responded / LA22 0LR – a small National Trust car park, alongside the lane leading north from the Bowness-on-Windermere ferry. The beach is 30m away across a meadow.

Red Nab car park SD 385 994 / beaten.parade.glad / LA22 0JH – a small lakeside National Trust car park located at the end of a steep, potholed lane.

Wray Castle NY 376 012 / teaching.notched.wasps / LA22 0JA – a major National Trust property, signposted for miles around. Park beside the castle (fills up quickly in summer) and follow paths 250m downhill to a shingle beach.

Ambleside RUFC NY 371 033 / basically.marked.herbs / LA22 0EN – Ambleside Rugby Club regularly offers 24-hour parking in its small car park. Accessing the water involves a carry of at least 500m. Walk south along the A5075 Borrans Road, then through a gate into Borrans Park. Follow the path around Galava Roman Fort, across Access Land, to the River Brathay.

Waterhead car park NY 376 032 / blinking.clef.kicked / LA22 0ES – a large National Park car park, with direct access to the beach and public slipway, across the A5075 Borrans Road. There is also a tiny car park at Ambleside Pier, 120m south.

Low Wood Bay Watersports Centre NY 385 019 / steamed.princely.goggle / LA23 1LP – a lakeside outdoor activity centre that offers parking and day launching.

Millerground Landing SD 402 988 / replace.impressed.deck / LA23 1EY – a lay-by with free parking, alongside the A592 Rayrigg Road. A choice of a footpath or permissive path lead 250m downhill, following a beck, to a beach and jetty. It fills quickly.

Rayrigg Meadow SD 402 984 / improves.punctual.acute / LA23 1BP – a public park with a car park, alongside the A592 Rayrigg Road. It's a 190m walk to the beach and public jetties.

Cockshott Point SD 395 964 / most.pollution.emeralds / LA23 3HE – park at Glebe Road car park, cross Glebe Road and follow the footpath 300m south to a beach on Cockshott Point.

Ferry Nab SD 397 959 / backfired.destined.persuade / LA23 3JH – walk 100m from the west end of Ferry Nab car park, to the public jetties. Launch at the public slipway alongside the Lake Warden's office. Busy.

Beech Hill car park SD 388 921 / bonds.sake.tradition / LA23 3LR – a large National Park car park, alongside the A592. Paths lead 100m to the beach, down steep steps.

◎ *Windermere from Gummer's How*

Windermere – southern

Trip Distance   18.3km / 11.4 miles
Start / Finish   Fell Foot Country Park SD 379 869 / proofread.accordion.intention / LA12 8NN

Description

"In making acquaintance with the lake it is desirable to begin with the tamer but still pretty S. end."
***Baedecker's Great Britain**, 1887*

The National Trust's Fell Foot Country Park provides convenient access to Windermere's southern tip. This seven-hectare site was once a fording point, controlled by Furness Abbey. Until demolition in 1907, Fell Foot villa overlooked the landscaped lawns which sweep down to the waterfront, where piers and castellated mock-Gothic boathouses now house a café. This peculiar miniature dockyard was constructed in 1869 for George Ridehalgh, to berth his steam yachts *Fairy Queen* and *Britannia*.

At the lake outflow, moraine (heaps of glacial till) and a bedrock spur hem in Windermere, forcing the course of River Leven through a tight bend. The river flows noticeably strongly at Fell Foot, especially so after recent rain. It is possible to paddle this river-lake downstream to Newby Bridge, a side-tour of nearly three kilometres; if the river is flowing well, the return paddle will be hard work. Below the five-arch bridge, which survives from 1651, is a weir and sluice, constructed in 1971 to regulate Windermere's level. Past Newby Bridge, the Leven is now popular with

white-water paddlers, but it once powered an industrial valley, including the north's first blast furnace, opened at Backbarrow in 1711.

Most will paddle across the River Leven to Lakeside, the cluster of quayside buildings on the western shore. Steer clear of any traffic, especially Windermere Lake Cruises' hefty steamer vessels. Lakeside is a busy interchange, where tourists transfer between the steamers and the Haverthwaite and Lakeside Railway's steam trains. Tourists have been doing this for over 150 years; Lakeside was developed by the Furness Railway Company, which operated from 1869 to 1965, also owning the steamers. They built the quayside pavilion; tiny traces of its Victorian heritage survive. The larger building behind is the Lakes Aquarium, and just to the north is the Lakeside Hotel.

The Windermere steamers

These are among Britain's most popular tourist attractions, shuttling a million tourists annually between Ambleside, Bowness and Lakeside. The steamer service (they now run on diesel) originated in the mid-nineteenth century, when two companies vied for the tourist trade, offering tours with brass bands on board. The competition was fierce: prices were slashed, touts became such a nuisance at Bowness that they had to be banned, and arson was suspected when the steamer *Lord of the Isles* was destroyed at Bowness Pier in 1850. In the 1870s, the Furness Railway Company took over the steamers.

Three of Windermere Lake Cruises' largest vessels are registered as National Historic Ships. MV *Tern*, a steam yacht launched in 1891, is recognisable by its long open deck and single chimney. MV *Teal* and MV *Swan* were built by Vickers at Barrow-in-Furness and launched in 1936 and 1938, respectively. In 1956, *Teal* carried Queen Elizabeth II. Both carry more than 500 passengers.

A fourth National Historic Ship is undergoing restoration at Windermere Jetty Museum. *Raven* was launched in 1871, a steam barge which transported cargo around the lake. She is the second-oldest ship registered with Lloyd's and the oldest retaining her original engine.

Following the western shore from Lakeside, there is an immediate contrast. In the eight kilometres to Ash Landing there are a succession of bays, headlands and small islands to explore, mostly wooded with little development.

These quiet shores were once a hive of industry. The woods were coppiced for charcoal burning and bobbin-making; behind Riddings Bay, not visible or accessible from the water, Stott Park Bobbin Mill is preserved by English Heritage as the last such working site in the Lake District. It's well worth a visit on a non-paddling day.

The next landmark is the YMCA Lakeside, established 1953 and among Europe's largest outdoor activity centres. The site extends over 160 hectares and spans two of Windermere's bays, about a kilometre of lakefront. The new (2020) £7 million Stoller Campus overlooks the first bay; the second bay used to be the North Camp but it was sold to developers in 2024. Between the bays is Costrells Rocks, a handful of shallow reefs, marked by red warning signs.

◎ Ling Holme

The island of Silver Holme, also known as Solva Holme, is 30m long and rears barely 3m above the water; like all of Windermere's islands close to shore, it's an outcrop of siltstone and mudstone (the Bannisdale Formation) which just about resisted being shredded to oblivion by the passing glacier's immense erosive power. In Arthur Ransome's books, this was 'Cormorant Island':

> *"'It's a secret,"* said Titty, *"but there is treasure there. Roger and I are going to discover it. The pirates put it there last night while I was anchored in Amazon.""*

Arthur Ransome, *Swallows and Amazons*, 1930

Beneath a fallen tree trunk in the island's centre, Titty and Roger uncover Captain Flint's box and rename the isle 'Treasure Island' on their chart. This all makes sense if you read the book!

Silver Holme is overlooked by Silverholme, an 1820 manor house which is now a luxury rental. The wooded reefs near its jetty are Harrop Rocks. Silverholme was home to floatplane pioneer Oscar Gnosspelius, who developed and tested his 'hydro-aeroplane' on Windermere, in 1911 achieving the distinction of Britain's first floatplane crash. Gnosspelius later (1925) married Barbara, daughter of W.G. Collingwood (page 159). Arthur Ransome, her earlier suitor, dedicated his book *Pigeon Post* to Gnosspelius and based the prospector character 'Squashy Hat' on him.

Windermere's western shore continues to lay on similar, delightful scenery: a solitary boathouse in the following wooded bay; the low outcrops of Grubbins Point and Crag Holme; the hidden inlet of 'Lazy Bay' at Little Baswicks ('Horseshoe Cove' in Ransome's *Swallowdale*, where *Swallow* was wrecked); and the island of Grass Holme. Grass Holme is a strip of carr woodland, barely rising above the water. It is ignominiously surrounded by a fence planted into the shallows to protect and restore the reedbeds, which surrounded it in the last century and presumably gave it its name.

Windermere – southern

Matson Landing

The road briefly comes close to shore at Hammer Hole, a jetty and houses which served Cunsey Beck's iron forges. Before the beck is reached, Rawlinson Nab, a prominent 8m high crag, narrows the lake to around 500m wide. Thomas West recommended Rawlinson Nab as one of his 'stations' (page 230) from which to best appreciate Windermere. Having paddled past the fallen trees angling into the water beneath this headland, a whole new vista is indeed unveiled, northwards: Storrs Temple, Claife Heights, Belle Isle and the fells beyond.

Ling Holme (Old Norse: heather island) is high-sided and craggy, guarding Cunsey Beck's inflow. This sizeable beck drains Esthwaite Water (page 166) into Windermere. It's hard to believe that this green and pleasant spot was, from 1712, the site of a water wheel-powered blast furnace.

Your passage to Ash Landing is marked by: submerged rocks at Carlew Crag and Sandy Nab; Fellborough, a sizeable shoreline villa overlooking Green Naze Wyke; and Matson Landing, where four boathouses line the shore close to the shallows of Matson Shoal. Ash Landing, this route's northward limit, is recognisable by a small bay and jetty, where the shores steepen notably, overlooked by castle-like Claife Viewing Station (page 119). It's possible to land here. Otherwise, this is the spot to cross to the eastern shore.

It's about 800m to the far shore, so be mindful of the weather conditions before deciding to proceed and, once committed, watch out for traffic! The crossing is punctuated by a pair of marked rocks at Bull Head (just south are another pair, Oven Bottom) and the island of Ramp Holme. All being well, you'll reach shore at Cannon Crag, a 3m-high outcrop, 250m south-east of Ramp Holme.

The first three kilometres of shoreline, stretching south, are a marked contrast to what you've enjoyed so far. Much of the waterfront is claimed by villas, mansions, hotels, modern 'Grand Designs'-style houses largely consisting of glass, and so forth.

Bowness dawn

Windermere – southern

> *"You might suppose as you sail along towards Bowness that you were passing by the suburban outskirts of some great city just over the hill."*

Hardwicke Rawnsley, 1905

All have their own boathouses, of course, ranging in style and scale from 'garden shed' to 'Tracey Island'. Exploring all of this isn't unpleasant. There is plenty to engage with and you can enjoy being a vicarious millionaire.

At Blackwell Bay, note the imposing white Arts and Crafts-style house, uphill beyond the green boathouse. This is Blackwell, designed by Mackay Hugh Baillie Scott in 1900 for Manchester brewer Sir Edward Holt. It's open to the public and well worth a visit; however, it's not accessible from the lake.

The Storrs promontory (Old Norse *storth*: thicket) is a highlight. Approaching, you spot the white Storrs Hall Hotel, formerly Storrs Hall. At the tip of the promontory, a stone jetty extends to an octagonal viewing station with four arched windows. This is the Storrs Temple, properly the 'Temple of Naval Heroes' but known locally as 'the Fishing House'. It was built in 1804, for Sir John Legard. The titular 'heroes' are named on the outside: Duncan, Howe, Nelson and St Vincent. All were a big deal, at the time, in the Anglo-French wars. Storrs Hall faces the lake across lawns on the promontory's south side.

The point where the shoreline bends southwards was Ransome's 'Houseboat Bay'. Bellman Landing, so-named as this was once a public launch spot, is marked offshore by Birkett Rock. The next two kilometres is more eye-wateringly pricey houses and boathouses. Broad Leys is the white Arts and Crafts-style house with three prominent window bays, fronted by lawns leading to a cluster of jetties. Built in 1898 by Charles Voysey, this has belonged since 1951 to Windermere Motor Boat Racing Club, the world's oldest, formed 1925. Harry Segrave and Donald Campbell were members. Since the 2005 speed limit, the club mostly races at Barrow-in-Furness, but a number of sustainable races are based here each year.

Storrs Hall Hotel

Storrs Hall

Storrs Hall was built for John Legard in the 1790s. It was enlarged between 1808 and 1811, by architect Joseph Gandy, for John Bolton; the completed mansion boasted Doric columns and a domed rotunda. Bolton was a Liverpool merchant enriched by the slave trade, notorious for having killed a man in a duel. He laundered his grubby wealth by spending his way into Cumbrian society; in 1825 he held a lavish Grand Regatta to celebrate Sir Walter Scott's birthday, with guests including Wordsworth and Southey. In the 1890s, the young Beatrix Potter attended parties at Storrs Hall and gathered fungi in the grounds; before literary success, she gained attention as a notable mycologist.

Beech Hill Hotel, not one of Windermere's more attractive buildings, looms above; from here, the shoreline rises steeply from the lake. Just past the hotel, steps ascend through woods to Beech Hill car park.

After rounding Dog Nab, stick a clothes peg over your nose: the industrial complex lining the shore is Tower Wood Sewage Treatment Works, which since 1915 has struggled to process Windermere and Bowness's ever-increasing waste. Paddle quickly past, to the canoe racks and climbing frames of Tower Wood Outdoor Education Centre.

The remainder of your paddle to Fell Foot is pleasant enough. The shores are largely mansion-free, replaced by chalets and caravans. Hill of Oaks and Avon Woods holiday parks stretch from Peartree Point to Blake Holme Nab, both reasonably obscured by Haws Wood.

Arthur Ransome sometimes described Blake Holme as *"the island most used as Wild Cat Island"* in his letters. However, this sizeable island does not match the description in *Swallows and Amazons* (no Hidden Harbour, for starters!): Peel Island on Coniston Water is undoubtedly

Blake Holme

the real Wildcat Island. Blake Holme also doesn't come close to Peel Island in ambience, being surrounded by mooring buoys and overlooked by holiday chalets.

Past Blake Holme Nab, you are treated to a largely undeveloped final two kilometres. The shoreline is often rocky; at Skirtful Crags, a few scraggy trees cling to a cluster of islets, extending 90m offshore. Gummer's How hogs the vista; this distinctive prominence rears above Windermere's southern tip, far more impressively than its modest 321m might imply. After paddling, it's well worth the two-minute drive and half-hour walk to ascend it, especially around sunset. The summit offers a commanding view along Windermere, closely resembling *Swallows and Amazons*' endpaper map, turned upside-down!

The lake narrows towards Fell Foot. Past the boathouses and landing stage, the River Leven's current may be very apparent.

📷 *Central Windermere*

Windermere – central

Trip Distance	6.5km / 4 miles
Start / Finish	Ash Landing car park SD 387 953 / noise.diverting.solves / LA22 0LP

Description

"The small isles here are but few in number – yet the best arithmetician of the party cannot count them."

John Wilson, *The Recreations of Christopher North*, 1842

Although there is plenty of interest along Windermere's shores, this paddle is all about the islands. The distance is short, but allow plenty of time for landing, picnicking, tree climbing, and so forth.

Ash Landing is recommended as the launch point as this small bay, with jetty, offers space and quiet; the eastern shore options are within chaotic Bowness-on-Windermere. Northwards from Ash Landing, Windermere's western shores steepen notably along Claife Heights, a wooded 200m-high backdrop. The forest originated, in the eighteenth century, as a million-larch enclosure planted for John Christian Curwen of Belle Isle.

Before launching, investigate Claife Viewing Station, the restored two-storey octagonal tower looming above the car park. Properly called Belle View, this oddity was built in the 1790s as a summer house for Reverend William Braithwaite. In 1802, the Curwens added the castellations,

neo-Gothic arches and coloured windows. The somewhat absurd 'Picturesque' movement was all the rage: visitors would view Windermere with their back turned, via a convex 'Claude glass' mirror (page 230). The coloured windows were supposed to add seasonal drama to the vistas. Robert Southey dismissed the tower as, *"in a style so foolish, that, if anything could mar the beauty of so beautiful a scene, it would be this ridiculous edifice"* (**Letters from England**, 1807).

The curving Ferry House promontory narrows Windermere to less than 500m. At its end, a cluster of buildings occupy the site of a former inn and meadow, where sporting events and regattas were held. The Ferry Inn became the Ferry Hotel in 1879, a girl's school in the 1940s and eventually home to the Freshwater Biological Association (page 252). For years, the promontory has been an unfinished building site; a new hotel may, or may not, emerge from this unholy mess.

Crow Holme is the island at the end of Ferry House promontory. Like all of the small islands in Windermere's central part, it is densely wooded and rises just a few metres from the water. It has also gone by the names Puppy Holme and Kennel Holme as, oddly, the Windermere Harriers once kennelled their foxhunt hounds here; corrugated iron debris on the island may be remnants of the kennels. The bay sheltered behind the promontory is Mitchell Wyke, usually filled with moored yachts.

Maiden Holme is a tiny one-tree affair, Windermere's smallest named island. It guards the approach to the Coatlap Point–Belle Isle gap; just 130m separates the grassy headland from Lakeland's largest island.

Belle Isle sprawls languorously across Windermere, its 1.1km length and 16 hectares almost diagonally bisecting the lake. Called Great Island or Longholme until 1781 and 'the long island'

📷 *The Pepperpot, Belle Isle*

in *Swallows and Amazons*, it is tree-lined all around, but clear in the centre.

Belle Isle is owned by the Curwens. Landing is not permitted and there is plenty of signage reminding you of this. Its southern tip, facing Coatlap Point, is narrow, with steep and overgrown shores. Paddling up Belle Isle's western side, a series of bays are revealed, each crammed with moored yachts: *"a placid backwater with a floating suburb"* (Norman Nicholson, ***Greater Lakeland***, 1969). A jetty extends into the second bay; glimpsed behind it is Belle Isle's cylindrical domed mansion, also named Belle Isle.

The Pepperpot

"The house makes the island belle; for it was the first mansion in the Lake District decided upon for picturesque reasons."

Nikolaus Pevsner, *The Buildings of England*, 1967

Belle Isle was possibly England's first circular mansion. John Plaw designed it for Thomas English, inspired by Rome's Pantheon. Building commenced in 1774, but it was mocked by locals, who dubbed it the 'Pepperpot'. William Gell scoffed that it looked *"exactly like a large tea shop canister"*.

Disheartened, in 1781 English sold Longholme island to the Curwens, whose wealth came from the Workington coal mines. They renamed it 'Bella Isle', after their daughter Isabella. Thomas White landscaped the grounds, planting trees on the island, to the horror of Wordsworth and others.

Isabella's cousin Fletcher Christian was born in Cockermouth in 1764. After news filtered back to Britain about his 1789 mutiny against Captain Bligh on the ***Bounty***, rumours persisted that he had returned and was hiding in Belle Isle.

📷 *Lilies of the Valley and Belle Isle*

Lilies of the Valley is the rather lovely name (if we overlook the fact that the plant is highly poisonous) for the twin islands halfway up Belle Isle's western side, both nearly 100m long. Wordsworth lauded, *"an Island musical with birds / That sang and ceased not; [and] a Sister Isle / Beneath the oaks' umbrageous covert, sown / With lilies of the valley like a field"* (**The Prelude**, 1850). Sadly, few lilies remain.

Belle Isle's second western satellite is Thompson's Holme, also known as Tommy Holme. It's a 300m arc, around a sheltered anchorage on its eastern side. A beach at the southern tip gives access to the perfect picnic spot, with a carved bench. Much of the island's woods are enclosed by fencing. Thompson's Holme is aligned north-east towards its own satellite, tiny Haw's Holme.

Next up is the hop of near-400m east-north-east from Haw's Holme to Hen Holme. This crossing is exposed to open water and wind from the north. If unsure, consider a more sheltered alternative route, perhaps heading south-east to Belle Isle. However, if the weather and lake are calm enough to paddle across, enjoy the glorious panorama of fells swaddling Windermere's northern half.

Hen Holme, a shrub-covered rock, is simply a staging post en route to Lady Holme. Approach Lady Holme cautiously, to circumvent and avoid consternating the considerable cormorant colony clustered in the high, dead branches above the southern beach. Lady Holme, also previously known as Chapel Holme or St Mary Holme, was topped in the thirteenth century by a chantry chapel.

> *"… small island, where survived / In solitude the ruins of a shrine / Once to Our Lady dedicate, and served / Daily with chaunted rites"*

William Wordsworth, **The Prelude**, 1850

The chapel must have been substantial, as the resident monks had rights to ten fishing nets. The only trace now is goose-shit-smeared steps, cut into a four metre high rock platform.

📷 *Hen Holme, Lady Holme and Rough Holme*

Rough Holme is a tempting 400m north, but this route now veers south, towards the passage between Belle Isle's eastern side and Bowness-on-Windermere. Approaching Bowness Bay, the western shore is dotted with wooden holiday park chalets, which encircle Fallbarrow Park, an 1834 Gothic mansion.

Bowness Bay is the waterfront of tourist resort Bowness-on-Windermere. Bowness's name is Old English: 'headland of bulls'. In **Swallows and Amazons**, it was 'Rio': *"The little town is known in guide-books by another name, but the crew of the Swallow had long ago given it the name of Rio Grande"*. Bowness expanded after the Kendal and Windermere Railway reached Birthwaite village, two kilometres north-east, in 1847. Landowners opposed further extension towards Ambleside, so Birthwaite was renamed 'Windermere' and hotels sprung up around the bay at Bowness, previously a quiet fishing and boatbuilding centre. Bowness and Windermere (still officially a village, despite a four-fold population increase from 1800 to 1921) duly merged into a single conurbation.

Royal Windermere Yacht Club (RWYC) occupies Bowness Bay's northern part. Formed 1860, it received a Royal Warrant in 1887. The Yacht Racing Association had rejected an application, airily noting that it *"had no jurisdiction over duckponds"*. The RWYC still races attractive wooden 17 foot 'fore-and-aft' rigged boats. These were introduced in 1904 at a cost of £100, more than the average annual salary; this was an exclusive club for wealthy amateur 'offcomers'.

Bowness Bay is undoubtedly the Lake District's busiest patch of water. Exploring by paddlecraft is an intense experience. Jetties are lined with hire boats and crowds throng around the steamer pier, with its Victorian Gothic ticket booth. Wordsworth scoffed, *"A person of feeling mind … [would be] disgusted with the bustle, the parade, and drest-out appearance …"* and, in 1830, 11-year-old John Ruskin recorded in his diary, *"dead cats & dogs, & the water is dirty from the quantity of boats continually sailing about the bay …"*. Ignore these naysayers: Bowness Bay is really not unpleasant!

Bowness-on-Windermere

Note the huge cream-coloured Belsfield Hotel, behind the pier. This was formerly Belsfield House, built in 1845 for Countess de Sternberg. From 1869, the mansion housed Henry Schneider, the mining and steel magnate behind Barrow-in-Furness's prosperity. Every morning, Schneider crossed his lawn, preceded by a butler carrying breakfast on a silver tray, to board his steamer *Esperance*. This shipped him to Lakeside, from whence the Furness Railway (which he co-founded) sped him, by private carriage, to Barrow. Quite the commute! SL *Esperance* is now in Windermere Jetty Museum (page 133).

Stars and stripes at Bowness

Bowness's oldest building is St Martin's Church, 100m from the shore along Lake Road. There has been a church here from at least 1203. The current iteration was consecrated in 1483 and restored in the 1870s.

Inside are all manner of intriguing things, not least the decorated rubble walls, adorned with strange texts. The east stained-glass windows were probably filched from Cartmel Priory, following its 1536 dissolution. These include three red stars and two red stripes on a white background: the coat of arms of George Washington, first US president! His ancestor John Washington was a local landowner. American legend dictates that their 'stars and stripes' flag was stitched together by Betsy Ross, inspired by Washington's arms.

In the graveyard, seek out the headstone of Rasselas Belfield of Abyssinia, died 1822: *'A slave by birth I left my native land / And found my freedom on Britain's Strand!'* Slave owner John Bolton (of Storrs Hall) is buried nearby: mixed messages!

The Windermere ferry, Mallard

Belle Isle's eastern side is less than 500m from Bowness Bay. Mid way between the two, Curlew Crag and Hartley Wife, marked rocks, peek from the water. A smattering of islets lines the larger island's shore. Fir Holme is possibly human built, joined to Belle Isle by causeway. Stake Holme, also called Snake Holme, is also close inshore. A pair of boathouses are followed by a small jetty, from where you enjoy the best view of Belle Isle house.

Robin the Devil

Belle Isle was defended during the English Civil War, by Royalist Robert 'Robin the Devil' Phillipson of Calgarth Hall. In 1645 it was bombarded, from Cockshott Point, by Colonel Briggs's parliamentary forces. After eight days, Robert's brother Colonel Huddlestone arrived and broke the siege. The brothers then tried to exact revenge by riding into Kendal's Holy Trinity Church while Briggs was at prayer. The congregation fought them off, Robert losing his sword and helmet in the process. These are still displayed in the church.

At The Narrows, Belle Isle and Cockshott Point are just 170m apart. Cross this busy highway with care! Cockshott Point is a wooded promontory on Bowness's fringes, with beaches offering a leg-stretch. A hangar built here in 1911 for seaplanes became the headquarters of the nascent Royal Navy Air Service. Complaints from Hardwicke Rawnsley and Beatrix Potter (*"There is a beastly fly-swimming spluttering aeroplane careering up & down over Windermere; it makes a noise like 10 million bluebottles …"*) got it moved, in 1916, to Hill of Oaks, near Blake Holme. Parson's Wyke, also called Parsonage Bay, is the bight between Cockshott Point and Ferry Nab. It is backed by Parson Wyke House, the 'Old Rectory' dating from the sixteenth century.

Ferry Nab is flanked on both sides by moored yachts, jetties and marinas. Every twenty minutes, the 30-year-old ferry *Mallard* chugs between Ferry Nab and Ferry House promontory. Give this 43m-long vessel a wide berth, not least because it can't avoid you: it is connected to two cables. It was slated to be replaced by an electric ferry in 2024; however, the council didn't get around to ordering it and *Mallard* will be in service for another five years. The ferry service has run for at least 800 years. Windermere Steamboat Museum has a preserved example of a ferry powered by 'sweeps': long oars. Steam and cables were introduced in 1870.

The fatal nuptials

In 1635 the ferry sank while returning a wedding party from Hawkshead; the ferryman, his forty-seven passengers and seven horses all drowned. The tragedy was mythologised by Richard Braithwaite in his 1636 poem *The Fatall Nuptiall*. His preamble explains: *"The Boat, either through the pressure and weight which surcharg'd her, or some violent and impetuous windes and waves that surpriz'd her, with all her people, became drench'd in the depths."*

Braithwaite, from Kendal, was the earliest 'Lake Poet'. His Wikipedia entry notes that he was also the first person to use the word 'computer' and describes him as *"the author of many works of very unequal merit"*. You be the judge of how much merit to award *The Fatall Nuptiall* ...

"See, see the leeking Vessell how it strives

And combats with the waves, to save their lives!"

Windermere Marina Village, a large marina, is reasonably well hidden at the back of Sourpool Wyke. Paddling south to Ramp Holme, the final island of the day, Chicken Rock and Hen Rock are successively passed, barely noticeable except for the marker posts and birds roosting upon them. At five metres high, Ramp Holme (Old English *hramsa*: garlic) is one of the more prominent small islands and worth a shore foray. It has also been called Berkshire Island and Rogerholm; it belonged in the eighteenth century to the Earl of Berkshire, who bred swans on it.

Ramp Holme is the staging point for the 600m paddle back to Ash Landing. Bull Head rocks punctuate this crossing, with Oven Bottom rocks seen a short distance south.

Wasn't that a great paddle?

Waterhead and Ambleside

Windermere – northern

Trip Distance	16km / 10 miles
Start / Finish	Waterhead car park NY 376 032 / blinking.clef.kicked / LA22 0ES

Description

"At the head, stands in lofty grandeur, and in full view, the high-towering ornaments of High-street, Kirkstone, Fair-field, and Helvellyn, which, in the early part of the season, are frequently covered with snow: to be able to picture the beauty, the grandeur, the loveliness, which on all sides presents itself, would require skill and comprehension very far surpassing any ever possessed by the writer."

James Gibson, *A Guide to the Scenery of Windermere*, 1843

Waterhead is the offshoot of Ambleside abutting the lake, a kilometre from the town's centre. The steamer terminal on Ambleside Pier was built in 1845, pre-dating the inns around the car park and also the hefty YHA Ambleside building to the south. Launching from Waterhead car park involves negotiating road traffic, aimlessly wandering tourists, feral wildfowl and also incoming steamers: an experience not unlike the classic computer game 'Frogger'.

📷 *Waterhead*

Ambleside

If you've never visited this Mecca for fleece jacket shoppers, you should know that, beyond the multifarious outdoor gear shops, there are a few points of interest. The eccentric, tiny seventeenth-century Bridge House which spans Stock Ghyll once housed a family of eight! Across Rydal Road is The Armitt, a museum, gallery and library, whose huge collection includes Beatrix Potter's fungi paintings and artefacts from Galava Roman Fort. The Knoll is close by, home from 1844 to social reformer Harriet Martineau; her 1855 *A Complete Guide to the English Lakes* was a more practical and grounded guidebook than those previously produced.

Having escaped Waterhead's piers and jetties, the National Trust's Jenkins Field offers a marked contrast, a beach-flanked promontory leading out to Holme Crag and a rocky islet. The A591 comes alongside at Dove Nest Bay; the Trust's Stagshaw Garden rears behind it, a semi-ornamental woodland on the flanks of 482m Wansfell Pike.

The large white hotel complex which follows is Low Wood Bay Resort & Spa. A £16 million refurbishment in 2017 added the marina and watersports centre. Local, Shawn Williamson, sculpted sixteen boulders, placed along the shoreline, into local fauna: fish, otter, swan and so forth. The hotel was built in 1850, on the site of a popular coaching inn. John Stuart Mill stayed in 1831 and wrote that the lake was, *"alternately of a deep lead colour; a beautiful iron-grey; a lightish blue; a glittering white sparkling with the rays of the sun"*. Further back, in 1800, Dorothy Wordsworth had something of a meltdown here:

> "I sate a long time upon a stone at the margin of the lake, and after a flood of tears my heart was easier. The lake looked to me, I knew not why, dull and melancholy, and the weltering on the shores seemed a heavy sound. I walked as long as I could amongst the stones of the shore."

Grasmere Journals, 1800–1803

📷 *Calgarth Park*

From Holbeck Point to Ecclerigg Crag, four successive mansions, all built for industrial barons complete with grounds landscaped by Lancastrian Thomas Mawson, parcel up the lake shore: Langdale Chase, Ecclerigg House, Brockhole and Cragwood House. Incidentally, they overlook Windermere's deepest part.

Langdale Chase, built c. 1890 in Jacobean style, is now a hotel. Neighbouring Ecclerigg House is privately owned.

Brockhole was built in 1897, in the Arts and Crafts style, for Manchester silk merchant William Gaddum. Beatrix Potter, cousin of Gaddum's wife, was a regular visitor. After a spell as a retirement home for Merseyside women, in 1966 Brockhole was bought by the National Park, and it became their Visitor Centre. Nowadays, the place is overrun by families drawn in by the huge adventure playground. Should you land and venture indoors, there is a café and 'Lake District Story' exhibit. Over three days in June, 10,000 swimmers take to the water at Brockhole: The Great North Swim.

Cragwood House, built 1910, is also Arts and Crafts style; it's now a hotel. At the lake shore, Ecclerigg Crag was inscribed with carved texts in the 1830s by Troutbeck stonemason John Longmire. You aren't supposed to land, but brushing the leaves aside reveals eccentric messages about topics as diverse as Wordsworth, the Corn Laws and the national debt. Nearby, a white cross rears from the water; this commemorates Ralph Thichnesse and Thomas Woodcock, young men drowned in 1853 when their boat overturned: *'Watch, therefore, for ye know neither the day nor the hour.'*

White Cross Bay is named for the above-mentioned cross, although it was previously Craams Bay ('Shark Bay' in *Swallows and Amazons*). At the rear of the bay are holiday park chalets, formerly the site of a flying boat factory! In 1940, during the Second World War, aircraft manufacturer Short Brothers relocated here, from Kent. Underwater metal rails survive, used to launch thirty-five Sunderland 'flying porcupines'. There are unconfirmed tales of scuttled flying boats on the lakebed.

📷 *The Langdale Pikes from Calgarth Park*

Trout Beck's wide, arcuate delta follows, which is this eastern shore's least developed stretch. A wide Georgian mansion looms behind the low-lying, marshy shoreline: this is Calgarth Park, built 1789 for Richard Watson.

The Bishop of Llandaff

Richard Watson (1737–1816) was a colourful figure, known by his Welsh flock as *"the bishop who lived in Westmorland"*, as he only bothered to visit Llandaff every three years. Watson mooted a scheme, thankfully never completed, to 'improve' Windermere by draining it. Watson published reactionary sermons such as ***The Wisdom and Goodness of God in having made both Rich and Poor***. Wordsworth responded with his ***Letter to the Bishop of Llandaff***, lauding the French Revolution, in which, of course, many bishops fled for their lives. However, the older, conservative, Wordsworth became a friend and regular visitor to Calgarth Park.

Trout Beck flows in through tangled carr wetland. Up to 204 million litres of water daily are extracted hereabouts and pumped to Kendal.

The sprawling farmhouse with large cylindrical chimneys, just past Trout Beck, is fourteenth-century Calgarth Hall. Legend has it (i.e. probably nonsense) that sixteenth-century magistrate Myles Phillipson got his hands on the place by inviting owners Kraster and Dorothy Cook for Christmas dinner, framing them for the theft of a silver cup and then sentencing them to be hanged. Phillipson was haunted at Calgarth Hall by the Cooks' screaming skulls, which, despite being thrown into Windermere and suchlike, repeatedly returned to terrorise him.

Meregarth

Behind Calgarth Hall, the community of Calgarth was constructed during the Second World War, for workers at White Cross Bay's Short Brothers factory. 'Short's Palaces', dubbed 'Chinatown' by locals, housed 200 couples and 300 singles.

The Windermere Children

Following the Second World War, Short's Palaces housed 300 Jewish children, survivors of the Nazi's Theresienstadt Ghetto. German-Jewish psychologist Oscar Friedman led the camp, which helped 'the Windermere children' recover from the trauma of the Holocaust. Icek Alterman, who had also survived Buchenwald and Auschwitz concentration camps, recalled canoeing on Windermere: *"We had arrived in paradise."*

At Meregarth, the Keldwyth boathouses are crammed side-by-side; there are at least nine, and more keep appearing.

Millerground Bay arcs around to the sixteenth-century stone ferry cottage at Millerground Landing, site of a former ferry to Belle Grange. The prominent hill behind the bay is 238m Orrest Head. In 1930, 23-year-old Alfred Wainwright, fresh off the train from Blackburn, summitted his first Lakeland fell:

"I stood transfixed, unable to believe my eyes. I saw mountain ranges, one after the other ... the shimmering waters of the lake below ... God was in his heaven that day and I a humble worshipper."

Alfred Wainwright, *Ex-Fellwanderer*, 1987

Wordsworth also rather liked the view; his description in *The Prelude* is on page 105. Those motivated to emulate Wainwright and Wordsworth can ascend Orrest Head direct from Millerground Landing, via a two-kilometre mix of footpaths and roadside walking. An

Windermere Jetty Museum

easier-to-attain viewpoint is Queen Adelaide's Hill, owned by the National Trust and rising just forty-five metres above the lake. This drumlin hillock was formerly Rayrigg Bank, until climbed by King William IV's widow in 1840. Rayrigg Meadow is at the hill's southern end, a public park. Rayrigg Hall, part-Tudor and part-Georgian, was the summer home of abolitionist MP William Wilberforce, who came here to escape visitors but complained, *"the banks of the Thames are scarcely more public than the banks of Windermere."*

Rough Holme lies 230m offshore. This 2m-high island is worth a diversion to explore, as it holds a secret: a large treehouse, perched high in its centre. This is, however, only accessible via the use of a ladder, or considerable ingenuity. Tuft Rock is marked to the south-east, offshore from Rayrigg Wyke.

Windermere Jetty Museum's large boatsheds and four long jetties mark the point at which this route crosses to Windermere's western shore. Landing at the museum is not permitted; however, a later visit is highly recommended.

Windermere Jetty Museum

Opened in 1977 and formerly known as the Steamboat Museum, this engaging attraction is crammed with historic vessels telling stories of leisure and work on the English Lakes. Their collection, showcased in 'dry' and 'wet' boathouses, includes: boats which belonged to Beatrix Potter and Arthur Ransome; *Esperance*, a model for Captain Flint's houseboat in ***Swallows and Amazons***; SL *Dolly*, the world's oldest working mechanically powered boat; and *Margaret*, the UK's oldest sailing yacht, built c. 1780 for the Curwens of Belle Isle. A third boathouse is given over to ongoing conservation and restoration work, which can be observed.

📷 *High Wray Bay*

Crossing to the western shore is a significant undertaking, a paddle of around 1.5km. That said, a succession of islands breaks up your passage, with no individual hop longer than 350m. Lady Holme, Hen Holme, Haw's Holme and Thompson's Holme are all outlined in the 'Windermere – central' route. If the conditions aren't right for the crossing, either turn back north or continue south and finish at Bowness.

The Crier of Claife

Crier of Claife, supposedly a monk who died of grief after rejection by a woman, is the only ghost marked on an Ordnance Survey map (the quarry at SD 386 982). One sixteenth-century night, a Bowness ferryman heard a cry on the Claife shore, and rowed across:

"He returned alone, ghastly and dumb with horror … in a few days he died, without having been prevailed upon to say what he had seen at the Nab. For weeks after, there were shouts, yells, and howlings at the Nab, on every stormy night."

Harriet Martineau, *A Complete Guide to the English Lakes*, 1855

A priest from Lady Holme attempted to banish the spook, using bell and candle. This exorcist was only able to confine it to the quarry, *"until men should walk dryshod across the lake"*.

Other Windermere things which go bump in the night include a spectral white horse, denoting a family death if seen crossing the lake surface, and creaks and groans coming from the ice when frozen: obviously, the restless souls of the wedding party lost in the 1635 disaster (page 126).

📷 *Wray Castle boathouse*

You should arrive at Windermere's western shore in the vicinity of Bass How; just north, jetties serve a small caravan site and Strawberry Gardens, a National Trust rental property. This side of the lake is a sharp contrast to the mansions lined up opposite; larch-covered slopes incline over two hundred metres above the water to Claife Heights, with little development beyond a shoreline track. Forest extends four kilometres north to High Wray Bay, and west across to Coniston Water, encompassing Esthwaite Water en route.

At Belle Grange Bay, a former ferryman's cottage with a belltower sits behind the jetty, which is alongside Bass Rock (just a rock). Here, the shoreline bends north-west, with the next landmark being the small headland of Red Nab, with its secluded car park.

Close to Pinstones Point, speed pioneer Sir Henry Segrave lost his life.

"Did we do it?"

Henry Segrave was a First World War pilot, shot down in 1916. Following the war, he won Grand Prix races and broke the land speed record at Daytona Beach, Florida. On Windermere in 1930, he set a new water speed record (98.76mph) in *Miss England II*, powered by twin 1800hp Rolls-Royce engines intended for air racing. However, the speedboat capsized, possibly after hitting a log. Of the three onboard, Segrave and his chief engineer were killed. Segrave's last words were, *"How are the two lads? Did we do it?"*.

High Wray Bay marks the start of the National Trust's Wray Castle estate. Wray Castle, a hefty neo-Gothic fantasy, peeks above the trees behind Watbarrow Point, overlooking Castle Bay. Around Watbarrow Point is Low Wray Bay; land here to check out the castle. The castle's grand and appropriately castellated double boathouse is hidden in an inlet a little further on, just before Wray Crag. Alongside is a rather wonderful miniature harbour, perfectly sized for paddlecraft.

Wray Castle

Wray Castle

Wray Castle looks not unlike something a child would construct from Lego; Nathaniel Hawthorne called it *"a great, foolish toy of gray stone"*. It was built, from 1840 to 1847, for Liverpool surgeon James Dawson, using £60,000 of his wife's gin trade wealth. Intended as a surprise for his wife, she reputedly hated it. Wordsworth, who usually railed against anything new, liked it.

Beatrix Potter's family rented Wray Castle in summer 1882. Hardwicke Rawnsley, then vicar of Wray Church, recognised the 16-year-old's artistic talent and interest in nature; he would eventually help her to publish *The Tale of Peter Rabbit*. Both were to become hugely influential in Lake District conservation: Rawnsley as a National Trust founder and Potter through bequeathing vast tracts of land to them.

The National Trust acquired Wray Castle in 1929, since when it has variously housed a youth hostel, the Freshwater Biological Association (page 252) and RMS *Wray Castle*: a training facility for merchant seamen. The Trust opened it to the public in 2014. It is worth walking up for a look, although the interior is largely gutted and primarily serves the function of sheltering screaming children on rainy days.

Windermere's north-western shores are a delight to explore; a succession of inlets, bays and craggy promontories keep the paddler guessing, all the way back to Waterhead.

📷 *Gale Naze Crag*

"… sometimes contracting the lake into the appearance of a noble winding river; at others retiring from it and opening into large bays, as if for navies to anchor in: promontories spread with woods, or scattered with trees and inclosures, projecting into the water in the most picturesque style imaginable; rocky points breaking the shore, and rearing their bold heads above the water; in a word, a variety that amazes the beholder."

Thomas West, ***A Guide to the Lakes***, 1778

Geology provides the reason for this engaging diversity; at least ten distinct bands of Windermere Supergroup Silurian slates slash across Windermere's northern part, the least erosive bands marked by promontories and crags. This effect is exaggerated at this north-western extremity, where highly resistant igneous Borrowdale Volcanics underlie Windermere. Put another way: Windermere has its head in the fells. From different points, paddlers are treated to grand perspectives of: the Coniston fells, the Langdale Pikes (the twin humps are unmistakeable), Loughrigg Fell, the Fairfield horseshoe, High Street and the Kentmere horseshoe.

Green Tuft Island barely qualifies as an island, but Bee Holme is more substantial, densely wooded and connected to shore by marshy carr, alongside the inflow of Blelham Beck. West of Bee Holme, Lily Bay is overlooked by the 1891 mansion of Pullwyke and its boathouse; both are mock-Tudor, both rentable by those with big pockets.

Low Grounds Point, Brock Crag and Seamew Crag guard the entrance to a secretive enclave: Pull Wyke and Sandy Wyke, twin bays where powerboats are banned in summer. Seamew Crag is a miniscule islet frequented by sea mews: kittiwakes.

Brathay Hall, set 350m back from Brathay Bay, is home to the Brathay Trust, a charity sending young people worldwide on expeditions. When constructed in 1788, it was not a hit with Samuel Taylor Coleridge: *"Mr Law's white palace – a bitch!"*. Watercolourist John Harden lived here from 1804 to 1833, with his friend John Constable a regular guest.

Windermere – northern

Brathay Rocks and Gale Naze Crag are both craggy promontories, extending southwards. The lovely inlet between is criminally blighted by the Brathay Trust's enormous twelve-bay boatshed, which resembles back-street garages.

The River Brathay flows into Windermere, between Gale Naze Crag and Brathay Neck. It's possible to explore 600m upstream to Croft, the 1830s house overlooking where the Rivers Brathay and Rothay merge. This was the eighteenth-century port of Clappersgate; annually, 1,500 tons of slate were loaded, and charcoal and gunpowder for the quarries were offloaded. Char supposedly swim up the Brathay (Old Norse: broad river) and trout up the Rothay (Old Norse: red river). Over 400 million m^3 of water flows into Windermere annually. The water entering here exits Windermere, via the River Leven, after nine months.

Brathay Neck is a swampy wetland fronting the National Trust's Borran's Field (Old Norse: heap of stones), site of Galava Roman Fort. Landing to explore is easiest from the River Brathay.

Galava Roman Fort

"At the upper point of Winandermere lies the carcase as it were of an antient city with great ruins of walls … the paved roads leading to it plainly bespeak it a Roman work."

William Camden, *Britannia*, 1586

Only the Furness sandstone foundations are visible, surrounded by grass-munching cows. R.G. Collingwood excavated the fort between 1913 and 1920, discovering that a turf and timber fort was first built c. AD 79. A second, stone fort was built c. AD 100, raised above flood levels by an earth platform. It was in use until at least AD 365. The fort had been burned at some point, and a tombstone hinted at violence: *'TO THE GOOD GODS OF THE UNDERWORLD / FLAVIOUS ROMANUS, RECORD CLERK, LIVED FOR 35 YEARS / KILLED WITHIN THE FORT BY THE ENEMY'*.

Borran's Field was the 'North Pole' in *Winter Holiday*, although the summerhouse described in Arthur Ransome's book no longer survives. Further around Waterhead Bay, Borran's Park was a segregated public bathing spot between the wars. The picnickers you'll encounter today are a sign that you've made it back to Ambleside.

Grasmere from Loughrigg

Grasmere

Length (km)	Maximum width (km)	Maximum depth (m)	Surface area (km²)	Catchment area (km²)	Height above sea level (m)
1.5	0.65	21.5	0.61	28.73	61

Trip Distance	3.5km / 2.1 miles
Start / Finish	Penny Rock Wood NY 342 060 / panic.bloomers.sweated / LA22 9SE

Introduction

"A beautiful image of stillness, clear as glass, reflecting all things – the wind was up & the waters sounding. The lake of a rich purple, the field a soft yellow, the Island yellowish-green, the copses Red Brown, the mountains purple."

Dorothy Wordsworth, *Grasmere Journals*, 1800–1803

A Grasmere paddle is a literal immersion in literary heritage. The years in which Dorothy and her brother William lived at Dove Cottage were their most creative period. Every nook and cranny of the lake gave inspiration to, or was referenced by, the Wordsworths and the eccentric coterie of writers (the so-called Lake Poets) whom they attracted to Grasmere.

Grasmere also happens to be simply gorgeous. Paddling around this small mere, marvelling at the *"stillness, clear as glass"* and relishing the silence and solitude is a precious experience, all the

more so because nearby Grasmere village is overrun by international tourists / literary pilgrims. Paddlers don't have to grasp the poetry* to feel poetic about Grasmere.

> "… one of the sweetest landscapes, that art ever attempted to imitate … this little unsuspected paradise."
>
> Thomas Gray, *Journal of A Visit to the Lake District*, 1775

Grasmere's name derives from the Old Norse *graes maer*: 'lake with grassy / reedy shores'.

*The author studied it at school, and still barely understands a word.

Access

Paddlecraft and rowing boats are allowed on Grasmere, powered boats are not. Landing is not permitted on The Island.

The National Trust leases the lake from the Lowther Estate. The Trust owns The Island, which was bequeathed to it in 2014.

Wildlife and environment

Look out for red squirrels in the mixed deciduous woodland along the shore; the Trust spends around £1,000 per year feeding them at Allan Bank.

There is a heronry of about four nests on The Island, established owing to the lack of disturbance. Grasmere is the best place in Lakeland to spot great-crested grebes; along the northern

📷 *Faeryland landing stage*

shore, look for their 'floating' nests, sheltered beneath bushes and fallen trees. The especially fortunate will witness their bizarre and endearing 'weed-dance' courtship ritual, in which a pair stretch their elongated necks high and present weed to one another.

A plan by the Lowther Estate to operate ten six-berth houseboats on the lake was ditched, after vociferous opposition, in 2020.

Invasive New Zealand pygmyweed has blighted the lake; follow the biosecurity practices outlined on page 34.

Launch points

Penny Rock Wood NY 342 060 / panic.bloomers.sweated / LA22 9SE – following the A591 south from Grasmere village, this is the second lay-by reached, 870m past the Daffodil Hotel and 320m past Banerigg Guest House. There is space for barely four cars: arrive early! Across the road, a gap in the wall accesses a narrow path leading 150m to a beach.

Penny Rock Beach NY 343 059 / alongside.assist.branch / LA22 9SE – the beach at Grasmere's southern point, alongside the River Rothay's outflow, is accessed by footpaths and bridleways, either side of the river, from the two large White Moss Common car parks, both operated by Lowther Estate. White Moss Upper car park is 1km away, across the A591. White Moss Lower car park is 1.1km away.

Faeryland Grasmere NY 333 071 / dreading.triathlon.factoring / LA22 9PX – a lakeside café, offering parking and launching for a fee; details are on their website. The café is reached, from Grasmere village, along Red Bank Road. As there is limited parking, they allow only three launch vehicles at a time.

A592 lay-by NY 342 064 / intensely.celebrate.pipeline / LA22 9SE – following the A591 south from Grasmere village, this is the first lay-by reached, 420m past the Daffodil Hotel. There is space for just three cars. Across the road is a low wall with a notable drop down to a

📷 *The Island*

small beach. Climbing down is awkward, especially so with a paddlecraft. Coupled with the traffic hazard, this spot isn't great.

Description

Penny Rock Wood has several small beaches to launch from. Shaded and hemmed by trees, they offer few hints as to Grasmere's nature until you paddle out, at which point pretty much the whole lake is revealed to you.

The paddle around Grasmere consists of a loop around the single, central, island, soaking up the fell views. The lake is roughly triangular, and you begin in the southern 'corner'. This appears to be walled off by Loughrigg Fell's bracken-covered slopes, latticed by paths and a perennial favourite for family walks. Combining a paddle on Grasmere with an ascent of Loughrigg makes for a fine adventure, especially enjoyed by the author and his daughter. Loughrigg is only 335m in height, yet when the ice flowed south, following the north–south aligned Coniston Fault, the hill's resistant Borrowdale Volcanics rock somehow withstood the glacier's pressure and redirected it into a sharp left turn. Hence, the River Rothay heads not south but north-east from Grasmere, flowing for a kilometre into Rydal Water (page 165), Grasmere's sister lake.

The River Rothay's outlet, where it babbles over a small weir, is hidden from view around a wooded corner. In 1950, rocks were blasted from the outflow to protect Grasmere village from flooding; this lowered the lake level. Penny Rock Beach is across the river. Picnicking on this gravel strand emulates the Wordsworths, who in July 1800 *"rowed down to Loughrigg Fell, visited the white foxglove, gathered wild strawberries … The ferns were turning yellow …"* (**Grasmere Journals**, 1800–1803).

The western, and longest, of Grasmere's three sides begins with Deerbolts Wood; deer appear at the shore around dawn, attracted by nomenclative determinism … and bolt, upon seeing you. The rest of the west is grassy fields extending to stony strands, punctuated by the occasional boathouse. Dale End Farm and its barns are the first of a series of stone properties (now pricey holiday lets) dotting the treeline behind the fields. The Wyke was home to the Mackereth family, friends of the Wordsworths; Sarah Mackereth was *The Westmoreland Girl* of William's 1845 poem, who, aged ten, rescued a lamb from flooded Wyke Gill: *"plunged into the torrent, / Clasped the Lamb and kept her hold"*. The craggy fell behind is 393m Silver How, *"A lovely name for a lovely fell ... rough slopes that delight the eye ... landscape artistry at its best"* (Alfred Wainwright, *The Central Fells*, 1958).

Grasmere's western half is barely 10m deep, the lakebed layered with 11 millennia of accumulated alluvium. Beneath is glacially scoured bedrock, revealing itself above the water's surface as The Island (also known as Grasmere Island, or Wordsworth's Island), a 12m-high and 200m-long hillock which withstood the ice and is now lushly wooded, including a huge, ancient oak. A stone barn, restored by the National Trust, stands near to the southern point.

Wordsworth's Island

"... hither does one Poet sometimes row

His pinnace, a small vagrant barge ...

... And beneath this roof

He makes his summer couch."

William Wordsworth, *Written With A Pencil Upon A Stone In The Wall Of The House, On The Island At Grasmere*, 1800

The Island was Wordsworth's favourite place to relax; as the oddly specific title makes clear, he wrote the poem above at the barn. *"Grasmere's lonely island"* was referenced in his first published work, *An Evening Walk*, 1793.

In an 1800 letter, Samuel Taylor Coleridge described an island bonfire with the Wordsworths, an activity which would not meet the National Trust's approval: *"... twigs heaved & sobbed in the uprushing column of smoke – & the Image of the Bonfire, & of us that danced around it – ruddy laughing faces in the twilight – the Image of this in a Lake smooth as that sea ..."*

The Island was sold in an 1893 auction. Hardwicke Rawnsley complained, *"... during the last two years the top of Snowdon, the island in the middle of Grasmere lake and the Lodore Falls have all come on to the market. Had such a trust as that now proposed been in existence, each of these places might have been obtained for the nation."* He was of course proposing the National Trust, which The Island's sale spurred him to form in 1895 (page 232).

Grasmere's north-west corner is a reedy inlet, frequented by swans and other waterfowl. Hidden at the head, where Wray Gill seeps into the lake, is 'Faeryland Grasmere', a wooden veranda-ed building and tea garden, with jetties. Previously known as Allonby's Boatyard, visitors have rented out rowboats here since the eighteenth century.

📷 *Penny Rock Wood, Loughrigg and Deerbolts Wood*

Fallen trees perched by cormorants indicate how shallow this lakehead is. Grasmere village lies beyond the lake's northern shore; it is shielded from view by the wetland reeds, willow and alder surrounding the River Rothay's delta.

The prominent building at the north-east corner, served by landing stages, is the Daffodil Hotel. From an 1857 royal visit until recent times, it was the Prince of Wales Hotel. Just beyond the hotel is Dove Cottage, modest home to the Wordsworths from 1799 to 1808 and then to Thomas De Quincey from 1809 to 1820. De Quincey wrote his account of addiction there, **Confessions of an English Opium Eater**. A visit is best left for after paddling; signs discourage launching or landing at the stone boathouse adjacent to the road. The boathouse was built in the early 1800s by William Pearson. Although Pearson was a schoolfriend of Wordsworth, the poet complained that it was ugly, *"not 200 yards"* from Dove Cottage.

Wordsworth did not approve of changes to Grasmere's eastern shore either. In 1800 he lauded its inaccessibility: *"A rude and natural causeway, interpos'd / Between the water and a winding slope / Of copse and thicket, leaves the eastern shore / Of Grasmere safe in its own privacy"* (**A narrow girdle of rough stones and crags**). In 1831, a causeway and road were constructed alongside the shoreline: the modern-day A591. The paddle back to Penny Rock Wood takes (slightly) less time than you'd imagine as the lake flows, albeit excruciatingly slowly, to the island's east. The only building overlooking Grasmere from the A591 is Banerigg, built in 1900 and a guest house since 1948.

The only thing left to mention is Helm Crag, best seen from Grasmere's eastern half. This modest (405m) but prominent fell (Wainwright: *"a midget of a mountain"*) presents as a neat pyramid, behind Grasmere village. It is unmistakeable, on account of the pinnacles jutting from its apex: 'The Lion and the Lamb'.

"Dear Valley, having in thy face a smile
Though peaceful, full of gladness. Thou art pleased,
Pleased with thy crags and woody steeps, thy Lake,
Its one green island and its winding shores."
William Wordsworth, *Home at Grasmere*, c. 1800

William and Dorothy

William and Dorothy Wordsworth were born in 1770 and 1771 respectively, in Cockermouth. After their mother died in 1778, William attended Hawkshead Grammar School and Dorothy was sent to Yorkshire relatives. By the time they were reunited in 1794, William had walked the Alps, rapturously immersed himself in revolutionary France (producing a French daughter in the process) and published his first poetry. The siblings lived in Dorset and then Somerset, where they met Samuel Taylor Coleridge. A creative bromance commenced, which thrived until 1810, when the latter's opium addiction drove the men apart.

In 1799, William and Dorothy returned home to Cumbria, renting 'The Dove and Olive Bough', a former inn beside Grasmere, *"the loveliest spot that man hath ever found"* (*A Farewell*, 1802). Their eight years here (*"plain living, but high thinking"*) made it famous as 'Dove Cottage', although this name came later. William productively churned out a new edition of the *Lyrical Ballads* (1801) with Coleridge, *Poems in Two Volumes* (1807) and two versions of *The Prelude* (1799, 1805), an autobiographical poem recounting his Cumbrian childhood.

The siblings' relationship was close: *"She gave me eyes, she gave me ears, / And humble cares and delicate fears"* (*The Sparrow's Nest*, 1801), awkwardly so after William married Mary Hutchinson in 1802. Dorothy has sometimes been sidelined to the bit-part of 'devoted spinster'. However, she was an accomplished poet and observer of the natural world in her own right. Thomas De Quincey noted upon first meeting her, *"some subtle fire of impassioned intellect apparently burned within"*. She produced the *Grasmere Journals* (1800–1803) and played a clear role in William's poetry (page 95).

From 1808, the Wordsworths lived in Grasmere village: at Allan Bank (National Trust) and, from 1811, the Old Rectory (since demolished). William gained the (pretty much honorary) job of Distributor of Stamps for Westmorland, receiving a salary for the first time in his life. They moved to Rydal Mount, near Rydal Water, in 1813, and remained there until death (William in 1850, Dorothy in 1855).

William's final years saw him morph from republican radical into reactionary conservative; he accepted the title of Poet Laureate in 1843 and scribbled NIMBY diatribes against change: *"Is then no nook of English ground secure / From rash assault?"* (letter to the *Morning Post*, 1843). Despite ranting against tourists (especially, *"the imperfectly educated classes"*), his most lucrative literary work was his *Guide to the Lakes*, a guidebook published anonymously in 1810 and regularly reprinted and updated, until 1835.

SY Gondola and Dow Crag

📷 *Torver Back Common and Wetherlam*

Coniston Water

Length (km)	Maximum width (km)	Maximum depth (m)	Surface area (km²)	Catchment area (km²)	Height above sea level (m)
8.7	0.79	56.1	2.78	42.47	46

Introduction

"Captain John was looking through the telescope … the blue lake under the clear summer sky stretched away into the big hills. Away to the south the lake narrowed and narrowed until it became a winding river through green lowlands."

Arthur Ransome, *Swallows and Amazons*, 1930

Visiting the Lake District at six years old, the author's Cumbrian aunt told him that his favourite book, *Swallows and Amazons*, was set on Coniston Water. I confidently / precociously pointed out that the book's lake didn't quite match (I'd spent hours poring over the maps) and the placenames were different. I have never forgotten my aunt's revelatory reply: *"Yes, but he had to have somewhere in mind when he wrote it"*.

Paddlers will discover that Coniston Water is still, absolutely 100%, the wild and unexplored lake in *Swallows and Amazons*. The shores are undeveloped and quiet, backed by low wooded fells, with the daunting peak of Kanchenjunga (sorry, the Old Man of Coniston) rearing behind. Wild Cat Island (sorry, Peel Island) is exactly as Ransome described, and can be visited.

The lake is explored here via two routes, respectively covering the woodland-shrouded southern and the fell-backed northern halves; a paddle around the whole thing would be at least 18km / 11 miles in length. A near-end-to-end trip between Coniston and Brown Howe car parks, perhaps shuttling utilising the X12 bus service, would be around 7.5km / 5 miles.

Coniston Water was home and inspiration to Victorian art critic and polymath John Ruskin and his devotee, antiquarian W. G. Collingwood, who in turn took Arthur Ransome under his wing. Post-war, the lake acquired international fame when Donald Campbell and *Bluebird K7* repeatedly broke the water speed record here, until his tragic death.

Coniston Water describes a very straight NNE–SSW course, slicing across the underlying Windermere Supergroup: Silurian mudstone, sandstone and siltstone. The glacier scoured a deep basin: the lakebed is below sea level. The shores tend to be rocky and steep-sided in the southern half and covered with gentler-inclined glacial clay beaches in the northern half.

Old maps called the lake Thurston's Mere or Thurstonmere. Thurston, or Thorstein, was probably a Norse settler. Coniston means 'King's Farm', from Old Norse *konungr* (king) and Old English *tun* (farm).

Access

Paddlecraft are allowed on Coniston Water, as are rowing and sailing boats. Powered craft are restricted by a 10mph speed limit; however, this rule is dropped in early November, when Coniston Power Boat Records Week takes place.

Fir Island and Peel Island have been owned by the National Trust since 1932 and landing is permitted.

Paddlers are asked to avoid a number of 'wildfowl areas': along the eastern shore, from north of Peel Island to opposite Brown Howe car park and also from Park Nab to High Nibthwaite; on the western shore, just south of Church Beck. Additionally, the National Park has designated six areas as 'vulnerable lakeshore', where care should be taken; most are private land, in any case.

Stay clear of the Coniston launches, *SY Gondola*, and their landing piers.

Wildlife and environment

The waters contain char, perch, pike and trout. A large array of wildfowl resides, winters or passes through, including Canada geese, cormorants, goldeneyes, great-crested grebe, greylag geese, mergansers and tufted ducks. Buzzards, peregrine falcons and sparrowhawks patrol the skies, looking for prey. Esthwaite Water's ospreys fish the lake; there are hopes that they will eventually nest here.

Roe and red deer reside within Grizedale Forest, on the eastern shore, and can be spotted enjoying an early drink. Red squirrels are seen, especially along the eastern shore abutting Grizedale Forest. Otters are a rare sight, but spottings have increased in the area from the northern end to Tarn Hows.

Invasive New Zealand pygmyweed has blighted the lake; follow the biosecurity practices outlined on page 34.

📷 *Bluebird K7, restored, at the Ruskin Museum in Coniston village*

Launch points

Brown Howe car park SD 291 910 / education.dishes.calculate / LA12 8DW – a large National Park car park, 50m from the lake shore.

Thrang Crag Wood lay-bys SD 290 913 / pixies.crumb.washroom / LA12 8EZ – four lay-bys line the A5084, between 300m and 1km north of Brown Howe car park. From the first, pass through a gate to a beach on Access Land. The second requires you to cross the road and pass through a gap in the wall. The others are directly lakeside. All fill up rapidly in summer.

Sunny Bank jetty SD 292 928 / tarnished.lace.blasted / LA21 8BJ – a rough parking area, signed 'Torver Commons', beside the A5084, 300m north of its bridge across Torver Beck. Follow the footpath 500m alongside Torver Back Common, descending 30m, to the jetty.

Coniston Boating Centre SD 308 970 / whiplash.ritual.awoken / LA21 8AN – a lakeside outdoor activity centre with a large car park. It charges for launching, from a day to a year.

Monk Coniston car park SD 316 978 / mouths.layers.slot / LA21 8AA – a lakeside National Park car park, with direct access to the water.

Machell Coppice SD 309 952 / fussed.village.comforted / LA21 8AD – a Forestry England car park, across the road from the lake. Sometimes closed for forestry operations.

Bailiff Wood car park SD 302 935 / upgrading.relishes.survive / LA21 8AX – a free car park, across the road from the lake shore.

Dodgson Wood car park SD 299 927 / youth.comforted.spices / LA21 8AX – a free car park, across the road from the lake shore.

Dales Wood lay-by SD 298 923 / jumbo.frozen.credit / LA12 8DW – a tiny lay-by beside a gate, across the road from a wooden pier. Only room for a couple of vehicles. Do not block the gate.

Amazon-Mavis at the Ruskin Museum, Coniston village

Low Peel Near lay-by SD 296 914 / egging.improvise.invent / LA12 8DW – a tiny lay-by beside stone bins, across the road from a gate. Only room for three vehicles. Either walk 80m south along the road to a beach or pass through the gate and cross the meadow (Access Land) to the water.

Lake Bank jetty SD 288 900 / initial.common.haystack / LA12 8EZ – a large lay-by beside the A5084, 300m north of Lake Bank. Follow a permissive path 200m through woods, negotiating a kissing gate, to the lake shore alongside the jetty.

Boon Beck SD 288 903 / shops.saddens.decreased / LA12 8EZ – a small parking area beside the A5084, 700m north of Lake Bank. Follow a path 200m across Access Land to the lake shore.

◎ *Mist on southern end of Coniston Water, from Coniston Old Man*

Coniston Water – southern

Trip Distance	7.5km / 4.5 miles
Start / Finish	Brown Howe car park SD 291 910 / education.dishes.calculate / LA12 8DW

Description

In summer, the pebble beaches fronting Brown Howe car park will be a hive of picnicking and paddling activity. Note the exposed tree roots, where waves have eroded the shoreline. Gazing up and down Coniston Water's narrow southern half, you have to strain your eyes to spot any buildings: Grizedale Forest's sprawling treescape completely envelops the far, eastern shore. The forest has expanded, since the first planting in the eighteenth century, to cover nearly 2,500 hectares; mostly spruce, larch and fir, but also native broadleaf trees. Only the summit of 335m Top o' Selside, the highest point between Coniston Water and Windermere, peeks above the treeline.

Paddling north to Oxen House Bay, the A5084 is at first close by, with a shoreline retaining wall. The road departs at the bay, which is formed by Torver Beck's arcuate delta curving out to further narrow the lake. An attractive vee-roofed boathouse sits just before the river mouth. Lake level allowing, it's possible to discreetly explore up-beck, passing beneath a vee-ed footbridge into a secret backwater.

Sunny Bank jetty, alongside an isolated boathouse, is the point where rugged Torver Back Common commences. Continuing north is tempting (and, if the lake is rough, a wise option);

however, following this route, the jetty is the springboard for the 650m paddle to the eastern shore. All being well, you'll touch land in the vicinity of Dodgson Wood car park, hidden across the lakeside lane.

> "The eastern shore turns out, when you get there, to be a chain of changes and surprises – rocks, knotts, nabs, coves, little bays and bulges of woodland."

Norman Nicholson, *Greater Lakeland*, 1969

A mix of woodland and pasture, with a wooden jetty marking the halfway point, line your passage towards the main attraction, 900m south: Peel Island. The island rears ten metres from the water, distinctive by its craggy Silurian mudstone and sandstone, which withstood the force of the passing glacier. The name possibly refers to a 'pele' tower; W.G. Collingwood thought that one stood here. Paddling around, shallow rocks and reefs shouldn't trouble your paddlecraft. The eastern side is a low cliff, and the south-western end is guarded by Calf Rock. This islet marks the entrance to a narrow inlet, where the mudstones have eroded a channel between steeply dipping sandstone beds. Millions of readers worldwide would instantly recognise this as Wild Cat Island's 'Hidden Harbour':

> "Slowly Swallow moved in among rocks awash. Then, besides the rocks awash, there were rocks showing above water. These grew bigger. Then there were high rocks that hid the eastern side of the lake, while the western side was hidden by a long rocky point sticking out from the island. It was almost like being between two walls ..."

Arthur Ransome, *Swallows and Amazons*, 1930

📷 *Approaching Peel Island*

If you land to explore (and why on earth wouldn't you?), you'll discover that the 90m-long island is, *"rocky and covered with heather and small stunted bushes, growing so thickly that it was not easy to push one's way through them"*, yet latticed with a myriad of paths leading to different levels and lookouts. It's a fabulous place for children, and their adults, to explore. The book's 'Lighthouse Tree' is present at the north end, planted by the Arthur Ransome Society after the original blew down. At the centre is a flat area within a deep cleft in the rocks, an ideal camp spot: *"With an island like that within sight, who could be content to live on the mainland and sleep in a bed at night?"*. Depressingly, National Trust signage notes that there has been *'anti-social behaviour'* here and hence patrol boats inspect the island, around dusk.

Ransome and Peel Island

Long before he immortalised it as 'Wild Cat Island', Peel Island was central to Arthur Ransome's life. His parents became engaged on the island, and in 1892 the Ransomes picnicked here with W. G. Collingwood and his family. Eight-year-old Arthur was inspired by Collingwood, who excavated 'Norse' remains on the island, and by his children's novel *Thorstein of the Mere*, in which a young Viking hides on the island. The adult Ransome would retreat here to write; Collingwood's youngest daughter swam from shore with proofs of *Edgar Allen Poe* tied to her head. In 1911, Ransome almost wrecked his boat while landing, inspiring John's accident in *Swallowdale*. Ransome took a sprig of Peel Island's heather to Russia and kept it with him throughout the Revolution.

Peel Island lies alongside High Peel Near, a craggy promontory which, along with the smaller headland Low Peel Near, encloses secluded Montague Wyke.

📷 *Anna's Nab*

To the south, a second successive pair of promontories, Park Nab and Anna's Nab, pinch Coniston Water through a hundred-metre gap.

Park Nab is occupied by Water Park Lakeland Adventure Centre, with an enclosed marina hidden from view on the north side and paddlecraft lined up on the south side's beach. The intriguing bit is Oak Isle, the high-sided island adjoined to Park Nab by a footbridge spanning a usually dry channel. Also known as Lake Holme, this is topped by a small cottage.

Slender, tree-covered Anna's Nab encloses Water End, Coniston Water's southernmost pool. The hummocky shores surrounding this lake-in-miniature are terminal moraines: glacial detritus which dammed and hence created Coniston Water. Landing and launching are discouraged at Nibthwaite Quay, the cluster of jetties and boathouses in the south-east corner; however, a public footpath leads to High Nibthwaite. This is just a hamlet, but in 1735 a water-powered furnace cast cannons here and in the nineteenth century it had a busy bobbin mill which served the cotton industry. Ransome holidayed at Laurel House, until a teenager. In his *Autobiography* (1976), he described his Nibthwaite Quay ritual:

> "I had to dip my hand in the water, as a greeting to the beloved lake or as proof to myself that I had indeed come home. In later years, even as an old man, I have laughed at myself, resolved not to do it again, and every time I have done it again."

The River Crake drains the lake, percolating through expansive reedbeds on both banks. If the river flow is not too strong, a discreet addition to your trip is recommended: Allan Tarn is 300m downstream, a delightfully secretive pool, where the Crake gathers itself before racing south to Morecambe Bay. Allan Tarn is better known as 'Octopus lagoon', where the Swallows staged a nighttime raid to capture *Amazon*. It was so-named as tentacle-like water lilies grabbed the children's oars. In the book, the river's flow is reversed:

> "Swallow moved up the Amazon River in the rapidly gathering dusk. There were walls of reeds on each side … Suddenly the river broadened into a wide, open pool, with tall reeds all round it."

Arthur Ransome, *Swallows and Amazons*, 1930

Back on Coniston Water and following the western shore north, Lake Bank jetty, the southern terminus of the Coniston launches, is directly opposite Anna's Nab. Bass Crag is the small promontory opposite Park Nab, with a marshy bay behind. Escaping the 'straits' on to the open water, you just need to pass a cluster of rather nice private residences hidden in small bays before returning to Brown Howe car park.

Arthur Ransome

Because of *Swallows and Amazons*, Arthur Ransome is indivisibly associated with Coniston Water and Windermere. However, his life took him much further afield. His childhood summers were spent at Coniston Water; his father dropped him in, to see if he would swim: he sank. During these holidays, Ransome met W.G. Collingwood, his future mentor (page 159). After attending Windermere's Old College, he moved to London to start a career in writing.

In 1903, Ransome returned to Lakeland. A chance meeting beside Copper Mines Beck reacquainted him with W.G. Collingwood and he made long stays at Lane End, learning to sail in their boat *Swallow*. After unsuccessfully proposing to at least two of Collingwood's daughters, Ransome married Ivy Walker. In 1913, he abandoned her and his daughter, to study folklore in Russia.

When the Russian Revolution erupted in 1917, Ransome stayed as a war correspondent for the British press. He became close to the Bolshevik leaders and wrote *The Truth about Russia* to garner international support for the Revolution. He was uncritical about Lenin (his chess partner!) and denied the 'Red Terror' executions. He even married Trotsky's secretary, Evgenia, in 1924. Lenin viewed Ransome as one of his *"useful idiots"*: naïve Westerners manipulated to his own ends. The British Secret Intelligence Service (MI6's precursor) reported that he was *"completely in the hands of the Bolsheviks"* and regarded him as a traitor yet recruited him as Spy S76. Whose 'side' was Ransome on?

Ransome returned to England, with Evgenia, in 1924. They lived at Low Ludderburn, near Windermere, where he wrote *Swallows and Amazons*. Published in 1930, its success led to eleven more classic novels. The 'Swallows' and the 'Amazons' were based on the Altounyans, the children of Dora Collingwood who had once spurned him. The books' unnamed lake combines features of both Coniston Water and Windermere. Responding to queries about specific locations, Ransome wrote, *"All the places in the book are to be found, but not arranged quite as in the Ordnance Survey's maps."*

During the Second World War, the Ransomes lived at The Heald, alongside Coniston Water. He was plagued by ulcers and mental health problems and, until his death in 1967, they moved repeatedly between London and Lakeland.

Torver Back Common and the Coniston Fells

📷 *Passing Bailiff Wood*

Coniston Water – northern

Trip Distance	12.1km / 7.5 miles
Start / Finish	Monk Coniston car park SD 316 978 / mouths.layers.slot / LA21 8AA

Description

Monk Coniston car park is so-named as, from the thirteenth century, the lands around Coniston Water's north, extending to Windermere, belonged to Furness Abbey. Similarly, Coniston village was originally called Church Coniston. The abbey, located to the south near Barrow-in-Furness, exploited the lake by burning charcoal and smelting iron ore at shoreline 'bloomeries'.

> *"The mountains at the head of the lake are great, noble, and sublime, without any thing that is horrid or terrible. They are bold and steep …"*

Thomas West, *A Guide to the Lakes*, 1778

It's impossible to ignore the Old Man of Coniston, the sprawling 803m bulk of ash and lava which rears beyond the far shore and overlooks the lake's length. The 'old man' is actually a high cairn (Celtic: *allt maen*). Arthur Ransome was carried up as a baby and the fell is better known, worldwide, as Kanchenjunga, summitted by the children in *Swallowdale*, *Swallows and Amazons*' 1931 sequel. The slate quarries and copper mines visibly scarring its flanks are where, in *Pigeon Post* (1936), the children prospected for gold.

Coniston Water's eastern shores first consist of tree-lined beaches, backed by sloping meadows. The farms and houses loosely spread behind form a (fiendishly complex and interconnected) 'Who's Who' of Lakeland history and culture; to make sense of the following, you may wish to grab a whiteboard and marker pen …

Tent Lodge occupies where Elizabeth Smith lived in a tent, eventually dying from tuberculosis, in 1806, at age 26. A friend of the Wordsworths, she was a brilliant linguist who taught herself nine languages. Poet Laureate Alfred Tennyson honeymooned at Tent Lodge in 1850 (also at Mirehouse, page 54) and stayed again in 1857, joined by his friend Charles Dodgson: better known as Lewis Carroll.

Paddlecraft are rented from the jetties fronting High Bank Ground Farm, which is also a café. More pertinently, this is 'Holly Howe', where the Walker children (the 'Swallows') stay in *Swallows and Amazons*. Ransome took inspiration for the characters from the children of Roger Altounyan, who holidayed here. Ransome and Altounyan bought dinghies (*Swallow* and *Mavis*) and sailed together. Behind High Bank Ground is Lanehead, now a yoga retreat but once home to W.G. Collingwood and family, who took Ransome under their wings. It was the model for 'Beckfoot', home of the 'Amazon' children.

The Coniston Collingwoods

William Gershom Collingwood (1854–1932) studied under John Ruskin at Oxford, and in 1875 moved to the Lake District to work as his secretary. Despite dedicating his life to serving the Victorian polymath, he was quite the polymath in his own right: writer, painter, designer, antiquarian and archaeologist, whose academic and creative work focused on the Lake District. His daughter Dora married Roger Altounyan (hence, the 'Swallows' were Collingwood's grandchildren) and his son Robin (1889–1943) became a noted philosopher and archaeologist, who excavated Galava Roman Fort, alongside Windermere.

Low Bank Ground and Thurston are successive outdoor centres, both fronted by jetties and accompanying paddlecraft racks. A solitary boathouse breaks up a quieter stretch of shoreline before the large, curved jetty serving Brantwood. Brantwood, the sprawling, cream-coloured, eighteenth-century house perched above, was home to John Ruskin. (See next page).

Around Beck Leven Foot headland, Coniston Water changes character. Although the road comes alongside the eastern shore, both shores of the lake's middle third are quiet and sparsely inhabited. Grizedale Forest spills to the eastern shore via a succession of deciduous woodland enclosures – Machell Coppice, Bailiff Wood, and Dodgson Wood – which, in truth, are indistinguishable without a map.

Fir Island, three metres high and smothered by trees, is home to a sizeable cormorant population. Fallen trees and other detritus connect it to the shore; paddling through the gap is only possible in high lake levels. The bungalow across the road, just before the island, is The Heald, Ransome's home from 1940 to 1945. He sailed his dinghy *Coch-y-bonddhu* from here, the model for *Scarab* in *The Picts and the Martyrs* (1943). It is now displayed in Windermere Jetty Museum.

📷 *Brantwood*

Ruskin at Brantwood

When the author first visited Brantwood as a Scout (in the 1980s), his Scout Leader made a memorable observation: *"This Ruskin fellow seems to have tried his hand at everything, yet not been especially good at anything"*. This is possibly unfair. John Ruskin was vastly influential in his lifetime, in a dazzling miscellany of fields: in no particular order, art, draughtsmanship, architecture, art history, literature, history, mythology, social reform, philanthropy, politics, economics, education, museology (I had to Google that one), botany, ornithology and geology. Although he was a critic, commentator and lecturer rather than a 'doer', his ideas are now regarded as ahead of their time, especially regarding the environment and sustainability.

Ruskin lived at Brantwood for 29 years, from 1871 until his death, from flu, in 1900. He expanded the house to accommodate his eclectic collections (books, drawings, paintings, specimens) and added the turret room looking out to the lake and the Old Man of Coniston. Regarding the view, he wrote in 1873, *"The scenery is — I think — the best in England"*.

Landing to visit is recommended, not just for the café: the house and gardens (including samples of Ruskin's collections, as well as his boat and carriage) are worth a couple of hours of your life. Pre-plan this excursion by bringing a clothing change: neoprene and Victorian high culture don't make for great synergy.

The Bailiff Wood car park is a quiet launch spot, albeit with a horrifying past. In 1997, divers discovered Carol Park's body 200m offshore. She had disappeared in 1976. In 2005, her husband Gordon was convicted of murdering her with his ice axe. He maintained innocence and, after the Court of Appeal had upheld his conviction, took his own life in prison in 2010.

📷 *Coniston Water Park*

The Cabin is a small bay, which happens to look out across Coniston Water's deepest point. Dodgson Wood car park, another secluded launch spot, marks the point where this route crosses to the western shore, weather and conditions allowing.

Your target during the 660m crossing is Sunny Bank jetty, located where Torver Beck's lower-lying delta intersects with Torver Back Common's slopes. Walkers are dropped off here by steamer or launch to walk the Cumbria Way, which parallels the shore north towards Coniston village. Torver Back Common is characterised by heather and bracken heathlands dotted with sparse, stunted trees. The A5094 is forced to bypass its 150m heights far inland, making for a wonderfully wild 'coastline'. The craggy waterline makes landings awkward, unless the lake level is low. From Moor Gill Foot, the Common is swathed in native broadleaf trees. It ends at the boundary of Torver Common Wood, where planted conifers encroach. Torver jetty serves a series of holiday parks, hidden inland at this point.

From Hoathwaite Landing to Lands Point, the woodlands fall back, and low-lying pastures line the shore. In summer, much of this is given over to busy campsites and you'll be joined by plenty of other water users. Just past Hoathwaite Beck, look for the low mound, rising barely two metres yet around thirty-five metres long: this is a slag heap. There are similar spoil tips in Water Park, marking the sites of 'bloomeries': ironworks. These date back to at least the fourteenth century, potentially even to the Vikings. The beaches are littered with 'clinker': dark slag rocks.

Lands Point is a notable headland. Coniston Hall shelters in the bay behind, a hefty farmhouse-mansion, in the National Trust's possession since 1971. The Le Fleming family owned the estate from the thirteenth century, although their mansion largely dates from the sixteenth. Ruskin sketched and evaluated Coniston Hall for its aesthetic qualities, in *The Poetry of Architecture* (1837). To the author's unaesthetic eye, the whole place looks, with its tall conical chimneys, not unlike Battersea Power Station. A large jetty fronts it, and the boathouse alongside houses Coniston Sailing Club.

📷 *Coniston village and Coniston Water*

Coniston village is fronted by two successive bird's foot deltas, where Church Beck and Yewdale Beck have deposited huge quantities of sediment, boosted by mining activity. Across Church Beck is the nearest thing to a bustling port on Coniston Water; piers serve SY *Gondola* and the Coniston launches, alongside the Bluebird Café and a pavilion hiring out boats. Coniston Boating Centre is behind. The café was rebuilt after damage in the 2009 floods. The original building dated from 1860, used by the Furness Railway Company to house the *Gondola* crew. It was used by Malcolm Campbell as a workshop during his 1939 water speed record attempts and a slate memorial outside commemorates his son Donald. Lake Road leads 800m to the village centre.

Coniston village

This small village is well worth a foray ashore.

John Ruskin lies in the church graveyard. Ruskin's headstone (he rejected the offer of burial in Westminster Abbey) is an elaborately carved Celtic cross, designed by W.G. Collingwood, who is also buried here. Campbell, along with his mechanic Leo Villa, is also commemorated by the slate seat, just along from the church, unveiled in 1968 by his daughter Gina.

The excellent Ruskin Museum has displays on local history, geology and mining. Roger Altounyan's dinghy *Mavis* (the inspiration for the fictional *Amazon*, later itself renamed *Amazon*) is on display. The Bluebird Wing houses *Bluebird K7*; the restored hydroplane came here in 2024 after an acrimonious twenty-year legal dispute between Gina Campbell and diver / restorer Bill Smith.

Yewdale Beck's delta is a veritable maze of channels and wooded islets. Water Head Pier is tucked behind, alongside Pier Cottage, a quirky three-storey boathouse. This was the Campbells' launch site during their record attempts; a diorama in the Ruskin Museum recreates the ramshackle scaffolding-pole-tent which housed *Bluebird K4*, then *Bluebird K7*.

The final stretch to High Water Head, Coniston's northern tip, passes the jetty of the Coniston Inn, a Victorian Gothic pile formerly called the Waterhead Hotel. Charles Darwin holidayed here in 1879.

"Here is an excellent Inn kept by Mr Braithwaite, where the party can … engage a boat for an hour on the water: the latter I should advise, as a row three miles down the lake will repay the trouble, but not further, as the scenery is tame below."

James Gibson, *A Guide to the Scenery of Windermere*, 1843

This route has indeed taken you three miles down-lake; he's wrong about the southern half, though.

SY *Gondola*

"A perfected combination of the Venetian gondola and the English steam-yacht … It may be said to be the most elegant little steam-vessel yet designed."

Carlisle Journal, 1860

Steam Yacht *Gondola* is the wonderfully eccentric Victorian launch plying the lake. This 42-ton vessel was built in Liverpool and launched in 1859. Its gondola shape, clipper stern and serpent figurehead were designed by Barrow industrialist and Furness Railway Company manager James Ramsden, after a tour of Venice.

Ransome steered it as a child, and, along with SL *Esperance*, it inspired Captain Flint's houseboat; the Ruskin Museum has an annotated postcard of *Gondola*, which Ransome sent to illustrator Clifford Webb.

"She was a long narrow craft with a high raised cabin roof, and a row of glass windows along her side. Her bows were like the bows of an old-time clipper. Her stern was alike that of a steamship."

Swallows and Amazons, 1930

Gondola served the lake (carrying 22,445 passengers in 1897) until 1939, when it was sold as a houseboat. Moored at Park Nab, it deteriorated and in 1963 it was swamped by a storm. It was then deliberately sunk, to preserve its iron plates. *Gondola* spent a decade on the lakebed before the National Trust raised it and had it restored at Barrow Vickers shipyard. It was relaunched in 1980. It now runs on sawdust, rather than coal.

The Campbells at Coniston

From the 1930s to the 1960s, father and son Malcolm and Donald Campbell were household names and media darlings, associated with flying the flag for Britain through daring speed record attempts.

Sir Malcolm Campbell, first man to exceed 300mph on land, also set water speed records on the Italian and Swiss lakes; however, in 1939 the political situation brought him to Coniston Water. His new boat *Bluebird K4* was launched at Pier Cottage by 18-year-old Donald, and Malcolm subsequently achieved a record of 141.74mph.

Donald picked up his father's mantle, and in 1955, on Ullswater, set a record of 202.15mph in *Bluebird K7*. Up to 1959, he set four further records on Coniston Water and, in 1964, he became the only person to break land and water speed records in the same year. However, in 1966 he repeatedly failed to achieve his water speed goal of 300mph, and the press turned on him, implying that he had lost his nerve. This seems to have rattled Campbell and on 4th January 1967, he made an all-out attempt to silence his critics.

The record-breaking rules required two runs over a marked kilometre, in opposite directions, with the average speed taken. *Bluebird K7* – boosted to generate 4,500lbs of thrust – registered 297mph on the southward run. On the return trip, just four minutes later, Campbell pushed the jet hydroplane further beyond its engineering and hydrodynamic limits (supposedly, 250mph). After passing Peel Island, *Bluebird K7* touched 328.12mph, before catastrophe: it left the water, performed a complete aerial backflip, cartwheeled along the lake's surface and finally sank. Campbell's final words, transmitted over intercom, were, *"I can't see a bloody thing. Hello, the bow's up. I'm gone."*

'Mr Whoppit', teddy bear mascot of both Campbells, was the sole survivor. Donald's remains (although not his head), along with *Bluebird K7*'s, were not recovered until 2001. His Union flag-covered coffin was carried to Peel Cottage on the launch MV *Ruskin* and he was buried in Coniston cemetery on 12th September, overlooked by the press due to the previous day's events.

Gina Campbell, seventeen at the time of her father's death, continued the family legacy by breaking the women's water speed record at Nottingham in 1984 and in New Zealand in 1990.

Other Lakes

Rydal Water

"Like a fair sister of the sky,
Unruffled doth the blue lake lie,
The mountains looking on."

William Wordsworth, *September 1819*, 1819

Paddling is not allowed on Rydal Water. That said … in the wetter months, it sees regular passage of paddlers descending the River Rothay from Grasmere to Windermere, and this appears to be tolerated. The author's first descent of this easy white-water river was in 1988, and the most recent was last week!

Rydal Water is almost bisected by islands. From north to south: a small rocky islet, Heron Island and Little Isle. Heron Island is adorned with an 1871 memorial to Crusoe, *'a noble Newfoundland Dog'* who belonged to the Flemings of Rydal Hall. Little Isle has a stone slipway and the remains of a stone hut. There are further islets, including Green Holme, at the outflow. These are overlooked by Thrang Crag, known as 'Wordsworth's Seat', as it was a favourite haunt of the poet in his later years, when he lived at Rydal Mount.

Thomas De Quincey stayed at Nab Cottage, the 1702 farmhouse alongside the A592. He got the owner's daughter Margaret pregnant in 1816 and, to the Wordsworths' disgust (she was his social inferior), married her. She endured his opium addiction, and they had eight children. Samuel Taylor Coleridge's son Hartley, another addict (alcohol), lodged here from 1840 until his death in 1849. He is buried at Grasmere, alongside the Wordsworths.

Elter Water

"Elterwater, which drains both of the Langdales, never quite makes up its mind when to cease to be a lake and begin to be the Brathay."

Norman Nicholson, *The Lakers*, 1955

Elter Water is actually three connected bodies of water: the pool seen alongside the Cumbria Way and also two lagoons to the west, which are hidden from view behind The Nab, a marshy island. The smallest of all the lakes, Elter Water was reduced to its current form in the nineteenth century, when Great Langdale Beck was straightened. It continues to shrink, being slowly filled by emergent vegetation and encroached on all sides by carr and wetlands.

Paddling is not allowed by the National Trust, on ecological grounds. However, paddlers commonly pass through as part of white-water river trips; the author, for example, has kayaked into Elter Water from both Great Langdale Beck and Little Langdale Beck, departing via the River Brathay. Note that Skelwith Force, a significant waterfall, lurks behind a bend on the Brathay, shortly after its outflow.

📷 *Esthwaite Water*

Esthwaite Water

"Once upon a time there was a frog called Mr. Jeremy Fisher; he lived in a little damp house amongst the buttercups at the edge of a pond."

Beatrix Potter, *The Tale of Mr Jeremy Fisher*, 1906

Paddling is not typically allowed on Esthwaite Water, a private fishery. It does, however, see plenty of rowboats and powered launches, hired out to anglers. Kayak fishing competitions have taken place on the lake, so perhaps the best chance of paddling on Esthwaite Water is to learn one end of a rod from the other. After years of being contracted out, the fishery lease returned to the Graythwaite Estate in 2024; it's not presently clear how this may impact the access situation.

Esthwaite Water has gentler shores than most of the other lakes: some farmland, some wetland. Agricultural run-off has made the lake highly eutrophic. Ospreys nest here. The peculiar blob-shaped headlands called 'Ees' (Old English: island) are drumlins.

Wordsworth attended Hawkshead Grammar School: *"… My morning walks / Were early; oft, before the hours of School / I travell'd round our little lake, five miles / Of pleasant wandering, happy time!"* (*The Prelude*, 1850). Beatrix Potter settled at Hill Top in Near Sawrey, now a National Trust property. She thought Esthwaite Water *"The most beautiful of the Lakes"* and set *The Tale of Mr Jeremy Fisher* upon it. The rowboat she kept on the lake has been restored and is in Windermere Jetty Museum.

📷 Rydal Water

The Western Lakes

Key to symbols used

⚓	Marina	🪨	Rock/reef
⌂	Boathouse	⊙	Iron Age hillfort
⛵	Sailing club	✲■+	Historical features
24 △	Campsite	+	Named church
🚐	Caravan park	●	Railway stations
🚐	Motorhomes only	■+	Monument/place of tourist interest
	Bunkhouse, camping barn or bothy		Area with restrictions
	Youth hostel		Restricted wildlife area
	Holiday park		Vulnerable lake shore
P	Car park	△	Start/finish launch point
	Café or pub	○	Alternative launch point

168

Buttermere north-west beach

The Western Lakes

The Screes – Bell Crag, Broad Crag and Whin Rigg

📷 *Wast Water from Lingmell*

Wast Water

Length (km)	Maximum width (km)	Maximum depth (m)	Surface area (km²)	Catchment area (km²)	Height above sea level (m)
4.8	0.78	79	2.78	42.47	64

Trip Distance	10.5km / 6.5 miles
Start / Finish	Countess Beck NY 151 054 / famines.plantings.frozen / CA20 1EU

Introduction

"The Lake was a perfect Mirror; & what must have been the Glory of the reflections in it! This huge facing of Rock said to be half a mile in perpendicular height, with deep Ravines the whole wrinkled & torrent-worn, except where the pink-striped Screes come in, as smooth as silk. All this reflected, turned into Pillars, dells, and a whole new-world of Images in the water! The head of the Lake is crowned by three huge pyramidal mountains."

Samuel Taylor Coleridge, 1802

Coleridge was blown away by Wast Water and its reflected fells. This letter to Sara Hutchinson (his unrequited love) was not hyperbole: everyone encountering this most dramatic of the English Lakes will feel the same awe. Paddlers get to experience Wast Water's astonishing Screes up close, and bask in the reflections of the *"huge pyramidal mountains"* including England's highest, Scafell Pike.

Herdies (herdwick sheep) at Wasdale Head Hall Farm

Wast Water is also known as Wastwater. Wast derives from Wasdale, from the Old Norse *vatn* (body of water) and *dalr* (valley). So, Wast Water means 'lake of the valley of the lake'!

Access

Canoes, kayaks, paddleboards and rowboats are allowed on the lake. Powered, sailing or fishing craft are not allowed. Paddlers are allowed in groups of no more than fifteen craft.

Direct queries to northandwestlakes@nationaltrust.org.uk.

Wast Water has been owned by the National Trust since 1979.

Wildlife and environment

Wast Water is the most oligotrophic of all the lakes; in other words, it has clear water and relatively little life within. It does contain brown trout and char, and black-headed gulls frequent the few islets. The lake is designated a Special Area of Conservation.

Up to four million gallons daily are pumped from the lake's exit, for cooling Sellafield's nuclear processes. In 1978, British Nuclear Fuels (BNF) proposed raising the lake with a weir, to extract an additional eleven million gallons daily. In 1980, a Public Inquiry rejected the plan (alongside similar plans for Ennerdale Water); it had emerged that BNF didn't really need the water.

Launch points

Countess Beck NY 151 054 / famines.plantings.frozen / CA20 1EU – a small lay-by adjacent to where the Gosforth road joins the west shore. More lay-bys are dotted along the road for the 2km up-valley towards Overbeck Bridge and also 650m down-valley, some notably further from the water. All fill up quickly at weekends. This shoreline is a Site of Special Scientific Interest (SSSI): don't park on the grass.

◉ *Countess Beck*

Overbeck car park NY 168 068 / task.informal.clerk / CA20 1ET – a National Trust car park with a donation box, alongside Overbeck Bridge. Cross the road to a beach.

Lake Head car park NY 181 075 / tango.responds.library / CA20 1EX – a large National Trust car park with a cash-only machine, popular with walkers ascending Scafell Pike. A 500m walk across Lingmell Gill bridge and then signposted down a track accesses Wast Water's northern beach.

Description

Countess Beck is a popular spot, as the lake is uncharacteristically shallow for some distance from the beach. Stepping stones access a tiny island, unless the lake level is high. Further offshore, Wast Water is *not* shallow. It's England's deepest lake, the dark waters plunging 79m, to 15m below sea level.

Paddling up-valley, the road is never far from the lake's north shore. At first, the shoreline beaches are backed by Greendale Mires SSSI, a rare peatland habitat, with the slabby, ice-scoured, slopes of Middle Fell rising behind.

A small boat shed is the north shore's only building, just before two successive becks flow in. Both Nether Beck and Over Beck are actively building arcuate (curved) deltas of volcanic boulders, flushed out into the lake. Overbeck car park is popular with scuba divers, who wade out into Wast Water's abyss. Somewhere down there is the infamous Gnome Garden (precisely what it sounds like) which three divers have sadly lost their lives searching for.

Behind Over Beck, 628m Yewbarrow stabs skyward, *"the shape of the inverted hull of a boat"* (Alfred Wainwright, *The Western Fells*, 1966). In any other context, Yewbarrow's fine symmetrical profile would be a scenic highlight, yet it is immediately upstaged by the loftier peaks arrayed around Wast Water's north end. This skyline, the finest backdrop of any English lake, inspired the National Park logo and was even voted 'England's Favourite View' in 2007. The distinct peaks

📷 *Yewbarrow, Kirk Fell, Great Gable and The Screes*

are: 802m Kirk Fell, 899m Great Gable, 807m Lingmell, 978m Scafell Pike and 963m Scafell. The building blocks of all these fells are sedimentary layers of lava, Borrowdale Volcanics, which make up the rugged heart of the Lake District, with granite occasionally intruded by immense igneous heat and pressure.

> *"We have heard of the pyramids of Egypt, built by the hand of man; but these are the Pyramids of the world, built by the Architect of the Universe."*

Thomas Wilkinson, *Tours to the British Mountains*, 1824

Great Gable is the stand-out performance, perfectly aligned with and framed by the lakehead and … well, its name says it all. Below its shapely apex are the cliffs famous among climbers for formations such as Napes Needle and The Sphinx. Lingmell Beck drains both sides of this ever-looming behemoth, joining Wast Water just as the road departs, via an overgrown and convoluted delta.

Coleridge's 1802 visit, mentioned above, included the first recorded ascent of England's highest mountain. This outing is generally regarded as the birth of fellwalking. Scafell Pike's summit is 978m (3209 feet) above sea level, precisely 2,999 feet above the lake. Nevertheless, it makes a less immediate impression than Great Gable, bookended as it is between Lingmell and Scafell, the latter (964m) appearing higher. Lingmell Gill descends to the lakehead from beneath Scafell Pike's summit cliffs, marking the most popular ascent route.

All this grandeur can be enjoyed from the wide stony beach arcing around Wast Water's head, formed and parcelled up by Lingmell Beck and Lingmell Gill's various channels. The keen-eyed will spot signs of longshore drift: SW gales funnelled along the lake (hopefully not today!) carry sufficient power to shift boulders, freshly deposited into Lingmell Beck's delta, along the shoreline.

At the beach's southern end, a track leads to Lake Head car park and the National Trust campsite. The *really* motivated could leave their paddlecraft on the beach and extend their lunchbreak with a Scafell Pike ascent. A more reasonable outing would be a stroll to Wasdale Head.

◉ *St Olaf's Church*

Wasdale Head

Wasdale Head is a hamlet 1.8km up-valley by bridleway or road, surrounded by *"stone walls apparently innumerable, like a large piece of lawless patchwork"* (William Wordsworth, *Guide to the Lakes*, 1835). A visit is recommended.

The Wasdale Head Hotel is a hub for outdoor adventurers. In the nineteenth century, it was the farmhouse home of Will Ritson, who sold liquor and was lauded as *'the biggest liar in England'*!

Across the road, St Olaf's is Cumbria's (and possibly England's) smallest parish church. Named for a Viking saint, four roof trusses reputedly come from a longship. It's something of a shrine for British mountaineers, with an image of Napes Needle (a rock spire on Great Gable) etched into a window and, outside, the graves of climbers and a memorial to Fell and Rock Climbing Club members fallen in the First World War. In their memory, the club donated Great Gable and the Scafells to the National Trust.

The best is still to come!

Turning on to the south shore, Wasdale Head Hall Farm occupies a brief, seemingly misplaced, shelf of green meadow, where 'Herdies' (Herdwick sheep) munch at the water's edge. Your attention will, however, be focused upon what lies ahead: The Screes. The entire south shore is a dauntingly steep incline, descending from the craggy summits of 608m Illgill Head and 537m Whin Rigg. Viewed from across the lake, this slope appears impressive, yet fairly uniform. Paddlers, privileged to explore this scarp close up, will discover that The Screes are anything but! The best analogy is opening one of those 'pop-up' birthday cards: an incredible three-dimensional wilderness is revealed, an absolute highlight of Lake District paddling. That said, the first kilometre is relatively mild: small streams trickle down greened-over slopes, with the gradient easing towards

The Screes

the lake shore. Both the greenery and the streams soon vanish, unable to gain purchase on the steepening scree.

What are The Screes? This wonderfully onomatopoeic word comes from the Old Norse *skríða*, meaning landslip: eroded and broken rocks, sliding down a mountainside. Paddling along the base of The Screes is an extraordinary experience: this steep (up to 45°) incline of jumbled rocks descends over 500 metres to the lake, where there is no base or shoreline to speak of, and so it instead plunges past and beneath you, far into the depths. Poet Norman Nicholson described this process, slowly ongoing since the glaciers retreated, more lyrically:

> *"a whole fellside has disintegrated, turning back into its own element, and seeping down to water which once shaped and raised it from mud to mountain."*

Norman Nicholson, *The Lakers*, 1955

The scree is not random. A pattern can be discerned, known as 'fall sorting', in which smaller rocks have come to rest higher on the slopes and larger rocks (a metre or more across) nearer, or beneath, the waterline. Furthermore, the scree splays down into Wast Water via numerous vast 'fans', with the scale of the waterline boulders varying between each. Sparse ferns and stunted juniper have colonised some fans; others are as bare as if they formed last week. This harsh Quaternary landscape is an SSSI.

There are no beaches or obvious landing spots. A footpath, occasionally discernible, threads across the rocks, above the shore. Walkers agree that one part is near-impassable.

The time of day will, literally, colour your experience. Until midday, The Screes are invariably in shadow. As the sun finally breaks over Illgill Head, its rays beam between the high crags and down the fans of scree, giving the sensation of your own personal stadium lightshow. By evening, The Screes' pink tinge is fully revealed: Coleridge noted, *"fine red Streaks running in broad Stripes thro' a stone colour."* In the nineteenth century, the iron-rich rocks were ground to make 'ruddle': red paint for marking sheep.

📷 *Lake outlet, River Irt*

Wast Water

Illgill Head rears above Wast Water's deepest part. Paddling towards its sister summit Whin Rigg, a series of increasingly prominent arêtes (or 'ribs') rises behind and between the scree fans, forming a shattered amphitheatre behind a wooded base. Wainwright regarded this as the Lake District's grandest fell frontage, which is no small accolade!

These crags and screes have claimed victims, with plane crashes in 1945 (a Grumman Avenger, three killed) and 1973 (a Piper Cherokee, four killed). In 1985, the remains of missing French walker Veronique Marr were discovered near Broken Rib. A massive search two years earlier had failed to locate her but had led to the discovery of Margaret Hogg (see The Lady in the Lake).

Whin Rigg's summit stands directly above the lakefoot. Here, Wast Water narrows into a hidden lagoon, encircled by trees and drained by the River Irt. The uninhabited building guarding the south shore is a pumping station extracting water for the Sellafield nuclear facility. It was first built, at the start of the Second World War, to supply the Royal Ordnance Factory at Drigg. The stone came from demolishing Down-in-the-Dale Farm, just downstream. Workers installing pipes in the 1960s saw *"something"* long and dark swimming in the deep and others since have reported spotting Wast Water's aquatic monster: you can't argue with science.

A boathouse stands on the opposite, north, shore. Low Wood extends along Wast Water's southern beach, occupying one of the low, rounded knolls which back the shoreline for the rest of your paddle. A change in geology is evident: this is granite, the so-called Ennerdale Intrusion. A hop ashore (or check out the island, shortly after) will reveal distinct striations where the ice, descended from Scafell Pike, scoured its way past.

Wasdale Hall is a distinctive half-timbered building, built in 1829 and a YHA hostel since 1968. Staying here cannot be recommended as, unfortunately, it is haunted. The Crinoline Woman walks the lake edge: the spectre of Isobel Rawston, a previous owner's wife whose daughter drowned in the 1820s. Should you encounter her … who you gonna call?

A tiny black-headed gull-frequented islet, which somehow resisted Wasdale's glacier, is the final landmark on the paddle to Countess Beck.

📷 *Yewbarrow*

The Lady in the Lake

In 1976, airline pilot Peter Hogg drove 300 miles from Surrey to England's deepest lake. In darkness, he rowed an inflatable to (so he believed) the lake's centre, and dumped his wife Margaret's body overboard, wrapped in a carpet weighted with a concrete slab.

In 1984, during the search for a missing French student, divers alerted police to a mysterious bundle at 34 metres depth; they had known of it for years, but not realised its significance.

Hogg had not rowed far enough offshore. Furthermore, his wife's body was easily identifiable by its *"wax-like"* preservation in the anaerobic deep water and by the fact that he had neglected to remove her wedding ring, inscribed with their names and wedding date. Asked by the police, *"Had you murdered your wife?"*, Hogg replied, *"Murder is not the right word. Certainly, she died. I think I strangled her."*

Margaret, an unfaithful wife, was described as *"a piece of erring humanity"* at the Old Bailey, and tabloids called her *"a cow"*. Hogg was found not guilty of murder and sentenced to three years for manslaughter.

Unfortunately, the lakes have repeatedly been utilised to dispose of female victims of male violence. See also, the fates of Sheena Owlett (page 193) and Carol Park (page 160).

Ennerdale Water, south-east corner

📷 *Angler's Crag and Crag Fell*

Ennerdale Water

Length (km)	Maximum width (km)	Maximum depth (m)	Surface area (km²)	Catchment area (km²)	Height above sea level (m)
3.8	1.2	42	3.01	43.46	113
Trip Distance	9.2km / 5.7 miles				
Start / Finish	Bleach Green NY 089 152 / painters.armrest.glassware / CA23 3AS				

Introduction

"Ennerdale is the least known, and, at the present time, the least likely to be visited of all the lakes … until Ennerdale has the benefit of carriage ways along its banks, it will remain comparatively a terra incognita to the tourist world."

Eliza Lynn Lynton, *The Lake Country*, 1864

Welcome to Wild Ennerdale! Ennerdale Water remains the only lake with no public road alongside; although accessing the water is relatively easy, it is the quietest lake to paddle upon, and is probably the least paddled of all.

Ennerdale Water is fifty-fifty divided between harder volcanic granite (the Ennerdale Intrusion) and more erosive Skiddaw Group (the 'Buttermere Formation'). Paddlers floating in mid-lake will experience this dual personality. The up-valley eastern half is narrow, confined within a trough gouged by glaciers descended from an imposing backdrop of fells. In the western

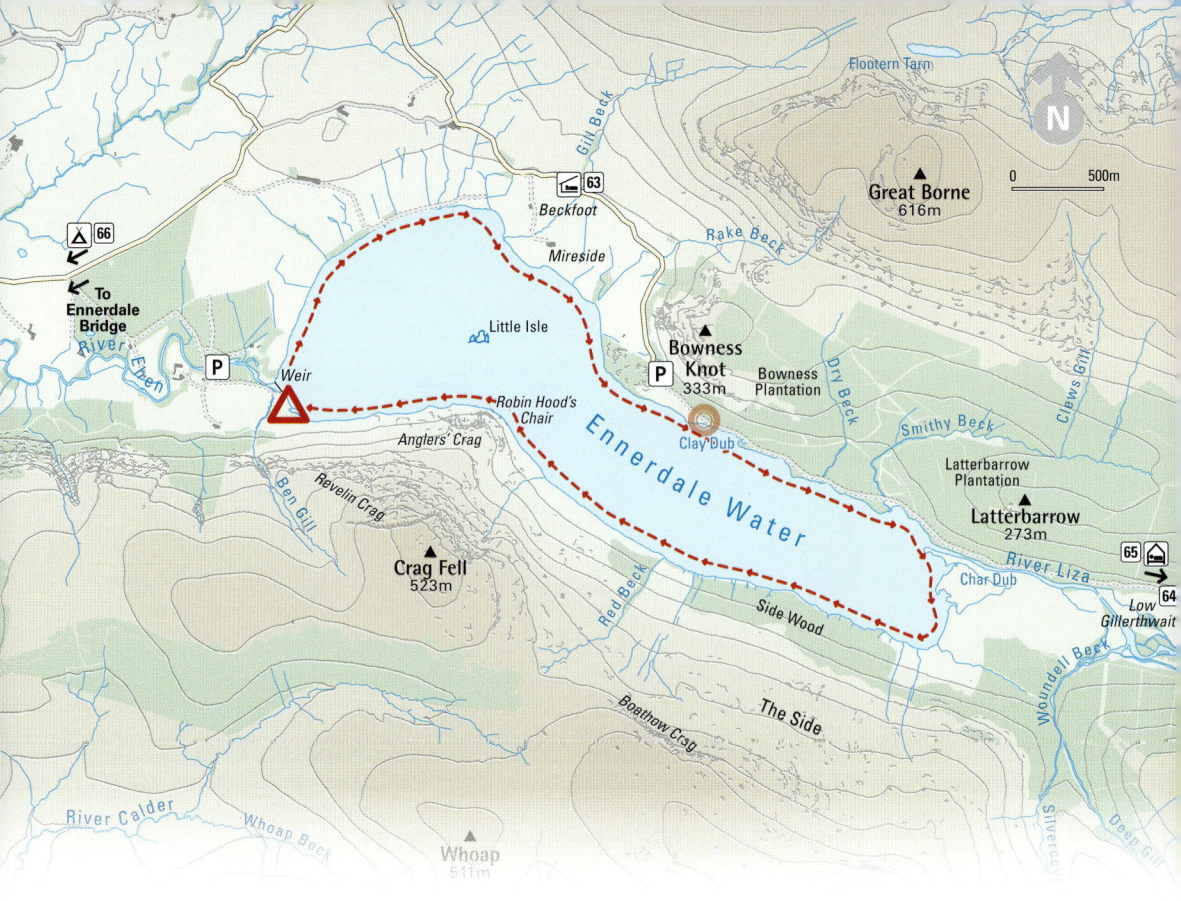

half, the water broadens towards the coastal plain's low horizons, where the glacier spread outwards. Coleridge described the lake as *"fiddle-shaped"*.

Splendidly, not much happens hereabouts; electricity didn't arrive until 1989! The lake has minor claims to fame: future US President Bill Clinton proposed to future US Presidential candidate Hilary Rodham, *"on the shore of this wonderful little lake, Lake Ennerdale … she said no"* and also the closing scenes of zombie movie *28 Days Later* were filmed here.

Ennerdale possibly means 'Anundr's valley' (Old Norse) or perhaps 'cold river valley', from the River Ehen (Celtic: cold) which drains it. Until recent times, the lake was also known as 'Broadwater'.

Access

Ennerdale Water is owned by United Utilities and is technically a reservoir, although no longer in use since 2023.

Canoes and kayaks are allowed to paddle; however, commercial groups or groups larger than five people need to request a permit from United Utilities (contact amber.thompson@uuplc.co.uk or phone 017687 72334). The permit is free of charge. As with the overwhelming majority of United Utilities' reservoirs, paddleboarding is banned, with no logical reason given. Likewise, swimming. Rowboats are allowed but boats with sails or motors are not.

📷 *Clay Dub*

Wildlife and environment

Ennerdale Water's reservoir status comes from the small weir at the River Ehen outflow, which, since 1902, has raised the level by a few feet. North West Water's 1978 proposal to build banks and a new weir raising the level by a further four feet were rejected at a 1980 Public Inquiry (alongside similar plans for Wast Water). 11-year-old April Roberts from Ennerdale Bridge Primary School gave evidence: *"We live by it, walk there and play there"*. United Utilities ceased extracting water in 2023 and is currently carrying out feasibility studies for removing the weir and infrastructure; this would mean lowering the lake level, similar to the plans underway for Crummock Water. No details are yet confirmed, beyond planning being completed by 2030.

Ennerdale Water is an SSSI. Its clear oligotrophic waters don't harbour much life; however, brown trout, char, eel and salmon are found. Red squirrels are commonly spotted among the shoreline trees, pine martens less commonly. The valley is home to around a hundred roe deer, with red deer visiting occasionally. Otters inhabit the River Liza, which feeds the lake. The 'Wild Ennerdale' partnership is considering introducing beavers into the river.

The Forestry Commission acquired Ennerdale in the 1920s, removing two thousand sheep from their heafs (pastures) and replacing them with a monoculture of Sitka spruce and Japanese larch:

> *"... a dark and funereal shroud of foreign trees, an intrusion that nobody who knew the Ennerdale of old can ever forgive ..."*

Alfred Wainwright, *The Western Fells*, 1966

The conifers still smother the valley and much of Ennerdale Water's northern shore; however, the Wild Ennerdale project has made significant progress in improving the look.

📷 *Great Borne and Bowness Knot*

Wild Ennerdale

Wild Ennerdale is a joint project between Natural England, the National Trust and United Utilities. It is a grand 're-wilding' scheme, ongoing since 2003, to reverse human impacts on Ennerdale and improve wildlife, habitats and biodiversity. Native broadleaf woodland (over 100,000 trees planted) and heather has replaced felled conifers, and harsh straight plantation lines have been blunted by planting along contours. Barriers along the River Liza have been removed, allowing it to flow unhindered. Sheep numbers have been reduced, to encourage plant regeneration. They are being replaced by Belted Galloway cattle; their trampling apparently improves habitat and species diversity.

Ennerdale is the only Lakeland valley where human influence has been significantly reversed. In 2022, it became a National Nature Reserve.

Further information about Wild Ennerdale can be found at The Gather community shop and café, in nearby Ennerdale Bridge.

Launch points

- **Bleach Green** NY 089 152 / painters.armrest.glassware / CA23 3AS – the lake shore beside the River Ehen outflow weir. Bleach Green car park (run by the National Park, free) is located 400m west, along a level track.
- **Bowness Knott** NY 112 150 / adopts.insulated.canal / CA23 3AU – mid way along the lake's northern shore. Bowness Knott car park (run by Forestry England, paying) is 330m north-west along a track, 25m higher up. It is sometimes possible to drive to the water's edge and quickly drop off paddlecraft, before parking.

📷 *Scoat Fell and Steeple*

Description

Having lugged or trolleyed your boat from Bleach Green car park, the reward is a fine view: the River Ehen burbles over a low weir, foregrounding the lake's clear waters and a fine fell panorama. The chain of, successively higher, fells seen from Bleach Green are Ennerdale's northern wall: tree-strewn Bowness Knot in the foreground, with Great Borne (also called Herdus) behind, leading to Starling Dodd, and then Red Pike, culminating with 806m High Stile. This alone makes for a fine backdrop. Yet … the best stuff is hidden from sight. Paddling north, following the boulder clay ridge damming Ennerdale Water's western end, the entirety of Ennerdale is revealed … and what a reveal! Looming beyond the lakehead is 892m Pillar. It's named for Pillar Rock, a 180m-high angular buttress which is partially visible from the lake. Pillar Rock's first ascent, by a local shepherd in 1826, is regarded as the birth of Lake District rock climbing. To the right / west of Pillar is Scoat Fell's broad cliff wall, but the limelight is stolen by Steeple, the pyramidal summit jutting from Scoat Fell. 'Pillar' and 'Steeple', the names say it all! These fells, the haunt of buzzards and peregrine falcons, are a constant companion (and distraction) while paddling around Ennerdale Water.

The western, down-valley rim of the lake is lined by trees, backed by beaches and, further around, a wall topped with a path. The Angler's Arms stood on these shores, surviving in various forms since Elizabethan times. It was demolished in preparation for the planned 1978 lake level rise (nixed by Public Inquiry). Edwin Waugh, a minor Victorian poet, launched from the inn for a night time row:

> *"In this sheltered corner little eddies of shimmering silver flit about,—the dainty Ariels of moonlit water … If there be magic in the world, it is this!"*

Edwin Waugh, ***Rambles in the Lake Country***, 1861

The Angler's Arms was the sole lakeside building; the next nearest are the white farm buildings of Beckfoot and Mireside, spotted uphill, either side of Gill Beck.

📷 *Revelin Crag*

Rake Beck marks the point where lush farmland switches to craggy outcrops extending to the water's edge; this is Bowness (Old Norse: curved headland). Behind is lumpy 333m Bowness Knot, an SSSI. Geologists get excitable hereabouts: around 475 million years ago, with unimaginable heat and pressure, granite of the Ennerdale Intrusion was fused with and baked the surrounding Skiddaw Group. The lake's narrowing showcases how this metamorphosed rock resisted the forces of glaciation.

Bowness Plantation's tall conifers smother the lakeside slopes. A track from Bowness Knott car park descends to the shore and follows it to the lakehead, and beyond up Ennerdale. It accesses Low Gillerthwaite Field Centre and the valley's two remote youth hostels; otherwise, it is closed to vehicles. If you find the occasional passing 4x4 to be intrusive, be grateful that an 1884 plan to blast a railway up-valley was defeated!

The small shallow inlet, overlooked by a picnic bench, is Clay Dub. Further east, Smithy Beck's name is a clue that ore, mined from Clews Gill further upstream, was once smelted here: Ennerdale may be a wilderness now but was once fully inhabited. From Smithy Beck to the River Liza's inflow at the lakehead, the conifers give way to Latterbarrow Wood's birch and oak. This ancient woodland, along with Side Wood on the opposite shore, is protected as an SSSI.

The River Liza's emergence into Ennerdale Water is a joy to behold. Cold, clear water flows powerfully into the lake from a channel known as Char Dub (a fishing reference), which is lined by shallow pebble spits. The free-flowing Liza has been restored by removing flood defences and retaining walls, allowing banks to erode and gravel shallows to build; this reduces sediment so that, even in spate flows, clear water enters the lake. Its name is Old Norse *lysa*: bright water.

Across Char Dub, a miniature woodland has been isolated by a maze of shallow and silted false channels and lagoons. These are filled with floating carpets of sphagnum moss and surrounded by marshy heathland covered with purple moor-grass. Resist the temptation to paddle in as you will potentially disturb this delicate ecosystem.

📷 *Little Isle*

Paddling south along the lakehead, you'll encounter a long gravel beach, backed by a gravel berm. If you stretch legs here (not Access Land), you'll notice that there is a higher terrace further back, which the lake sometimes floods up to. The grasslands behind the lake were the site of Woundell Beck Vaccary, a medieval cattle farm; it's fitting that Belted Galloways now graze here.

The Demon Dog of Ennerdale

In 1810, Ennerdale was terrorised by the 'Demon Dog'. This seemingly supernatural creature preyed, by night, on livestock, killing around 400 sheep. After it was eventually cornered and shot, *"T' girt dog"* was found to resemble a lion and weigh 51 kilos! It was possibly a (now extinct) Tasmanian tiger, escaped from a circus.

Ennerdale Water's southern shores are (if it is possible) quieter, only frequented by occasional walkers following the Coast to Coast Walk National Trail. Side Wood is rather lovely, a smattering of gnarled and mossy deciduous trees scattered along the first two kilometres. The high drystone wall lining this fellside, below Boathow Crag, is a clue that this was formerly a park for deer and wild boar, The Side.

Below 523m Crag Fell, opposite Bowness, the south shore rounds a corner and the lake opens out. Angler's Crag is an outcrop of Crag Fell, rearing 100m above the lake. It in turn has its own outcrop, Robin Hood's Chair: a 22m-high eminence at water level (what it has to do with the legendary outlaw is anyone's guess). When the lake level is low, Little Isle is revealed offshore, in mid-lake, *"The haunt of cormorants and sea-mew's clang"* (William Wordsworth, ***Guide to the Lakes***, 1835).

📷 *River Ehen at Bleach Green*

The islet, still the haunt of cormorants and sea mews (kittiwakes), resisted the glacier's erosive force, because of the underlying Skiddaw Group rocks being baked hard (see Bowness Knot, above). It has a peculiar round depression in the centre, possibly human-made.

The final kilometre to Bleach Green is overshadowed by Revelin Crag, a jumble of oddly shaped towering pinnacles.

The River Ehen below the weir is home to the endangered freshwater pearl mussel, so don't splash around in the shallows.

"The magic of the place is this,
Its solitude and silentness:
Streams rush and tempests wail;
But other sounds are few, and deep
The silence is that loves to sleep
In the solitudes of Ennerdale."
Annie Armitt, **Ennerdale**, 1878

📷 *Crummock Water from Red Pike*

Crummock Water

Length (km)	Maximum width (km)	Maximum depth (m)	Surface area (km²)	Catchment area (km²)	Height above sea level (m)
4.1	0.9	43.9	2.5	62.69	96

Trip Distance	9.5km / 5.9 miles
Start / Finish	Rannerdale Knotts NY 162 183 / plantings.fixtures.soccer / CA13 9UZ

Introduction

"There is scarcely anything finer than the view from a boat in the centre of Crummock Water. The scene is deep, and solemn and lonely; and in no other spot is the majesty of the Mountains so irresistibly felt as an omnipresence."

William Wordsworth, ***Guide to the Lakes***, 1835

Wordsworth knew what he was talking about: he grew up down-valley at Cockermouth. Crummock Water is a delight to paddle, the author's personal favourite of the western lakes. Nearby Buttermere soaks up the tourist crowds, allowing you to appreciate Crummock in peace. Crummock's undeveloped shores mean that the geomorphic forces which formed and shaped it are clearly on display. Rugged fells rear skyward, directly from both shores; this is perhaps the best of the lakes for combining paddling and fellwalking adventures.

Greylag geese over Crummock Water

Crummock means 'little crooked one' and derives from Celtic (*kukro*: crooked), referring either to the lake's slightly bent shape or to the River Cocker which drains it.

Access

No motorised craft are allowed on Crummock Water. Paddlers are allowed, in groups of no more than ten craft. There is no limit on the total number of craft on the water.

The National Trust, which purchased the lake in 1935, requires paddlers to purchase a permit to paddle. The cost in 2025 was £5 per craft per day. Day permits can be bought from the (coin-only) machines in the Trust's car parks at Buttermere (CA13 9UZ) and Lanthwaite Wood (CA13 0RT). You can also buy permits via the PayByPhone phone app; enter the code 804483. Note that there is zero phone reception in the valley.

Annual permits, which also cover Buttermere and Loweswater, can be bought via the National Trust website; Google 'boating and fishing in the Buttermere valley'. You can also call the Trust's North and West Lakes office on 017687 74649 or email northandwestlakes@nationaltrust.org.uk. The cost in 2025 was £65 (£100 for fishing).

Wildlife and environment

A dam and weir, built in 1879 to supply water to Cockermouth and Workington, raised the lake's level. United Utilities ceased extracting water in 2023 and plans to remove the dam and restore the lake's natural character. The lake level will be lowered by around 1.35m and will subsequently rise and fall more naturally after rainfall, with a range of about 1.5m.

The lake contains char, perch, pike and trout, with salmon and sea trout arriving in summer. Greylag geese nest on the shores. Canada geese, goosanders and oystercatchers nest on the

📷 *Launch point below Rannerdale Knotts*

islands; avoid these during nesting season, March to September. The lake is part of the River Derwent and Bassenthwaite Lake Special Area of Conservation.

Invasive New Zealand pygmyweed has been detected in Crummock Water since 2023. Follow the biosecurity practices outlined on page 34.

Launch points

Rannerdale Knotts NY 162 183 / plantings.fixtures.soccer / CA13 9UZ – a small roadside beach beside a wall leading into the lake. Small car park (free) 100m north, along and across the B5289.

Hause Point NY 162 182 / glassware.condense.powerful / CA13 9UZ – a tiny lay-by on the B5289, alongside a rocky spur plunging into the lake.

Woodhouse Islands NY 167 177 / escapades.repeating.nightlife / CA13 9UZ – a beach, divided by a wall. Either launch directly below the road or use the permissive path through the gate. Three parking bays and limited lay-by parking along the B5289.

Wood House NY 168 173 / ribcage.looms.rattled / CA13 9UZ – a quiet beach accessed by a 500m downhill walk starting at the back of Buttermere National Trust car park (paying), along a woodland footpath and then a permissive path.

Lanthwaite Wood NY 151 208 / tanked.sharpens.novelist / CA13 0RT – a beach reached by a 780m walk along a level footpath track from the National Trust car park (paying) alongside Scalehill Bridge.

Cinderdale Common NY 161 194 / prompting.commended.sketches / CA13 9UZ – a small beach accessed by a 150m walk from a small car park (free). Cross the B5289 and follow it north to a gate leading to a narrow downhill path. There is a second car park beside Cinderdale Beck, 100m further south.

Woodhouse Islands launch point

Description

The tiny beach below Rannerdale Knotts is a dramatic launch point. A drystone wall trails into the water, leading your eye towards the crag-and-scree flank of 512m Mellbreak, rearing above the far shore.

At Hause Point, a stone's throw to the south of the beach, 355m Rannerdale Knotts plunges into the water. The road clings to the fellside and you should watch out for swimmers jumping off ledges! This spot has a chilling past. In 1988, Kevin Owlett waded and swam out dragging his wife Sheena's body, cabled to a plastic barrel and car cylinder head. When he flooded the barrel, Karma intervened and he was almost dragged below with his wife. Divers discovered Sheena three weeks later, and Owlett confessed to murder.

Crummock Water's lakehead is characterised by long beaches, scattered islets and river deltas. The islands, and the low hill of Nether How, are remnants of a band of Skiddaw Group mudstone which withstood the glacier as it gouged out the valley.

The three Woodhouse Islands occupy the corner where the road heads away from the lake, a popular launch spot. Trees cling to a single grassy islet. The other 'islands' are rocky reefs. Wood House overlooks the isles, a National Trust property rented out as holiday accommodation.

Mill Beck, the bubbling stream flowing through Buttermere village, emerges into the lake via a small pebbly delta. Mill Beck's delta is actually vastly larger; the alluvial fan washed down from 839m Crag Hill spans the entire valley, severing Crummock Water and Buttermere into separate lakes.

Buttermere is just a kilometre up-valley, hence Crummock's southern end is backed by the same impressive fells which dominate that smaller lake. Fleetwith Pike is the distinctive ridge-back at the head of the valley, the 899m dome of Great Gable rears behind Hay Stacks, and the hanging valleys of High Crag, High Stile and Red Pike form a continuous wall ending above

Scale Island

Crummock itself. Red Pike's name comes from its reddish haematite (iron ore), baked by the Ennerdale Intrusion.

The twin Holme Islands, the haunt of nesting geese, are smothered with dense growth of stunted birch, juniper and sessile oak. They mark Crummock's southern corner, where Buttermere Dubs flows in. This small river flows just one kilometre from Buttermere, squeezed, by Mill Beck's alluvial fan, along the valley's southern edge. It's possible to paddle up and explore the interweaving delta channels.

Scale Island is even more overgrown than the Holme Islands; gnarled and stunted trees splay outwards from this miniscule perch. Its name comes from Scale Beck, which also splays outwards into the lake, via a wide boggy delta fan. Waves have eroded a wide beach of pink granite boulders, washed down from Red Pike. The Lake District's earliest tourists were ferried here, to visit Scale Force.

Scale Force

Lakeland's highest waterfall is hidden 1km away from the lake and 100m uphill, on Scale Beck. Scale Force's 38m plunge is confined within a glistening green chasm. It is guarded by a lower waterfall which must first be scrambled past; this is only safe and practical in dry conditions, when the beck is low. Swimming in Scale Force's tiny plunge pool is an intense experience.

"On its margin, as if more peculiarly to adorn this enchanting spot, hang in graceful order both the willow and the ash. Its moist walls are covered with the soft hand of nature with every sweet variety of moss, herb and flower, which form innumerable pictures beyond the reach of art to imitate such excellence."

Stebbing Shaw, *A Tour in 1787*, 1788

📷 *Low Ling Crag*

Low Ling Crag turns out to be quite the landform. A pebble spit reaches out to this low-lying reef, narrowing the lake so that Hause Point is just 420m away. The spit has curved beaches on either side, making it the Lake District's only tombolo. The tombolo was formed when waves refracted around the crag, depositing the facing beaches. Geomorphology nerds will notice that the north beach pebbles form a steeper berm, on account of the longer 'fetch' down the lake. Low Ling Crag itself is a *roche moutonnée*, smoothed by glacial ice flow on the up-valley side, rough-edged on the down-valley side. More pertinently, this is the perfect lunch spot, backed by High Ling Crag with grand views along Crummock.

Despite being a relatively low fell, Mellbreak certainly makes its presence felt. *"Its one allegiance is to Crummock Water"* (Alfred Wainwright, *The Western Fells*, 1966). The 1.5km paddle along the west shore is overshadowed by Mellbreak's steep slopes, cliffs and screes, extending to the water's edge as beaches of talus: eroded fragments of Skiddaw Group slates, broken from the fellside and washed by waves on to the lake margins. The Iron Stone is a tiny lone islet, its name referencing haematite ore discovered in medieval times; at several points, the spoil from long-defunct mining works trails to the beach.

Crummock Water's down-valley, northern end is contorted and narrowed by two landforms: Peel 'hill' and the alluvial fan from Park Beck.

Peel, named for a double-moated 'pele' tower which once stood here, is actually a drumlin, a mound of glacier-deposited sediment. Waves travelling Crummock's length have eroded a low cliff.

Park Beck flows from Loweswater (both the lake and village), entering Crummock via a canalised channel, alongside a Victorian pump house, surrounded by railings. Either side of Park Beck, a low concrete wall forms the shoreline, extending to the lake's northern tip, where the River Cocker escapes by lapping over two adjacent weirs, with fish ladders overlooked by footbridges. In normal flows, there is little risk of being swept over.

Plans for Crummock Water

All of this will change! Canalising Park Beck caused problems: sediment washed down the beck, focused upon a single outflow spot, and formed an overlong curved spit, curving towards the lake's northern tip. The beck's focused flow, so close to the lake outlet, makes the River Cocker more flood prone. United Utilities plan to remove the concrete wall, restore Park Beck into a multi-channel delta and dismantle the dam and weir at the River Cocker outflow. All of this will presumably cause significant disruption, although the work will be carried out in the quieter winter months. It seems likely that vegetation will take years to re-colonise the shoreline down to the predicted 1.35m lower lake level; it may well all look a bit grim. At time of publication, United Utilities have resubmitted their plans and delayed their planned 2025 start on this work.

The beach beside the River Cocker is a popular spot, close to the Lanthwaite Wood National Trust car park. The woodlands, adorned by an attractive boathouse, shroud the shore below Lanthwaite Hill, one of Thomas West's 'stations' (page 230). Look out for the roe deer who graze hereabouts, surreptitiously. However, the eye will be drawn upwards to the pyramidal bulk of 851m Grasmoor, the highest of the north-western fells, looming above Crummock's eastern shore.

Grasmoor changes profile as you paddle south, becoming an intimidating gully-rent wall before shifting aside to reveal the adjoining summits. The prominent pyramid which appears after Cinderdale Common is 660m Whiteless Pike.

"Of all the scenes in the Land of the Lakes, that from the middle of Crummock is assuredly the grandest."

Robert Southey, *Letters from England*, 1807

Cinderdale Beck was named for long-vanished 'bloomeries', where iron was smelted. It marks the point where the 'secret valley' of Rannerdale reaches the lake shore, its ancient delta now occupied by Rannerdale Farm. The farm is just a stone's throw from the beach below Rannerdale Knotts.

The Secret Valley

Each spring, an amazing bluebell carpet adorns Rannerdale. By legend, it is fed by blood spilled in battle, one flower for each death. Nicholas Size's 1930 novel *The Secret Valley* invented the story of how, 1,000 years ago, Viking chief Boethar ambushed and massacred the Earl of Carlisle's encroaching Normans when they entered Rannerdale from Crummock Water.

📷 *Blake Fell and Burnbank Fell*

Loweswater

Length (km)	Maximum width (km)	Maximum depth (m)	Surface area (km²)	Catchment area (km²)	Height above sea level (m)
1.7	0.56	16	0.6	8.19	125

Trip Distance	3.6km / 2.2 miles
Start / Finish	Loweswater–Lamplugh road lay-by NY 128 217 / garden.influence.yelled / CA13 0SU

Introduction

"Lowes Water ... exhibits a sweet rural landscape, the cultivated slopes being ornamented with neat farm houses and trees."

Jonathon Otley, *A Concise Description of the English Lakes*, 1823

Shhh, don't tell anyone about Loweswater! This tiny, compact, beautiful lake gets completely overlooked. Loweswater is tucked away up a side valley from that of Buttermere and Crummock: most visitors simply aren't aware it exists. It nestles between relatively small fells, occupying a trough carved by a glacier heading north-west and seawards; however, Loweswater is actually the only one of the English Lakes to drain 'inwards', towards the centre of the National Park.

The author is lucky enough to live just minutes away from Loweswater. He can regularly be found there at sunrise, lapping the lake on his surf ski.

The name derives from the Old Norse *Laufs saer*, meaning 'leafy lake' or possibly 'Lauf's lake'.

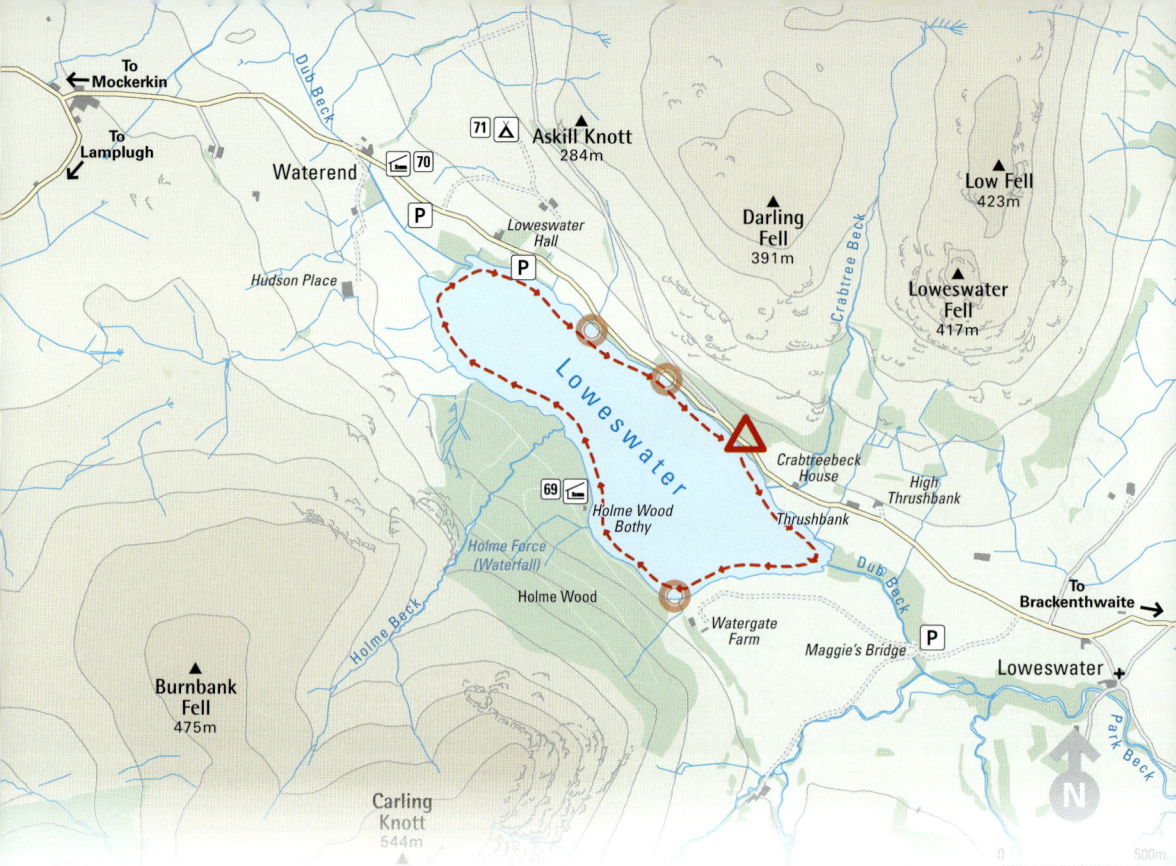

Access

No sailboats or motorised craft are allowed on Loweswater. Paddlers and rowboats are allowed. There is, however, a limit of four craft on the water at any one time. The National Trust, which owns Loweswater, notes, *"generally it doesn't get too busy so this isn't normally an issue"*.

The Trust requires paddlers to purchase a permit to paddle. The cost in 2025 was £5 per craft per day. Day permits can be bought from the (coin-only) machines in its car parks at Buttermere (CA13 9UZ) and (more convenient for Loweswater) Lanthwaite Wood (CA13 0RT). You can also buy permits via the PayByPhone phone app; enter the code 804483. Note that there is usually zero phone reception around Loweswater.

Annual permits, which also cover Buttermere and Crummock Water, can be bought via the National Trust website; Google 'boating and fishing in the Buttermere valley'. You can also call the Trust's North and West Lakes office on 017687 74649 or email northandwestlakes@nationaltrust.org.uk. The cost in 2025 was £65 (£100 for fishing).

Wildlife and environment

Loweswater contains perch, pike and trout. Waterfowl include greylag geese. Holme Wood, lining the southern shore, is home to red squirrels and badgers.

The lake is highly eutrophic (nutrient rich), and in summer months it can suffer from blooms of cyanobacteria, better known as blue-green algae. This has been caused by farming practices within

Loweswater's catchment, including outflow from septic tanks. The Loweswater Care Partnership, later part of the West Cumbria Rivers Trust, was set up to address these issues. It has made much progress towards its aim of Loweswater achieving 'good' ecological status by 2027.

Invasive New Zealand pygmyweed has been detected in Loweswater since 2023. Follow the biosecurity practices outlined on page 34.

Launch points

- **Loweswater–Lamplugh road lay-by** NY 128 217 / garden.influence.yelled / CA13 0SU – approaching from Loweswater village, this is the first of three small lay-bys along Loweswater's north shore. It is directly waterside. There is space for just two cars.
- **Loweswater–Lamplugh road lay-by** NY 126 219 / exotic.penned.savers / CA13 0SU – this second waterside lay-by also has space for two cars, but it is somewhat rougher.
- **Loweswater–Lamplugh road lay-by** NY 123 221 / plod.generated.nervy / CA13 0SU – this third and final lay-by is located where a wall and path lead down to the lake. Again, just two cars.
- **Watergate Farm** NY 126 211 / wasps.bottled.meant / CA13 0SU – Maggie's Bridge car park is run by the National Trust and is free. It's a 900m walk to the lakeside at Watergate Farm, along a wide, level track.

Description

The northern shore is lined by a band of trees whose branches trail in the water, broken up by small beach launch points. Paddling a short distance offshore allows you to orientate yourself. Loweswater is hemmed in on this northern side by Loweswater Fell (just to be confusing, there is another Loweswater Fell, to the south-east). Opposite, twin hills rise beyond the plantations of Holme Wood: Blake Fell and Burnbank Fell. The fellside trees were apparently planted in the form of the 'Loweswater pheasant', with a beak, eye and wing becoming visible in autumn … judge for yourself … the author can't make it out!

The lake's south-east end is backed by a fine array of higher, steeper fells, notably Mellbreak and Grasmoor. Logic would dictate that this is the lakehead, but actually Loweswater is back-to-front and this is the down-valley end. Regardless of the grand backdrop, the shores around the south-east end comprise green farmland and meadows, with walls and fences leading down to the water.

Crabtreebeck House is the first of the *"neat farm houses"* seen, white-painted and dating from 1660. It is hard to visualise now, but in 1828 this bucolic homestead was the scene of an ecological and human catastrophe. A dam serving a lead mine failed:

> *"… the whole of the water it contained rushed into Crabtree Beck … John Tyrrel, the master, who was in bed with his wife and a young child, was so much terrified by the sound, that he rushed down to the front door with the young child in his arms, into the torrent, and both were swept down into Loweswater Lake and drowned."*

John Askew, *A Guide to the Interesting Places in and around Cockermouth*, 1866

Holme Wood

Dub Beck percolates from the lake through tangled carr woodland, towards Maggie's Bridge car park. In its lifespan of under three kilometres, Dub Beck accumulates further streams to become Park Beck and passes Loweswater village (and the splendid Kirkstile Inn) before emptying into Crummock Water.

The National Trust's Watergate Farm sits at Loweswater's southern extremity. Prior to paddling being allowed, the Trust rented out rowboats here. The farm is partly rented out as holiday accommodation and partly a ranger station for managing adjacent Holme Wood.

Paddling alongside, beneath, and occasionally among the trees of Holme Wood is a highlight of exploring Loweswater. Although Holme Wood's upper slopes are coniferous plantation, the lakeside is a mixture of alder, ash, chestnut, oak, lime and sycamore, carpeted by bluebells in spring. Paddle quietly, as this is the haunt of red squirrels, owls and spotted flycatchers. Holme Wood Bothy is this southern shore's sole building, a former fish hatchery now used as a (somewhat rustic) holiday rental. Holme Beck's broad alluvial fan covers much of this shore, the trees dangling above and extending into the water, as carr.

The woodland ends at a fence trailing into the water, the boundary of Hudson Place Farm. An eighteenth-century farmhouse and modern barns are fronted by marshy meadows, grazed by Belted Galloway cattle. The farm looks across Loweswater's north-west extremity, where a wetland of reedbeds, white water lily and water lobelia obscures Dub Beck and other small streams trickling *into* the lake. They should, by rights, be flowing *out*, this being the lake's seaward end. However, Loweswater's glacier deposited a moraine (gravel) ridge which dammed the valley, reversing the drainage.

The wetland merges into yet more carr, as the north shore is rejoined. Before returning to your launch beach, it's tempting to linger and explore this unworldly drowned forest, hidden in a quiet corner of a quiet lake in an almost unknown corner of the Lake District.

◉ *Buttermere*

Buttermere

Length (km)	Maximum width (km)	Maximum depth (m)	Surface area (km²)	Catchment area (km²)	Height above sea level (m)
2	0.59	28.6	0.91	18.68	103

Trip Distance	4.8km / 3 miles
Start / Finish	Buttermere's north-west beach NY 174 164 / grid.vitamins.elders / CA13 9UZ

Introduction

> *"Blessed by an idyllic setting in the shelter of majestic fells and graced by mature woodlands, Buttermere is a foretaste of heaven … And its shining jewel is its lovely lake, mirror of an enchanting landscape."*

Alfred Wainwright, *Wainwright in the Valleys of Lakeland*, 1992

St James' Church, built upon a rock in Buttermere village, has a memorial to Alfred Wainwright beside the window looking across the lake to his favourite fell, Hay Stacks. Following his death in 1991, Wainwright's ashes were sprinkled around Innominate Tarn*, at Hay Stack's summit. It's not hard to grasp why the great fellwalker and guidebook author chose Buttermere as his final resting place. Even by Lake District standards, this lake is breathtakingly beautiful to behold (and paddle), its glassy waters symmetrically mirroring an extraordinary amphitheatre of looming

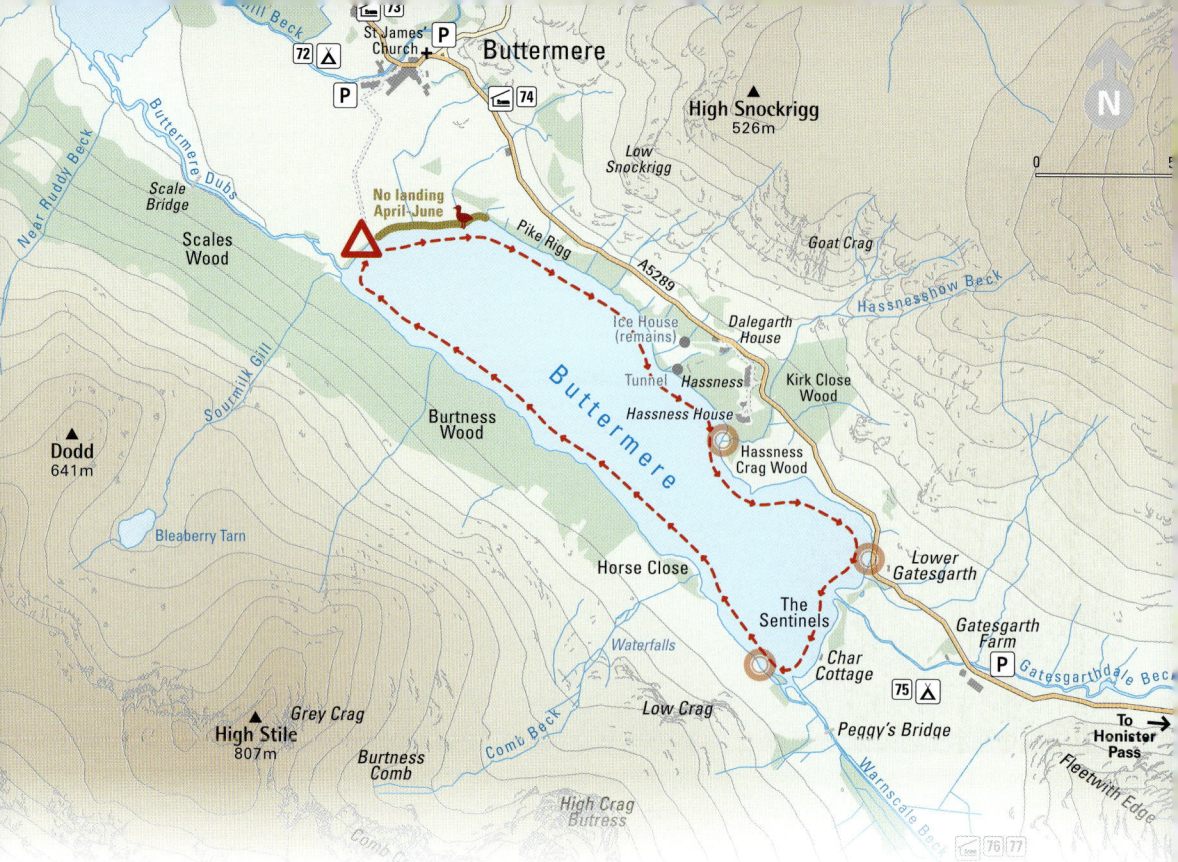

cliffs and peaks. W.G. Collingwood summed Buttermere up: *"nature's art for art's sake"* (*The Lake Counties*, 1902).

Buttermere's diminutive size means that it doesn't take long to paddle around. However, factor in time spent picnicking upon shingle beaches, soaking up the views. Any sense of solitude can feel hard won: while paddler numbers are small because of both the National Trust's restrictions and the awkwardness of accessing the water, the shoreline paths are hugely popular with walkers.

The ridiculously quaint name could literally mean 'butter lake' (Old English *butere*: dairy pastures). Alternatively, it could be Old Norse, 'Boethar's lake' or perhaps referring to huts (*búðar*) beside the water.

* If you were wondering, Innominate Tarn doesn't drain into Buttermere: instead, Ennerdale Water is diluted Wainwright.

Access

No motorised craft are allowed on Buttermere. Paddlers are allowed, in groups of no more than ten craft. There is no limit on the total number of craft on the water.

The National Trust, which purchased the lake in 1934, requires paddlers to purchase a permit to paddle. The cost in 2025 was £5 per craft per day. Day permits can be bought from the (coin-only) machines in the Trust's car parks at Buttermere (CA13 9UZ) and Lanthwaite Wood

📷 *Fleetwith Pike*

(CA13 0RT). You can also buy permits via the PayByPhone phone app; enter the code 804483. Note that there is zero phone reception in the valley.

Annual permits, which also cover Crummock Water and Loweswater, can be bought via the National Trust website; Google 'boating and fishing in the Buttermere valley'. You can also call the Trust's North and West Lakes office on 017687 74649 or email northandwestlakes@nationaltrust.org.uk. The cost in 2025 was £65 (£100 for fishing).

The section of the north shore, east of the north-west beach launch point, with a permissive path leading along it, is closed from 1st April to 30th June. This is to protect ground-nesting sandpipers: avoid landing here.

Wildlife and environment

Buttermere contains brown trout, char, perch and pike. Sandpipers lay their speckled eggs on the northern shore's pebble beaches. Highland cattle graze the southern shore, which is lined by alder, oak and Scots pine.

Invasive New Zealand pygmyweed has not reached Buttermere, despite being present in Crummock Water and Loweswater. Follow the biosecurity practices outlined on page 34.

Launch points

Buttermere's north-west beach NY 174 164 / grid.vitamins.elders / CA13 9UZ – the wide beach spanning Buttermere's north-western end is 650m from Buttermere village, accessed along a bridleway track. Buttermere National Park car park is behind the Buttermere Court Hotel; arrive early to secure a space. Buttermere National Trust car park is a further 400m, uphill, along the B5289 in the Cockermouth direction (down-valley). Free parking is available 200m or more in the opposite direction, in the lay-bys extending along the steep road uphill from St James's Church.

◉ *Dalegarth*

Hassness Crag Wood NY 186 157 / protected.clearcut.picturing / CA13 9XA – a beach accessed by a 200m-long footpath descending across a footbridge and through woodland from a lay-by on the B5289. Approaching from Buttermere village, the lay-by is on the left, just after passing a bus stop and the entrance to Hassness Country House, beside a sign for 'Folders Wood'. There is space for just three or four cars.

Lower Gatesgarth NY 191 153 / liberty.costumed.masters / CA13 9XA – a beach directly alongside the B5289; however, there is no parking. Gatesgarth Farm car park is 500m along the road in the Honister Pass direction (east).

Buttermere south shore NY 186 150 / comforted.learns.freshest / CA13 9XA – launch where the wall ends and the Access Land begins. Reached by a 1km-long bridleway path from Gatesgarth Farm car park, crossing Warnscale Beck via Peggy's Bridge and then turning right to reach the south shore.

Description

The bridleway track from Buttermere village reaches the lake where a fence trails into the water. On a wet day, the noise and spectacle of Sourmilk Gill will dominate the senses. This torrent originates from Bleaberry Tarn's hanging valley, 400m above, cascading through Burtness Wood *"like a white ribbon bisecting the mountain"* (William Gilpin, ***Observations***, 1786) to join Buttermere at the beach's western end. On clearer and drier days, 648m Fleetwith Pike commands the attention; this is the fell perfectly framed and mirrored at Buttermere's opposite end, symmetrical in profile and bisected by Fleetwith Edge, the prominent ridge aligned to point directly into Buttermere. Geologists also get excited by this view: a 'suture line' slices across Fleetwith Edge, dividing the older, more erosive Skiddaw Group on its lower half from the craggier Borrowdale Volcanics on its upper half.

📷 *Hassness*

The long, stony beach stretching along the north-west shore has been eroded by waves travelling the lake's length, exposing tree roots. Paddling to Buttermere's northern shore, be mindful of the ground-nesting sandpipers mentioned above.

The northern shore begins with Pike Rigg woods, backed by High Snockrigg fell and the cliffs of Goat Crag. A meadow interrupts the trees, then you reach a rock outcrop with a tunnel blasted through; this is the Hassness Estate. Nineteenth-century Manchester mill owner George Benson commissioned the tunnel so that he could walk the shore without straying. The original eighteenth-century Hassness House burned down c. 1900 (remains of its ice house survive, near the lake). In the 1920s, Swiss Chalet-style Dalegarth House was built on the spot and a new Art Nouveau Hassness House was constructed, nearer the lake; this is the wide white building prominently visible above Hassness Crag Wood from around the lake. The two houses underwent various roles in the twentieth century, including a sanitorium for *'habitual drunkards'* and use by Manchester merchant Sydney O'Hanlon as *'a gentleman's sporting retreat'*. For the past sixty years, Hassness House has been a hotel serving rambler groups.

Hassness promontory is a D-shaped delta, its wide beaches deposited by Hassnesshow Beck. It directly faces the delta of Comb Beck, across the lake, pinching Buttermere to just 300m wide. Geomorphology nerds can tell you that Hassness has the larger delta because the Skiddaw Group rocks above are more erosive than the Borrowdale Volcanics drained by Comb Beck.

At Lower Gatesgarth, the B5289 briefly descends to the water's edge. A magnificent line of venerable, ancient Scots pines (*Pinus sylvestris*, Britain's only native pine tree) stands along Buttermere's south-eastern shoreline, either side of Gatesgarth Beck. Known as 'the Sentinels', these trees are Buttermere's signature landmark and a perennial favourite with photographers. Fleetwith Pike looms 600m behind, filling the sky. The road ascends Honister Pass, beneath Fleetwith's precipitous northern face; the levels and scars of Honister Slate Mine (still working) can be spotted. In certain light, Buttermere's waters have a green hue, on account of the slate dust flushed down-valley.

◎ *Char Cottage*

The lone, ramshackle, white building beneath the shoreline Scots pines is Char Cottage, named for the lake's rare arctic fish (a post-glacial survivor) and built as a bothy for fishermen. Behind, Gatesgarth Farm's meadows were a vaccary (cattle farm) in the thirteenth century, with a herd of sixty cows; this possibly explains Buttermere's twee name. The backdrop to all this is, however, anything but twee.

> *"Fleetwith to the eastern, and Scarf on the western side; a hundred mountain torrents form never-failing cataracts, that thunder and foam down the centre of the rock, and form the lake below."*

Thomas West, ***A Guide to the Lakes***, 1778

Warnscale Beck descends via the above-mentioned waterfalls, tumbling from the grand amphitheatre spanning between Fleetwith Pike and Hay Stacks. Slopes of Skiddaw Group rocks are topped by crags and summits of Borrowdale Volcanics. Hay Stacks's name is perhaps explained by its jumbled array of rounded knolls with no obvious summit, a dishevelled fell. Coleridge was awed by the scene and described *"an enormous round basin mountain-high of solid stone cracked in half and one half gone"* in an 1802 love letter to Sara Hutchinson. Incidentally, Warnscale Beck is now something of an Instagram celebrity: good-looking 'influencers' (and, also, the author) selfie themselves swimming in the 'infinity' pools below the cliffs, reached by bridleway from Gatesgarth Farm.

Warnscale Beck flows into Buttermere's southern corner, also the point where the bridleway from Scarth Gap Pass (from Ennerdale) reaches the lake. Highland cows graze the shore here, gentle hirsute creatures despite the intimidating horns. Despite transportation from Scotland, presumably they feel at home in this locale!

In evenings and winter afternoons, the paddle along Buttermere's southern shore will be in shadow. A literal wall of conjoined peaks blots out the sunlight, rising directly from the lake shore; High Crag, High Stile and Red Pike are fronted by three successive spurs (High Crag Buttress, Grey Crag and Dodd) with waterfalls spilling from the glacial cirques nestled between

📷 *Northern corner of Buttermere*

them: Burtness Comb and Bleaberry Tarn. This is quite a lot to soak in, in just two kilometres of paddling.

"No mountain range in Lakeland is more dramatically impressive than this, no other more spectacularly sculptured … This is superb architecture."

Alfred Wainwright, *The Western Fells*, 1966

Horse Close, Comb Beck's delta, is covered by plantation. As you paddle past the beck's outflow, enjoy a view, glimpsed between the conifers, of the beck's waterfalls leading right up the fellside.

Burtness Wood swathes the remaining, steepening, shoreline back to your start point. Buttermere's north-west beach is backdropped by a fine panorama of Grasmoor and Whiteless Pike.

Sourmilk Gill's white-water flumes end at Buttermere's western corner, which is also the point where Buttermere Dubs passes beneath a footbridge to flow out of the lake. Crummock Water is just a kilometre away; paddlers with river experience have explored this winding stream into the larger lake*. The alluvial delta (all deposited by Buttermere village's Mill Beck) separating the two lakes covers a rock band underneath; the lakes have their own glacially scoured troughs, even though, in aeons past, they were joined.

That was a short paddle, but you'd be hard put to name a more impressive one.

* It's not without hazards and obstacles, so proceed with caution!

St James' Church, Buttermere village

The Maid of Buttermere

In his guidebook *A Fortnight's Ramble in the Lakes*, Joseph Budworth extolled Buttermere's attractions … the highlight being 15-year-old landlord's daughter Mary Robinson. With no apparent grasp of privacy or propriety (or safeguarding), Budworth lauded her *"full eyes and lips as sweet as vermillion"*. Ogling the 'Maid of Buttermere' became a tourist itinerary fixture; Budworth pompously warned the child not to let celebrity go to her head.

In 1802, Robinson's inadvertent fame / exploitation attracted 'the Honourable Colonel Alexander Hope', brother of an earl, to Buttermere. Hope courted Robinson and, within days, married her. 'Hope' was then, sensationally, identified as commoner John Hatfield, who was wanted for theft, fraud and forgery (and now, bigamy). Hatfield fled, abandoning Robinson, who was pregnant. After capture, he also became something of a tourist attraction: while awaiting hanging at Carlisle, he was visited by Coleridge and Wordsworth.

Robinson's child died of pneumonia. She was remarried, to a Cumbrian farmer, and is buried at St Kentigern's Church in Caldbeck.

"… the Maid of Buttermere,
And how the spoiler came, 'a bold bad Man'
To God unfaithful, children, wife, and home,
And wooed the artless daughter of the hills,
And wedded her, in cruel mockery
Of love and marriage bonds."

William Wordsworth, *The Prelude*, 1850

High Snockrigg

Fleetwith Pike, Buttermere – Skiddaw Group and Borrowdale Volcanics

Culture and Landscape

The Story of The Lake District

"… the whole of the country, its past and its present, its men, its plants, its rocks, its animals, are one."

H. H. Symonds, *Walking in the Lake District*, 1933

📷 *Whiteless Pike beside Crummock Water, Skiddaw Group*

Geology

The mountainous landscapes within which the lakes sit are highly diverse, despite this being a relatively small area. This is because of the variety of different rock types, formed in differing ways at different times, underlying and surrounding the lakes.

Commencing nearly half a billion years ago, a succession of rock layers were deposited on top of one another. From oldest to newest: the Skiddaw Group, Borrowdale Volcanics and the Windermere Supergroup. Additionally, molten rock was 'intruded' (squeezed in) among these layers, the main intrusions being the Ennerdale and Eskdale Granites. Additional rock layers certainly topped all of these; however, the forces of erosion effectively shaved the upper layers away, exposing the older layers to the surface in three distinct bands. These cross the Lake District diagonally south-west to north-east, with the oldest layers spanning the north-west and the youngest spanning the south-east. The Ennerdale and Eskdale Granites slightly mess up this neat picture by (literally) intruding along the western edge.

"There stands the base and root of the living rock,

Thirty thousand feet of solid Cumberland."

Norman Nicholson, *To the River Duddon*, 1944

SKIDDAW GROUP

The Skiddaw Group, the Lake District's oldest rocks, originates from 485 million years ago (mya) in the early Ordovician period. The rocks were laid down as a sequence of sands, silts and clays on the floor of the relatively deep Iapetus Ocean (south of the equator) and today appear as a range of darkish and flaky mudstones, sandstones and siltstones. The Skiddaw Group underlies Crummock Water, Loweswater, Buttermere, Bassenthwaite Lake and Derwent Water, as well as the lower halves of Ennerdale Water and Ullswater. Later Devonian mountain-building events altered these mudstones to slates. The Skiddaw Group slates' friable qualities mean that its fells tend to have weathered into rounded profiles (although, no one seems to have told Blencathra).

BORROWDALE VOLCANICS

The Borrowdale Volcanics, which make up the central Lakeland fells, and the contemporaneous and more northerly Eycott Volcanic Goup, are more youthful. They were deposited around 450 mya in the late Ordovician period, when intense volcanic activity around the Iapetus Ocean's rim buried the Skiddaw mudstones in lava and ashes. These were mostly compressed into hard, resistant rocks called andesites and tuffs; for example, the knobbly Langdale Pikes, rearing unmistakeably behind Windermere, originated as layers of ash. Borrowdale Volcanics underlie Wast Water, Thirlmere, Haweswater, Brothers Water, Elter Water, Rydal Water and Grasmere, as well as Ullswater's and Windermere's southern and northern tips, respectively. These are the most acidic of the lakes, as the rock doesn't buffer the effects of naturally acidic rain or (reducing) human pollution well. Their impermeable nature also helps to explain why such severe flooding happens in Borrowdale. Borrowdale Volcanics give rise (literally) to the Lake District's highest and most spectacular mountains, eroded into craggy peaks: the Old Man of Coniston, Helvellyn, the Scafells. They also underlie the overwhelming majority of upland tarns.

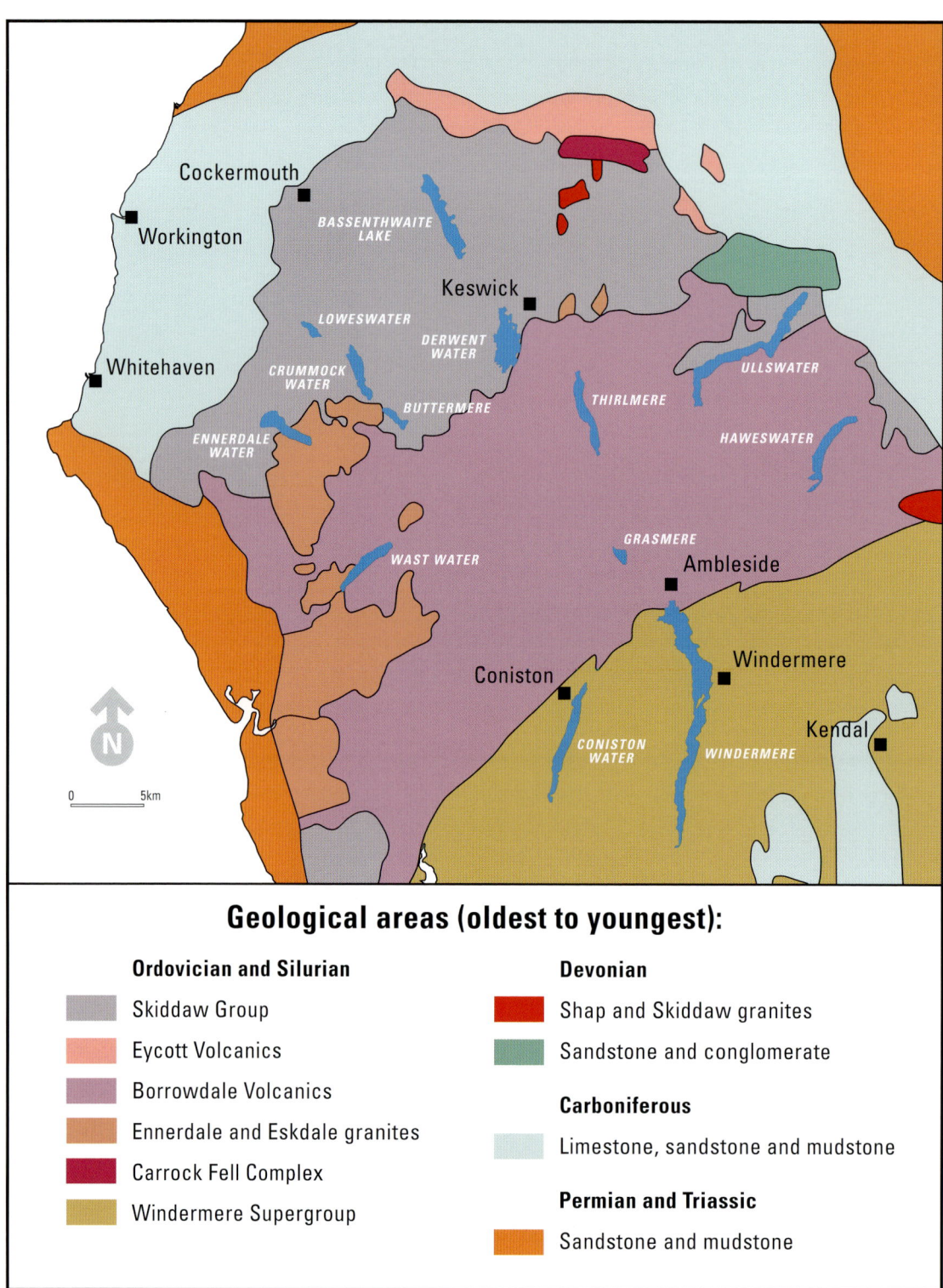

ENNERDALE AND ESKDALE GRANITES

The Ennerdale and Eskdale Granites are the magma chambers which fed the Borrowdale Volcanic eruptions, during the Ordovician period. The granite originated beneath the earth's crust as a batholith: a chamber of magma which was intruded (literally, squeezed in) among the other rock groups, and subsequently exposed by 'uplift' and erosion. The subsurface extent of these chambers is in the region of 1,500km^2! The Eskdale Intrusion touches Wast Water's southwest tip (barely). The Ennerdale Intrusion underlies Wast Water's western part and Ennerdale Water's south-eastern half, and it also touches Buttermere's north-west corner. The granite is pigmented with iron and often gives a pinkish hue to walls and buildings constructed from it.

WINDERMERE SUPERGROUP

The Windermere Supergroup dates from around 420 mya, during the Silurian period. The grand name encompasses a series of sedimentary slates – mudstones, sandstones and siltstones – along with some limestone. These were deposited atop the Borrowdale Volcanics, four to five kilometres thick, in a shallow basin of the Iapetus Ocean. Esthwaite Water, Coniston Water and all of Windermere barring its northern tip sit atop the Windermere Supergroup. These rocks have been heated, folded, faulted and eroded, and they now present as rounded, rolling fells of relatively low height; those spanning between the lakes are known as the Furness Fells.

Metamorphism, Faults and uplift

Around 420 mya, the Iapetus Ocean closed up, as the landmasses of Laurentia and Avalonia joined together. This was a final stage of the Acadian Orogeny, a (50-million-year-long) mountain-building event in which the earth's crust was compressed and folded. The heat and pressure from this event are most clearly seen in the Skiddaw and Windermere Groups, where slates formed. This is when the Shap and Skiddaw Granites were emplaced. Magmatic heat from a further, concealed mass of magma created the Crummock Water aureole: a ring of altered rocks surrounding the body of magma. This altered the Skiddaw Group around Crummock Water and explains why those fells have a notably craggier appearance.

The pressure from the orogeny created a series of fracture lines running through the Lake District's rocks, known as faults. This matters to us, as the water and ice which later eroded out the Lake District's main valleys generally followed these faults, exploiting the path of least resistance. For example, Grasmere and Thirlmere were formed on the Coniston Fault, and Ennerdale Water on the Rossett Gill Fault.

Around 60 mya, the North Atlantic Ocean began to open up and the formation of the world's modern major mountain ranges got underway. These grand events had a less grand side-effect: the resulting pressure of the magma beneath the Atlantic Ocean caused the Lake District region to be modestly uplifted, just a few millimetres annually. As the land gradually rose, the surface rock layers were eroded, removing an eventual thickness of around a kilometre! This uplift was complete by 25 mya, exposing the rock bands we see today. Rivers had incised valleys deeply into the uplifting rock, *"the cartwheel of dales and ridges"* (Norman Nicholson) radiating outwards from the centre.

📷 *Skiddaw in winter (not the actual Ice Age!)*

The formation of the lakes

"It has been said that when God made England his finger touched but did not press, but that is not true of Cumbria. He pressed there all right. What is more, he used his nails. And the nails were ice."

Norman Nicholson, *Portrait of the Lakes*, 1964

THE ICE AGES

The Quaternary period began 2.5 mya ... and we are living in it today. Through the Quaternary, Lakeland has been repeatedly covered by ice. Seabed deposits indicate up to fifty distinct periods of ice cover. The main British ice sheet flowed south from Scotland, parting around the (uplifted) Lake District. This allowed Lake District ice to successively expand and retreat radially, with glaciers – rivers of ice, moving at a glacial pace – scouring out the earlier proto-valleys.

The Devensian glaciers

The last glacial period, known in Britain as the Devensian, began around 115,000 years ago and sculpted the Lakeland we recognise today. When the Devensian ice reached its maximum extent around 22,000 years ago, a dome of ice up to a kilometre thick covered the region. The summits of the highest fells possibly peeked above the ice sheet as 'nunataks'.

The valley basins which would eventually be occupied by the lakes were shaped via two key processes: 'plucking' was the fracturing and breaking apart of rock under the ice's relentless pressure, and 'entraining' was carrying away the rock which itself acted as a scouring pad which smoothed the valley floor and sides. The Lake District glaciers were of a (relatively) fast-moving and highly abrasive type known as 'warm-based', in which the base of the ice is near to melting point, with meltwater underneath lubricating its motion down-valley.

The ice retreats

By around 15,000 years ago, the ice had completely retreated (i.e. melted). It then returned on the higher fells, 12,900 years ago. This was the Loch Lomond Stadial (cold period), possibly triggered

Bowness Knot beside Ennerdale Water – the left side is Skiddaw Slates, the right side is Ennerdale Granites

by meltwater changing Atlantic circulation patterns and / or volcanic eruption-related cooling. This ended abruptly, 11,700 years ago, when temperatures rose 10 degrees within a few decades.

Basins

"A day of violence … in the dales the rock was gouged into hollows, for lakes to gather, where the keels of glaciers had sliced and scoured their beds."

H. H. Symonds, ***Walking in the Lake District***, 1933

The English Lakes first filled up in 'basins': areas of 'over-deepening' where glaciers had scoured deeper into the valley floor than they did down-valley.

The glaciers poured from the fells via staircases of ice. Where the gradient was steeper, the ice increased velocity and thinned ('extending flow'). Where the gradient was less steep, the ice slowed and backed up ('compressional flow'). Basins formed at the junctures between extending and compressional flow. Basins could also be created by the pressure from side-valley glaciers joining the main glacier; for example, Ullswater's deepest basin is directly below Glencoyne.

Between 10 and 12,000 years ago, the lakes appeared in their current form: long 'ribbon' lakes, flooding the basins. Ullswater, Windermere and Esthwaite Water have multiple basins, while the rest occupy a single basin.

In areas where extending flow commenced, the ice was stretched across bedrock, forming *roches moutonnées*: polished rock with a distinctive drop-off at the down-valley end, where plucking has occurred. Many of these survive as islands.

Damming the lakes

The retreating glaciers deposited vast quantities of boulder and clay till, ground out from the surrounding fells. These heaps of rubble, known as moraines, still litter the valley floors. Coniston Water, Windermere and Ennerdale Water are examples of lakes dammed by 'terminal' moraines, dumped at the end point of glaciers, raising their water levels beyond just their basins.

Alluvial fan separating Crummock Water and Buttermere

Some of the lakes were dammed by alluvial fans which blocked entire valleys: masses of sediment carried down from the fells by side-streams and strewn across valley floors. Brothers Water and Loweswater were formed in this way. The pairings of Bassenthwaite Lake and Derwent Water, and Crummock Water and Buttermere, were both originally single lakes, separated eventually by alluvial fans.

Alluvial fans which have not (yet) dammed the lakes are called arcuate (curved) deltas.

Incidentally, there were other lakes! The upper part of Borrowdale, Kentmere and Longsleddale all once hosted lakes, since infilled by silt and sediment. All of the existing lakes will follow suit … eventually.

What lies beneath?

The lakebeds consist of accumulated debris atop the basin's bedrock. The complexity of this debris has only recently begun to be unravelled. Seismic surveys have revealed that although Windermere's current depth is 64m, the solid rock is at least 110m, possibly 160m, beneath the surface. This is topped by 16 distinct moraine layers (from successive ice retreats), a 15m band of clay layers (these grow thinner, with increased organic content, towards the top), further moraine debris (from the Loch Lomond Stadial) and, finally, 11,700 years' worth of organic sediment: in the southern basin, a 40m-thick layer of gunk.

St Herbert's Island and Rampholme Island (drumlins), Derwent Water

Drumlins

The glaciers of the Loch Lomond Stadial deposited drumlins: oval-shaped mounds of glacial till on the valley floors, aligned in the direction of the ice flow. Geologists suspect, but aren't certain, that these formed *beneath* the glaciers. The retreating ice left behind a peculiar 'basket of eggs' topography of drumlins across the Solway Plain, extending up-valley to lakes such as Bassenthwaite Lake, Derwent Water and Crummock Water. The drumlins are recognisable within these lakes as rounded headlands and islands. Further south, Esthwaite Water is also heavily shaped by drumlins.

Castlerigg Stone Circle

History

"These lakes and inner vallies are unadorned by any of the remains of ancient grandeur, castles, or monastic edifices, which are only found upon the skirts of the country."
William Wordsworth, *Guide to the Lakes*, 1835

The Lake District was only 'discovered' a few hundred years ago! At least, as we think of it: a place of leisure among natural beauty. Although humans have settled and worked this mountainous landscape for millennia, their farming and industry left few grand traces in terms of buildings and monuments. It was only late in the eighteenth century that Lakeland resonated with contemporary aesthetic sensibilities, and visitors flocked to the newly dubbed 'Lake District'.

Note: the county of Cumbria, which encompasses the Lake District, has only existed since 1974, prior to which it was divided between the counties of Cumberland, Westmorland and Lancashire. To simplify things, the region is referred to as Cumbria throughout this book.

Prehistory

Signs of prehistoric human activity around the English Lakes are scarce; most of their traces are found on Cumbria's coastal fringe. The earliest evidence of humans is flints uncovered in limestone caves at Allithwaite, south of Windermere, dated to 11,000–9,500 BC. These Palaeolithic Cumbrians hunted red deer and elk in a landscape swathed with deciduous forest up to the 750m contour: alder and willow along the lake shores, oak and ash in the valleys and pine and birch on the high ground.

Hunter-gatherers of the Mesolithic era (9,600–4,000 BC) left virtually no trace of their activities, beyond a chert blade discovered beneath Ambleside's Galava Fort.

THE NEOLITHIC

Neolithic farmers (4,500–2,350 BC) had far greater impact on the landscape. Stone axes of polished volcanic green tuff were quarried from Scafell Pike and, sensationally, a precipitous gully in the Langdale Pikes. These seemingly had religious significance: they appear across the UK and Ireland, accounting for 27% of all axes found, and often seem more decorative than practical. It's no coincidence that lakebed pollen samples have revealed the 'elm decline', around 4,000 BC; forest cover was significantly reduced, by human activity and climate change.

Stone circles, *"circles of rude stones attributed to the Druids"** (William Wordsworth, *Guide to the Lakes*, 1835), appeared at Lakeland's fringes. The exception is fabulous Castlerigg, a hundred-metre-diameter circle of Skiddaw Slates megaliths constructed c. 3,200 BC, several kilometres east of Derwent Water.

A further, little understood, Neolithic legacy is rock carvings such as the 'cup and ring' marks first discovered around Rooking, near Ullswater's head. Over thirty more sites have subsequently been identified; the fact that many are located close to the heads or feet of lakes such as Grasmere and Crummock Water has led to speculation that they were waymarks for navigation.

* *Nothing whatsoever to do with the Druids, who showed up in the Iron Age.*

◎ *Galava Roman Fort*

BRONZE AND IRON AGES

The Bronze Age (2,500–700 BC) saw the proliferation of stone cairns and burial chambers on the lower fells; Askham Fell, overlooking Ullswater, is peppered with these, alongside The Cockpit stone circle.

Archaeologists aren't sure who Iron Age (800 BC-AD 100) Cumbrians were. The Carvetti tribe seems to have lived in the north and the Setantii in the south. The Romans thought these were part of the Brigantes tribe (named after the goddess Brigantia), which spanned Northern England. They appear to have spoken Cumbric, a Celtic language, seen in placenames like Derwent and Crummock. Whoever they were, they accelerated woodland clearance and lived in palisaded settlements of roundhouses such as those, still discernible by their platforms, at Maiden Castle near Ullswater. Their hillforts were sparsely distributed, and modest in scale, relative to the Southern England giants. The hillforts of Dunmallard, guarding Ullswater, and Peel Wyke, overlooking Bassenthwaite Lake, are wooded over. Castle Crag, dominating Borrowdale up-valley of Derwent Water, and Castle Rock, looming down-valley from Thirlmere, remain clear and are well worth visiting.

History

THE ROMANS

> *"The Roman Eagle was once proudly carried over our hills … trippers can picnic on Borrans Field at Waterhead amid the ruins of Galava."*
> William Rollinson, *A History of Man in the Lake District*, 1967

Although the Romans 'conquered' Britain in AD 43, it wasn't until c. AD 71 that they advanced into the north, to pacify the Brigantes. Galava Fort (page 138) was built at Ambleside as early as AD 80. Cumbria effectively became a military zone, garrisoned by auxiliaries from around the

◉ *St Bega's Church*

Empire. Hadrian's Wall, the epic coast-to-coast frontier line constructed from AD 122 across Cumbria's northern border, was supplied via High Street, a road departing from Windermere at Galava and traversing above Ullswater to reach Brocavum Fort, near Penrith.

Traces of enclosed farms and fields, as well as lake sediment records indicating two centuries of intense deforestation from AD 200, show that life went on in Cumbria. No villas have been discovered, but it has been suggested that Galava's commander may have constructed one beneath Belle Isle's current house.

THE MIDDLE AGES

Early medieval kingdoms, saints and Vikings

We no longer call AD 410–1066 the 'Dark Ages', but this doesn't change the awkward fact that details about the centuries following the Roman withdrawal are extremely hazy. The author is a history teacher, used to tackling heavy-duty historical texts; nonetheless, merely the Wikipedia summary of this period almost gave him a brain aneurism. The people of the region spoke a Celtic language, calling themselves *combrogi* ('country-men'), the origin of 'Cumbria'. That said, it's questioned whether there ever was such a thing as Celts / Celtic culture, in Britain at least. By the fifth century, according to Welsh sources, Cumbria may have been part of the kingdom of Rheged, which may or may not have existed. Cumbria was, possibly, later absorbed into the kingdoms of Northumbria and then Strathclyde, the timescales and geographical extent of both events being hotly disputed (i.e. no one has a clue).

Christianity arrived in the form of missionary 'saints', about whom we only know legend and hearsay: St Kentigern / Mungo is said to have founded Keswick's Crosthwaite Church in AD 553, St Patrick supposedly preached at Patterdale, St Herbert resided on his Derwent Water island (page 67) and St Bega gave her name to the church beside Bassenthwaite Lake (page 53).

Copeland Forest, a medieval hunting ground, Ennerdale Water

"It was the Norseman, above all others, who bred the dalesman, and gave him his bone, his language, and his way of life."

Norman Nicholson, *The Lakers*, 1955

The impact of the Vikings, who settled from the Isle of Man and Ireland in the late ninth and tenth centuries, is much clearer. Although they left little physical evidence beyond the remarkable slender carved cross at Gosforth (approaching Wast Water), they signed their presence in Old Norse placenames, especially on the high ground. They appear to have introduced Scandinavian farming practices, moving their animals with the seasons.

THE NORMANS

"In this year King William with a great army went north to Carlisle … and thereafter came south hither and sent thither a great multitude of churlish folk with women and cattle, there to dwell and till the land."

The Anglo-Saxon Chronicle, 1092

Following the 1066 Norman Conquest, Cumbria was left alone until 1092, when William the Conqueror's son, William Rufus, invaded. Seventeen motte and bailey castles encircled the region, none close to the lakes. Instead, Norman barons parcelled Lakeland into 'forests': private hunting grounds for deer and wild boar. Copeland Forest spanned Ennerdale Water to Wast Water.

Monasteries

The big change brought by the Normans was the establishment of religious houses: monasteries, priories and abbeys. Although sited around the fringes, they had a huge impact on the Lakeland landscape, through exploiting resources and developing farming and industry on their landholdings. St Bees Priory, for example, owned Ennerdale and Loweswater. They enclosed land and drained lakeside wetlands for 'grange' farms, their main income coming from sheep farming. Walls known as felldykes (also, intacks, fellgarths, headgarths or ring garths) ran around valley

Mine waste at Brandlehow Bay, Derwent Water

sides to separate the upland grazing; these boundaries are still highly visible. Wool was transported for export via packhorse roads. Cattle ranches known as 'vaccaries' (Latin *vacca*: cow) were established beside Ennerdale Water, Wast Water and Buttermere.

The largest and wealthiest religious house was Furness Abbey (near Barrow-in-Furness), founded by the Cistercians in 1127. Their 12,000-hectare estate extended between Windermere and Coniston Water, and northwards into Borrowdale. They were licensed to fish with nets on the lakes, and they operated over 250 'bloomeries': small ironworks. Lakeshores were deforested and alders coppiced, to produce charcoal for smelting iron and bark for tanning leather.

Reivers

> *"The Scots invaded England ... laying waste everything as far as Furness ... Especially were they delighted with the abundance of iron which they found there."*
>
> *Chronicle of Lanercost*, 1314–1315

The Scottish victory at the Battle of Bannockburn in 1314 commenced two centuries in which Cumbria was effectively (as with the Roman period) a militarised frontline, England's 'West March'. The wealthy monastic lands were a prime target; Furness Abbey was ravaged by King Robert ('The Bruce') in 1322. The raids continued: an endless succession of cross-border raiders known as 'Reivers' (Old English: robbers) pillaged and ravaged Cumbria. Church towers were fortified and stone 'pele' towers sprang up, including possible examples at Peel Island and Crummock Water.

THE EARLY MODERN ERA

Mines Royal

After gold was discovered near Derwent Water, Elizabeth I created the Company of the Mines Royal in 1564, wresting mining rights away from the unreliable Earl of Northumberland. She astutely imported outsiders to work the mines: German engineers, led by Daniel Hechstetter. They

Glencoyne Farm, Ullswater – dating from the seventeenth century

were empowered to *"search, dig, try, roast and melt all manner of mines and ores of gold, silver, copper and quicksilver"*, with a tenth of the precious metals going to the monarch. The Germans settled on Derwent Isle (for their safety) and opened up workings around Derwent Water, Skiddaw, Helvellyn and the Old Man of Coniston.

Statesmen farmers

The 1536–41 Dissolution of the Monasteries saw the religious houses' estates sold off. Many of the new landowners were non-noble yeoman farmers. Over two centuries, this emergent 'statesman' class increased cattle and sheep populations by 50% and grew in wealth by around 70%. After Scotland's King James VI became England's James I, the Reiver raids ceased and the resulting stability enabled the Great Rebuilding: from 1650 to 1720, the statesmen farmers replaced their timber-framed cottages and outbuildings with buildings of local stone. These farmhouses and barns, often combined in a single, long structure, remain a ubiquitous and integral part of the landscape. The sandstone lintels above front doors commonly display a date and three initials: surname, husband and wife's forenames. To explore a well-preserved example, visit the National Trust's Townend, located two kilometres east of Windermere at Troutbeck; this was home, from 1626 until 1943, to the Browne family.

The statesmen enjoyed a degree of autonomy and independence, answering to no one but the local vicar, who was usually comparatively impoverished. William Wordsworth later romanticised them:

> *"Towards the head of these Dales was found a perfect Republic of Shepherds and Agriculturists … this pure Commonwealth … an ideal society …"*

William Wordsworth, *Guide to the Lakes*, 1835

Stott Park Bobbin Mill, Windermere

THE INDUSTRIAL AGE

Turnpikes and enclosure

The *Turnpike Acts* of the 1750s authorised trusts to collect tolls, to pay for road improvement. In Lakeland, the 1715 and 1745 Jacobite risings (page 63) provided an additional roadbuilding impetus. A turnpike was under construction through central Lakeland by 1768, opening up Windermere, Grasmere, Thirlmere and Derwent Water. It's now the A591.

Two factors led enterprising / unscrupulous landlords to enclose (wall off) 'common' lands on fells: the French Revolution caused food prices to soar, and livestock was recognised as more profitable than arable farming. Over 20,000 hectares had already been enclosed when the 1801 *General Enclosure Act* allowed landowners to go ahead without parliamentary approval. Some, such as Henry Lowther, Earl of Lonsdale and owner of Ullswater, enclosed their estates to 'improve' them using modern methods, for example, 'sweetening' fields using lime and slag. Most of the drystone walls which lattice Lakeland were built 1760–1850 and are identifiable by their notable size, straight walls and rectangular / square outline.

Mills, mines and fisheries

Furness Abbey had already made Furness (southern Lakeland) into Lakeland's main industrial centre. By the Industrial Revolution's onset, the Furness forests had largely been cleared and given over to sheep. The iron bloomeries were soon rendered obsolete by Windermere's blast furnaces, opened in 1711 at Backbarrow and 1712 at Cunsey Beck. Large-scale iron production led to re-planting of Furness, for charcoal. Coppiced trees were harvested to manufacture bobbins for the north-west's textile mills; a working bobbin mill is preserved at Stott Park. Boats plying Windermere and Coniston Water supplied ore and charcoal for the ironworks and bobbin mills and also saltpetre and sulphur for gunpowder works at Low Wood, near Backbarrow.

📷 *Ennerdale Water plantations*

Lakeland mining expanded in scale, boosted by railway links to achieve peak output in the late nineteenth century: copper at Coniston; slate at Honister above Buttermere; graphite at Derwent Water; lead at Greenside, above Ullswater.

Through the nineteenth century, the largest lakes saw industrial-scale fish extraction. 21 companies operated on Ullswater, netting an incredible 12,000 schellies at a time. Windermere's char were hoovered up by 113 seine netting sites. Unsurprisingly, fish populations crashed, with Windermere's last commercial fishery closing in 1921.

Forestry

Plantations of non-native conifers notably transformed the Lake District landscape, enraging the likes of Wordsworth and Wainwright. The first appeared in the early 1800s, but the twentieth century saw this trend reach its apogee. In 1907, Sitka spruce was planted around Thirlmere, to reduce sediment flow into Manchester's newfangled water supply. The Forestry Commission (FC) was founded in 1919 to boost Britain's strategic timber reserves, depleted by the First World War. The FC smothered entire valleys beneath larch and spruce: Thornthwaite Forest and Dodd Wood beside Bassenthwaite Lake, Grizedale Forest between Windermere and Coniston Water, all of Ennerdale by 1930. It even felled native broadleaf woodlands, such as oaks alongside Bassenthwaite Lake at Wythop, to make space for conifers. By 1934, 1,250,000 larch and 5,000,000 spruce had been planted.

OFFCOMERS: THE DISCOVERY OF THE LAKE DISTRICT

"All the world comes to the Lakes"

William Wordsworth, letter in 1819

The Lake District was 'discovered' in the late eighteenth and early nineteenth century by an eclectic parade of visiting gentry, writers, artists and aesthetes, who paved the way for eventual mass tourism. Cumbrian poet Norman Nicholson dubbed these 'the Lakers' (*"separate, alien, self-conscious"*), noting that people had lived and worked in this landscape long before their home

The Wordworths' graves, Grasmere

was patronisingly 'discovered'. These 'offcomers' imposed their own perspectives, often ignoring or supplanting the ways in which locals interacted with the landscape. The Lake District we enjoy today is as much of a constructed concept, as a place.

The first visitors

> *"I Rode almost all the waye in sight of this great water ..."*

Celia Fiennes, *Through England On a Side Saddle*, 1698

Fiennes, a remarkable woman who rode through every English county, was perhaps the first Lake District tourist. Journalist Daniel Defoe briefly visited Lakeland's fringes shortly after, seeing enough to dismiss it as *"barren and wild, of no use or advantage either to man or beast"* (*A Tour Thro' the Whole Island of Great Britain*, 1724). It was decades before this view was reappraised, by Dr John Brown. He toured Borrowdale in the 1750s, and described Derwent Water:

> *"Rocks and cliffs of stupendous height, hanging broken over the lake in horrible grandeur, some of them a thousand feet in height, the woods climbing up their steep and shaggy sides ..."*

Description of the Lake and Vale of Keswick, c. 1753

Thomas Gray read Brown's letter, published as a pamphlet, and in 1769 was inspired to make his own Derwent Water visit:

> *"The Vale of Elysium ... the most delicious view, that my eyes ever beheld ... the shining purity of the Lake, just ruffled by the breeze enough to shew it is alive, reflecting rocks, woods, fields, & inverted tops of mountains."*

Journal of A Visit to the Lake District, 1775

Gray's writings (published posthumously) became, effectively, the first Lake District guidebook. The continental Grand Tour became difficult following the French Revolution, and interest increased in England's natural beauty; the visitor floodgates opened, and have not closed since!

📷 *Claife Viewing Station, Windermere*

The Picturesque tourists

Gray was an adherent of the 'Picturesque' movement, which reduced landscapes to picture-format. The aim was not to enjoy views, but to assess their aesthetic merits based on arcane criteria. These tourists would view the lakes, with their back turned, through a convex 'Claude glass' mirror, intended to alter the natural scene into the style and format of sixteenth-century landscape painter Claude Lorrain.

William Gilpin spearheaded the English movement, visiting the newly dubbed 'Lake District' in 1772. Here, he (over)reacts to Derwent Water:

> *"Here is beauty indeed—Beauty lying in the lap of Horror! … Nothing conveys an idea of beauty more strongly, than the lake; nor of horror, than the mountains."*

William Gilpin, *Observations*, 1786

In his 1778 *A Guide to the Lakes*, Jesuit priest Thomas West defined 21 'stations' from which tourists should evaluate the lakes, via Claude glass; his book remained in print for 50 years. Windermere's Claife Viewing Station occupies one of West's stations.

The visitor experience was further enhanced, as early as 1773, by firing cannons to create echoes, from boats on Ullswater and Derwent Water: hence, generating more 'horror'.

The Romantics

Cumbrians William and Dorothy Wordsworth moved to Dove Cottage at Grasmere in 1799 (page 145). Their friend Samuel Taylor Coleridge settled at Greta Hall in Keswick, the following year. The two men had just published **Lyrical Ballads**, a collection of poems advocating a new approach to life: the 'Romantic' movement. They believed a connection with nature and wild places improved people, promoting imagination and creativity (*"… from emotion collected in tranquillity"*). Radically, they advocated that these emotions and experiences were for everyday folk, not just the social or cultural elite. Their move to the Lake District was an attempt to live out their ideals, in (relatively) modest circumstances. Rather than appreciating the landscape from

Dove Cottage, home of William and Dorothy Wordsworth, Grasmere

afar (or via a ridiculous mirror), they personally interacted with it, tramping across the fells and rowing on the lakes.

A coterie of writers followed their lead: Thomas De Quincey, Robert Southey and Hartley Coleridge all settled in the Lake District. In 1817, they were dubbed the *"Lake Poets"* by critic Francis Jeffrey, *"the School of whining and hypochondriacal poets that haunt the Lakes"*. Fellow Romantic Lord Byron stayed away: *"There is a narrowness in such a notion, / Which makes me wish you'd change your lakes for ocean"* (**Don Juan**, 1819). Nevertheless, they heavily influenced, and continue to influence, the way that people perceive and interact with the Lakeland landscape.

The leading Romantics, who had of course promoted and publicised the Lake District, came to resent others intruding into their chosen paradise. Coleridge raged against guidebooks, *"All authors of tours … Damned liars"**, and Wordsworth became an unashamed reactionary, despite quietly profiting from his own bestselling guidebook.

Painters such as J.M.W. Turner and John Constable were also influenced by the Romantics, painting the Lake District's natural landscapes as they perceived them; this was a radical departure from the idealised and over-dramatic depictions of Lakeland by earlier visitors such as Joseph Farington and Thomas Gainsborough.

* This guidebook excepted.

The steam merry-go-round

In 1847, the modern world caught up with the Lake District, when a railway line reached Birthwaite, two kilometres from Windermere. The Coniston Branch was completed in 1859, the Cockermouth–Keswick–Penrith line in 1864, and the Lakeside Branch in 1869. All of these lines were originally built to serve industry (especially mining) but came to be used by, and reliant upon, tourist visitors. In 1876, John Ruskin railed against railways, which he claimed were, *"making a steam merry-go-round of the lake country"*. He may have had a point: by the late 1880s, 80–100,000 tourists passed daily through Windermere Station (Birthwaite, renamed).

Mansions and middle classes

The early visitors' writings paved the way to ever-increasing numbers of visitors, gradually moving down the social scale as the railways democratised travel.

Renewed interest in England's natural beauty led the wealthy to indulge themselves by snapping up lake shore property and constructing lavish, sometimes garish, mansion-villas; early adopters included Joseph Pocklington at Derwent Water (page 62) and the Curwens on Belle Isle (page 121). They were joined, through the nineteenth century, by the north-west's bankers and industrialists, who commuted to their Windermere villas at weekends. Built to help the super-rich relax away from the smoke of Manchester or Bolton, most now survive as hotels; Brockhole became the National Park Visitor Centre. The mansions were set amid landscaped gardens; the wild Lakeland backdrop needed to be tempered by an artificially engineered sylvan foreground. Royal Windermere Yacht Club was formed as an exclusive club for these privileged offcomers.

The middle classes increasingly favoured the Lake District for their holidays, ranging from Beatrix Potter's family who rented places like Wray Castle for the summer, to those of more modest means who frequented new guesthouses at Bowness, Keswick and Ambleside. They were joined, from the early twentieth century, by the *hoi polloi*, working people who rarely had the money or time to explore far beyond 'steamer' trips taken from the Windermere and Coniston railheads.

PRESERVING THE LAKE DISTRICT

"a sort of National Property, in which every man has a right and interest who has an eye to perceive and a heart to enjoy."

William Wordsworth, *Guide to the Lakes*, 1835

Long before the National Trust and National Park became a reality, Wordsworth mooted ideas about preserving and protecting the Lake District.

The vicar of Crosthwaite

The key figure in making such ideas a reality was Hardwicke Drummond Rawnsley (1851–1920), vicar of Wray Church from 1877, then of Keswick's Crosthwaite Church from 1883. He campaigned tirelessly to preserve the Lake District, beginning in the 1870s and 1880s by opposing lakeside railway proposals: *"the loss is altogether out of proportion to the gain; and what is more, the loss is sustained by the whole nation"* (article in *The Spectator*, 1883). He campaigned against, but later supported, the Thirlmere dam (page 78).

In 1883, Rawnsley set up the Lake District Defence Society (LDDS). Not everyone was delighted. *The Cumberland Pacquet* opined, *"A handful of enthusiasts had taken the Lake District under their protection and had resolved that the inhabitants should be shut out from the world and the conveniences of modern travel."*

The LDDS was the forerunner to the National Trust, which Rawnsley created in 1895, alongside solicitor Robert Hunter and social reformer Octavia Hill. He, his co-founders and over 90% of the original membership were from outside Cumbria and the Trust (as today) had a distinctly middle-class tinge to it. Rawnsley didn't help when he patronisingly suggested, *"Inhabitants of the dales are not the safest guardians of their lovely home"*.

Although the Trust is often associated with stately homes and cream teas, it was founded to acquire and protect Lake District land. Its original acquisitions were around Derwent Water.

These landholdings were boosted by huge bequeathments such as those from Beatrix Potter (page 69) and the Fell and Rock Climbing Club (page 176). It's now the National Park's largest landowner, managing 45,000 hectares, a fifth of the total.

Friends against plantations

> *"Many now preach the gospel 'Preserve the countryside'. Let us then preserve it in the best possible way, by teaching as many as we can to use and value it; not by locking it up, or by making a museum of it ..."*
>
> H. H. Symonds, *Walking in the Lake District*, 1933

School headteacher Reverend Henry Herbert Symonds was a force of nature in conserving the Lake District and promoting public access. He played early roles in the Rambler's Federation and nascent Youth Hostels Association, in 1933 published a Lake District guidebook heavily focused on championing public access, and in 1934 proposed *"some thoroughly national group of Friends of the Lake District"*. Friends of the Lake District (FOTLD) was launched at a rally in Keswick that year, a still-influential charity and pressure group.

FOTLD's first success came in 1935, against the FC. It presented a petition and Symonds published ***Afforestation in the Lake District***, an enraged polemic against *"the serried ranks of conifers"*. Plantations planned for Wasdale and Buttermere were thankfully halted.

The National Park

The National Park concept hails back to Wordsworth's *"national property"* idea: pretty radical when first written in 1810. The 1932 Kinder Trespass returned the concept to the national discussion. A 'Council for National Parks' was established in 1936. Following the Second World War, the 1949 ***National Parks and Access to the Countryside Act*** was passed by Clement Attlee's Labour government; H. H. Symonds helped to shape the legislation.

The Lake District National Park was the second to be created, in 1951. It was formed with two stated purposes:

1. Conserve and enhance the natural beauty, wildlife and cultural heritage of the Lake District.
2. Promote opportunities for the understanding and enjoyment of the special qualities of the National Park.

The National Park has the unenviable task of deciding how best to balance these purposes against Lakeland's chief economic activity, tourism. In 2024, there were 17.73 million visits against a resident population of 40,478.

Wildlife and Environment

"The lake was perfectly still, the sun shone on Hill and vale, the distant Birch trees looked like large golden Flowers – nothing else in colour was distinct and separate but all the beautiful colours seemed to be melted into one another."

Dorothy Wordsworth, *Grasmere Journals*, 1800–1803

Paddling the English Lakes, nature is a constant companion. Their waters and shores host a diverse range of habitats, teeming with life, interlinked by intricate ecosystems. Living creatures, large and microscopic, have adapted to the lakes since the ice retreated, sometimes uniquely to a particular lake. Human activity has also impacted on the lakes' wildlife and environment; the Lake District's UNESCO World Heritage Site designation makes it clear that for all its wild beauty, the modern landscape is 'agro-pastoral': farmland. Paddlers are privileged to engage with this complex natural history in a unique manner; your paddlecraft treads lightly and leaves no trace, offering access to remarkable natural places and breathtaking wildlife encounters.

Rock and scree, Place Fell, Ullswater

Habitats

"… a multiplicity of symmetrical parts uniting in a consistent whole. This is everywhere exemplified along the margins of these lakes."

William Wordsworth, ***Guide to the Lakes***, 1835

Paddlers will experience a mosaic of habitats around the English Lakes. These habitats don't exist in isolation: they physically overlap one another and are interconnected and interdependent.

Lakes

OLIGOTROPHIC AND MESOTROPHIC

Some lakes host less life than others. Some are oligotrophic, meaning the water has low nutrient content and is less productive. Others are mesotrophic, meaning they host moderate levels of nutrients and are more productive.

Oligotrophic lakes have fewer nutrients because of their rocky shores and catchments, resulting in less diversity of life within the water and fewer birds around it. Wast Water tops the scale with 73% of its shores being rocky, explaining its clear, alkaline waters. The other notably oligotrophic lakes are Ennerdale Water (67%), Buttermere (50%) and Crummock Water (48%).

Mesotrophic lakes are those where the retreating glaciers deposited alluvial clays on the valley floor; Bassenthwaite Lake, Derwent Water and Windermere are clear examples. Their shores became rich in life, with meadows, woodlands and wetlands, supplying nutrients to diverse and plentiful life within the lakes themselves. Esthwaite Water is by far the most nutrient-rich lake; it's perhaps unsurprising that it is now a private fishery, with paddlers banned. As 46% of its drainage is farmland, Esthwaite is at risk of becoming eutrophic: rich in nutrients to the point at which bacteria consume all oxygen.

IN THE WATER

Beneath the lake surfaces, life thrives, largely unseen. This is best understood as a 'food web', in which a vast range of organisms exist interdependently upon one another.

At the microscopic level, bacteria, fungi and single-celled protozoa feed off dead organic matter, particularly on the lakebed. In summer, microscopic algae, floating plants known as phytoplankton, photosynthesise light in the lakes' warm, less dense, surface layer (the epilimnion), oxygenating the water. These algae give the water a greenish-brown hue. As they die and sink to the lakebed, their decomposition deoxygenates the denser, cooler lower layer (the hypolimnion). With the beginning of autumn, the cooling of the epilimnion and stronger winds cause the layers to mingle, bringing fresh nutrients to the surface and returning oxygen to the depths.

Invertebrate creatures, called zooplankton, get a look-in next. These are a huge range of organisms, generally translucent, although just about visible to the naked eye, which filter-feed phytoplankton algae from the water. The zooplankton are in turn eaten by small fish, including char.

Macroinvertebrates encompass a huge diversity of creatures. They are visible to the naked eye. Some live purely in the water, such as freshwater shrimp and gastropods (freshwater snails), and

Hydrosere at Bowness Bay, Bassenthwaite Lake

others emerge to reproduce, such as caddisfly, dragonfly and mayfly. They help to break down organic matter, feeding on algae and plant material.

With these microscopic and macroscopic organisms forming the basis of nutritional supply (i.e. lunch), the food web spreads out to encompass larger organisms: newts, fish, eels, toads, birds, otters … up to the magnificent ospreys which swoop down to swipe whole fish from the water.

Hydroseres

Hydroseres are the zone of transition from deep water to dry land ecosystems. They encompass diverse habitats, less so when the shore area is rocky or steep.

A hydrosere begins in the deepest water where light penetrates, generally about six metres in depth. Here, aquatic plants, known as macrophytes, colonise the lakebed. Submerged plants include: shoreweed, grass-like and able to resist wave action; stonewort, algae which likes silty lakebeds; and quillwort, whose spirally arranged quill-like leaves colonise stony areas.

In shallower water around three metres in depth, emergent macrophytes begin to, well, emerge: plants rooted to the lakebed, with long stems extending to the surface. White and yellow water lilies flower colourfully, while the leaves and long stems of pondweeds and Canadian waterweed (a well-established invasive non-native species) provide sustenance for waterfowl.

In shallows up to a metre deep, reed swamps take root. Common reed and other marsh plants such as bottle sedge, bulrush, club-rush, reed-grass and water horsetail extend up to three metres from the water. On stony shores, reed canary-grass predominates. This habitat is especially vulnerable to erosion; many reedbeds are protected 'no-paddling' zones and Windermere's Grass Holme has seen its reedbeds almost disappear. The reedbeds trap sediment, which gradually accumulates.

Fen and carr are the penultimate stages of the hydrosere. Organic mud settles. Plants with creeping roots (rhizomes) firm up the gunk into marshy soil, which is further augmented by leaf

Side Wood, Ennerdale Water

detritus from marsh plants such as purple loosestrife, marsh marigold and meadowsweet. Finally, alder, downy birch and willow colonise, forming carr (wet woodland). Carr is low-canopied and tangled growths, the closest thing in the Lake District to mangrove swamp. For an example, explore Thirlmere's Wyth Burn.

The hydrosere's end-stage is dry woodland, on land formerly occupied by deep water. Each hydrosere stage is part of the biological infilling process, as plants die and sediment accumulates: lake shores are extending and the lakes are shrinking. Esthwaite Water's North Fen has moved fifty metres south over two centuries. A former chain of lakes in the Kentmere valley has been completely infilled. The process is apparent in sheltered bays such as the Derwent Water's Otterbield Bay, at lakeheads such as Loweswater's Waterend, around deltas such as Windermere's Trout Beck and all around small lakes such as Elter Water.

Woodlands

"The woods consist mainly of oak, ash and birch, and here and there wych elm, with underwood of hazel, the white and black thorn, and hollies; in moist places alders and willows abound; and yews among the rocks."

William Wordsworth, *Guide to the Lakes*, 1835

After the ice retreated, forests carpeted Lakeland, to the 750m contour. A thousand years ago, humans had largely felled it. Only traces of the post-Ice Age wildwood survive, in high, inaccessible locales, notably Young Wood, above Mungrisdale. All lakeside woodland today has either regenerated or been planted, often for coppicing.

About 10% of the Lake District is now wooded. Half of this is conifer plantations planted over the past two centuries. Ancient semi-natural woodland is that which has been undisturbed for 400 years; there are about 20,000 hectares of this. This takes the form of carr (wet) or broadleaf (i.e. deciduous) woodland.

Upland heath, Crummock Water's western shore

Native broadleaf woodland

Lakeshores are lined with broadleaved woodlands of ash, silver birch, hawthorn, hazel and oak. Sessile oak is the most common, thriving on the region's acidic rocks. Many of the trees have been historically coppiced, evidenced by multiple stems growing from older bases. These woodlands generate their own damp, moist climate: these are temperate rainforests, part of Britain's Atlantic oakwood. Fine examples include Buttermere's Scales Wood, Ullswater's Glencoyne and Hallinhag Woods and Ennerdale Water's Side Wood. Although mostly coniferous, the Furness forests spanning from Windermere to Coniston Water have plenty of deciduous woodland. Lakeland's finest examples are agreed to be in Borrowdale, especially Great Wood, Lodore Wood and others along Derwent Water's eastern shores.

Ground flora is a mixture of bilberry, bracken, brambles and wildflowers such as wild daffodils and bluebells. This soggy sub-arboreal world is, however, the kingdom of the bryophytes: mosses, liverworts and hornworts. These seedless plants carpet the landscape. The damper the surrounds, the greater the diversity: Borrowdale has 136 species! To appreciate their ubiquity, stroll up the ravine of Derwent Water's Lodore Falls. Lichens are also an important element of the rainforest, colonised on rocks but predominantly on trees, especially birch and Great Wood's big 'maiden' oaks. Incidentally, when sheep are present … almost none of the above applies, they munch *everything*.

Plantation

These dark, foreboding forests are mostly the legacy of the Forestry Commission's (FC) twentieth-century exploits (page 250). Another culprit is the National Trust, who latterly had a policy of introducing spruce and larch into native broadleaved woodland; during the 1940s much of Buttermere's Burtness Wood was converted to conifers.

The plantations are made up of Douglas fir, larch, and Norway spruce: fast-growing trees planted densely, with profit in mind. The result is sterile forest floors supporting a limited range of wildlife, due to lack of light. The positives are that raptors such as goshawk, merlin and sparrowhawk favour these environments, and that red squirrels find sanctuary from greys. Larch is also, admittedly, attractively colourful in spring and autumn.

The FC now varies its planting patterns. To encourage biological diversity, around Ennerdale Water's and Thirlmere's shores, younger and older trees are mixed and cleared spaces introduced; the younger plantations are favourable to small mammals such as mice and voles (attracting owls and other raptors) and the spaces are favoured by larger mammals like badgers and roe deer.

Fellsides

This section outlines habitats found where fells descend to the lake shore. It's worth remembering that these seemingly wild and untamed upland ecosystems were created by prehistoric axes, followed by the voracious appetites of sheep.

UPLAND HEATH

Upland heath is peat moorland colonised by dwarf shrubby plants, especially heather species: bell, cross-leaved heath and ling. Alongside these are bearberry, bilberry, cowberry and crowberry. When these plants flower, dwarf shrub heath becomes a riot of colour. Invertebrates such as beetles and spiders thrive, feeding ground-nesting birds such as curlews, golden plovers and skylarks. Probably the best examples of this habitat are seen along Crummock Water and Buttermere's western shores.

Heathland developed as a result of tree felling and sheep-grazing, which reduced soil nutrient levels and increased soil acidity, supporting heather. If undisturbed, heathland reverts to woodland, while if overgrazed, it becomes smothered with bracken and gorse; an obvious example of the latter is rough and unkempt Torver Back Common, alongside Coniston Water.

ROCK AND SCREE

Lakeshore crags and scree slopes offer habitats inaccessible to the all-devouring sheep. Mosses and liverworts thrive in damp, sheltered gills and ravines. Ledges, rocks and scree give haven, barely, to flowering plants such as starry saxifrage, herbs such as alpine lady's mantle and a range of ferns: fir clubmoss, parsley and polypody.

Higher above the water, thickets of juniper cling to scree and loose rock. This sprawling shrub, established for example on Place Fell at Ullswater, is reputed to ward off evil. Could be worth knowing.

The high crags are, of course, the birds' prerogative. Ringed ouzel, stonechat and wheatear nest in cracks and crevices. Raptors such as buzzard and peregrine falcon hunt from inaccessible nests and ravens haunt high eminences; there are about thirty-three Raven Crags in Lakeland, the most spectacular being above Thirlmere. There are also many Eagle Crags (and Eel Crags, meaning the same). Sadly, the last golden eagle, nesting above Haweswater, died in 2015.

Canada Goose, Ullswater

Wildlife

A handful of the Lake District's star species is outlined below.

Fish

Although largely hidden from view, three species of fish are worth knowing about: vendace, schelly and char. All are glacial relics, stranded when the ice retreated. All, inevitably, are under threat: by historical overfishing, by introduced species such as roach, by pollution and, latterly, by climate change.

VENDACE AND SCHELLY

Vendace and schelly are whitefish, resembling herrings. Vendace are especially rare, only found in Bassenthwaite Lake and Derwent Water. They had disappeared from Bassenthwaite by 2001, but returned in 2014 following work to restore the water quality.

Schellies are found only in Ullswater, Haweswater and surrounding tarns, including Red Tarn, England's highest. The Haweswater fishery kills (sorry, 'culls') cormorants to protect schellies, despite their decline being caused by water abstraction.

CHAR

> "Big as a small trout rather slendere and the skin full of spots. Some reddish, and part of the whole skinn and the finn and taile is red … the inside flesh looks as red as any salmon."

Celia Fiennes, *Through England On a Side Saddle*, 1698

Salvelinus alpinus, the char or Arctic charr, is trout-like, blue-grey or green-brown and covered in colourful spots. The key distinguishing feature is the pink-red belly; the name derives from the Celtic *ceara / cera*: blood-red. Char are found in nine of the ten deepest lakes; the Ullswater population was exterminated by the 1927 Keppel Cove Disaster (page 99). Char populations have evolved genetic variations between the lakes, with those of Ennerdale Water being most distinct. Char has the most northerly distribution of any freshwater fish, with the Windermere population at its southernmost extremity. They survive because of thermal stratification, feeding on zooplankton in the colder hypolimnion layer.

Potted char was regarded as a delicacy, enjoyed in decorated Windermere charr pots, which are now desirable collectors' items.

Nineteenth-century overfishing, twentieth-century phosphate pollution, and now climate change have all pushed char to the brink of extinction in Lakeland; their future is uncertain.

Birds

The range of birds inhabiting or visiting the lakes and their fell, wetland and woodland shores is vast, requiring far more volumes than this one to cover thoroughly. Just a summary is offered here.

Many birds utilise the lakes as safe havens: island nesting spots, overnight or overwinter roosts, and, in the case of seabirds, a sheltered retreat when the sea is too rough. Oystercatchers and sandpipers (known locally as 'willy wickets') nest and breed on stony shores. Swallows and

Peregrine falcon, from 'The Birds of Great Britain', 1873

◎ *Osprey, Wikimedia Commons*

martins nest and feed off insects along lake margins. Wetland reedbeds shelter coot nests and are feeding grounds for reed buntings and reed warblers; listen for their respective 'teu' and 'churr' sounds. Woodlands host redstarts, redpolls and willow warblers, while carr provides nesting spots for wildfowl, including swans and geese.

The oligotrophic lakes are attractive to 'fish-eaters' such as cormorants, goosander, great-crested grebes, herons, red-breasted merganser (known as 'sawbills' because of their serrated bill, evolved to grasp prey while diving) and, the overlord of all, the osprey. Waterfowl 'dabblers' feed off the invertebrates and aquatic plants: coot, goldeneye, mallard, pochard, teal, tufted ducks and wigeon.

PEREGRINE FALCONS

This 250kph raptor nests on crags between the 350m and 600m contours. Spotting one hunting above the water, a blue-grey blur, is a common occurrence. There are around a hundred pairs in the Lake District: Europe's highest density. Peregrines nearly didn't make it: pesticides and persecution reduced numbers to just six pairs. Egg thieves, dogged 'collectors' who seemingly lacked something fundamental in their human psyche, were determined to wipe them out. When a nest was re-established at Falcon Crag above Derwent Water in 1970, a 24-hour 'crag watch' was necessary to guard the nest, with Keswick Mountain Rescue sleeping on the cliff. The nest has gone on to produce dozens of chicks.

OSPREYS

Seeing an osprey plunge on to a lake surface, at 125kph, wings drawn back and claws extended forward to grasp some unfortunate fish, is an unforgettable experience. About a fifth of the time, the osprey is successful; the sign of this is rather laboured attempts to take off again. Ospreys are unmistakeable by their crooked 1.8m wingspan, hooked beak and razor-sharp talons, not to mention their huge size: the largest raptor in Lakeland's skies. Ospreys hunt above the lakes, early morning and late evening, June to August.

Water Vole, Wikimedia Commons

Ospreys returned to the Lake District (and England) in 2001, nesting at Bassenthwaite Lake (see page 49). They have since established themselves across the region, including three nests at Esthwaite Water. Half a dozen pairs are nesting here at the time of writing. Those at Foulshaw Moss, south-east of Windermere, have their own webcam.

The ospreys arrive from late March and lay eggs in late April. Hatchlings emerge in early June. In early September, the ospreys migrate back to West Africa, a 5,000km odyssey which has been tracked; it is accomplished in an incredible 20 flying days, with daily legs reaching 430km.

Mammals

Less commonly encountered mammals include the dormouse, wood mouse and the now extremely rare pine marten. They all find shelter in native broadleaf woodlands.

SHREWS AND VOLES

The water shrew is widespread across the English Lakes. Despite being up to 17.5cm in length, this dark-grey shrew is hard to spot. It lives in burrows and swims along the surface among wetland and carr, hunting for invertebrates.

Water voles were once widespread but are now critically endangered and have disappeared completely from all but Lakeland's southernmost fringes. They have suffered from shoreline erosion (they live in burrows) and, especially, predation by non-native minks. This rotund, chestnut-brown creature, up to 36cm in length, is often mistaken for the brown rat (grey-brown, with a more pointed nose).

OTTERS

Otters were once bountiful enough in the Lake District that bounties were paid for killing them. They were hunted with hounds (legal until 1981) and made into hats. Otters clung on until the

Otter, Wikimedia Commons

1960s, when organochloride pesticides almost exterminated them nationally. Otters have spent the past few decades tentatively recolonising the Lake District from Scotland, starting with the northern lakes. They are now commonly spotted in all lakes. Ecologists don't as yet have any idea of the population size, and it has been suggested that their increasing visibility – on the waterfront at Bowness-on-Windermere, for example – is a sign that they are struggling for food sources.

RED SQUIRRELS

"This is a Tale about a tail – a tail that belonged to a little red squirrel, and his name was Nutkin."
Beatrix Potter, *The Tale of Squirrel Nutkin*, 1903

The Lake District is among England's few remaining enclaves where red squirrels cling on. Grey squirrels, an invasive non-native species introduced in the 1870s, out-compete them for food and, worse, carry the deadly parapox virus. Greys are expanding their range in the south, but reds are still a common sight along the northern and western lakes' woodland shores. Reds have a small advantage: greys don't like coniferous woods, whereas reds are happy inhabiting both broadleaved and coniferous woods; it's no coincidence that the author has encountered reds most frequently at Bassenthwaite Lake, Thirlmere and Ennerdale Water. They can swim! In 1901, Beatrix Potter was inspired to write *The Tale of Squirrel Nutkin* after witnessing this at Derwent Water.

Red squirrels are often encountered on the ground, gathering and burying seeds for the winter. Chewed pine cones and scratch marks on bark are signs of nearby dreys, their spherical nests, built in the forks of trees, especially oak. Their 'kittens' are born in litters of two or three in the spring and are blind at birth.

Across Lakeland, roadside signs read, *'Red squirrels: slow down'*. Should they even be allowed to drive?

Red squirrel, Wikimedia Commons

DEER

"The wild aristocracy of the Lakes"

Norman Nicholson, *Cumberland and Westmorland*, 1949

Spotting deer drinking at the lakeside is a rare experience, gifted only to early risers who paddle quietly. Two species of these beautiful and retiring creatures are found in the Lake District: red and roe deer.

Red deer are Britain's largest land mammals, standing over 1m tall at the shoulder. They are rust-red, turning brown in winter, with short tails and widely branched, multiple-pointed antlers. Those on the fells from Thirlmere to Haweswater are strays from Martindale Deer Forest, and they descend, in winter, to the shores of Ullswater. A second population lives in the forests between Windermere and Coniston Water. These Furness deer are darker and have larger (160kg!) stags, boasting 14 or 16-point antlers. Stags compete during their autumn rut, asserting their dominance with awesome and intimidating roaring. Paddlers on Ullswater will hear them bellowing across the lake from Place Fell, receiving replies from the far shore.

Roe deer are about 70cm tall at the shoulder. They are also rust-red, but turn grey in winter, and have a distinctive white patch on their bum, no tail, and no more than three points on their antlers. They are widespread, but with populations centred on the Furness forests and High Street. They feed on brambles and undergrowth, thriving wherever everything hasn't already been eaten by sheep.

HERDWICK SHEEP

"No obstacle is too great to prevent a Herdwick, which has been sold and removed a dozen or more miles away, returning to its native heaf."

F.W. Garnett, *Westmorland Agriculture 1800–1900*, 1912

Herdies at Wasdale Head Hall Farm

There are about 50,000 Herdwicks in the Lake District, concentrated in the centre and west. They outnumber humans! Although not the only sheep hereabouts (there are three million in Cumbria), 'Herdies' are an iconic part of the landscape, instantly recognisable by their white 'smiling' faces and thick, bristly, grey fleece. Young Herdwicks, known as 'hogs', are black, or rusty brown.

Herdwicks are ideally adapted to the landscape and climate. They shrug off severe weather, forage effectively on heather, bilberry and bracken and, amazingly, don't even need fences. Herdwicks are attuned to graze and remain in their own 'heaf' territory, possibly by smell. Farm sales stipulate that herds cannot be moved.

Hardwicke Rawnsley and Beatrix Potter recognised their centrality to Lakeland culture and heritage: Rawnsley founded the Herdwick Sheep Association in 1899, and Potter stipulated that the 15 farms and 1,600 hectares which she bequeathed to the National Trust upon her death in 1943 should continue to be grazed by Herdwicks.

Despite this being the 'wildlife' section, Herdwicks are no such thing. They are a domesticated and non-native species, probably introduced by Vikings (Old Norse *herdvyck*: sheep pasture); their DNA suggests a common ancestor in Orkney and Scandinavia.

Everyone loves Herdwicks. (Who wouldn't? They smile.) However, some have questioned their impact, and that of sheep in general, upon the Lake District. Centuries of overgrazing has reduced soil health, denuded the fells of grassland and wildflowers, stifled woodland regeneration and, overall, created today's artificial landscape of heather and bracken. The awarding of World Heritage Site status in 2017 cemented this situation, being largely predicated around preserving the Lake District as an agro-pastoral landscape. *The Guardian* (who else?) warned that the Lake District had been ossified into, *"a Beatrix Potter-themed sheep museum"*. Although 're-wilding' is controversial (the **Daily Telegraph** calls it a *"religion"*), various schemes have borne fruit. For example, no sheep have been grazed above Derwent Water's Falcon Crag since 1999; there has already been a dramatic return of wildflowers and oak, juniper and willow.

Cormorants on Lady Holme, Windermere

Environmental issues

Like any modern natural environment, the English Lakes face significant challenges, all a result of human activity. The good news is that these issues are largely well understood and measures are underway to mitigate or reverse them.

Plantations

Lakeland's non-native coniferous forests hugely reduce wildlife diversity and can increase lake acidity. Modern forestry management is more sympathetic, with treelines softened, trees diversified with native broadleaves, and actions taken towards carbon capture and storage.

Pollution and run-off

> *"I want my children to be able to return to these same places one day with their children. I want them to be able to boat across Lake Windermere like we did, without worrying about getting sick or being surrounded by hazard signs."*

Sir Keir Starmer, 2024

Pollution is undoubtedly the greatest immediate threat to the English Lakes.

TREATED SEWAGE

Towns and villages (and sometimes caravan parks) discharge treated sewage effluent into the lakes. This raises phosphate levels, nutrients which encourage the growth of cyanobacteria: better known as blue-green algae (page 32). This causes eutrophication: an increase in nutrients to the point at which bacteria consume all oxygen and insufficient light penetrates the water.

From the 1950s to the 1980s, phosphate levels increased 15–20 times in Windermere's south basin. Even the deepest water was deoxygenated and the char were endangered. The 1991 installation of phosphorus removal apparatus led to instant improvement. However, phosphate levels are rising again, and its north basin has seen oxygen levels decline by 9.1%, compared with the 30-year average; this is a source of current conflict (page 109).

FARMING

A significant source of pollution is run-off from farming practices since the Second World War. The key culprits are artificial, inorganic fertilisers used on lakeshore grasslands and cattle shed slurry: both leach nitrogen and phosphorus into lakes. A further issue is insecticides used in sheep-dipping, which have sometimes been dumped into becks, killing invertebrates. Solutions applied include banning the more noxious chemicals, avoiding applying fertiliser in wet times, and building retention tanks for slurry. The Loweswater Care Project has borne success, the Centre for Ecology and Hydrology's partnership with Loweswater farmers.

MINING

Mining has left a legacy of pollutants. An extreme example is the heavy metals discharged into Ullswater by the 1927 Keppel Cove Disaster (page 99), which poisoned swans well into the twenty-first century. The spoil heaps on Derwent Water's south-western shores remain unveg-

📷 *Blue-green algae on Windermere*

etated because of noxious chemicals within. Core sampling of Bassenthwaite Lake's bed revealed cadmium, lead and zinc deposited over centuries, from the Newlands and Coledale Valley mines. Coledale's Force Crag Mine operated until 1990. In 2015, a water treatment plant was installed beside Coledale Beck, below the lowest adit; this now filters out 90% of metal pollutants.

ACID RAIN

Two centuries of sulphur dioxide entering the atmosphere from the North West's coal-burning industries caused sulphuric acid rain. This impacted most severely on lakes underlain by Borrowdale Volcanics and Eskdale Granite: these non-absorbent rocks don't buffer acid well. Improved air quality has led to some recovery over thirty years, but nitric acid rain, from petrol burning, is still a problem.

Erosion

Land erosion leads to organic and soil silt being washed into the lakes, stifling invertebrate life and aquatic vegetation. The causes can be walkers on footpaths, ploughing and, the key culprit, overgrazing by sheep. Shoreline erosion can reduce a biodiverse reedy shoreline to a sparse pebbly beach. This can be caused by powerboat wash, but also footfall; paddlers need to be conscious of where, and how carefully, they land.

Invasive species

The key invasive non-native species blighting the lakes is New Zealand pygmyweed (*Crassula helmsii*), a fast-spreading yellowish-green plant with succulent leaves. Brought to Britain in 1911 to oxygenate fishponds and aquariums, it is now banned but was discovered in Derwent Water in the 1990s and has subsequently spread to about half of the lakes. The weed has many negative impacts, for example smothering the gravel beds where endangered fish such as vendace spawn. Note the biosecurity guidance on page 34.

📷 *Thirlmere's plantations*

Other issues

Climate change is impacting upon the lakes in insidious and not yet fully understood ways. Since the 1980s, Windermere's average annual surface temperature has risen by over a degree centigrade. Warmer water means less dissolved oxygen supporting invertebrate life. Cold-water fish such as char (which require water below 8°C) and vendace will eventually be forced to relocate further north to survive – except that they can't: it's a lake.

Ever since the creation of the Thirlmere dam, water abstraction has been a hot topic. Although the creation of new dams seems unlikely (Ennerdale Water and Crummock Water are having theirs removed), the demands of industry and an increasing population may put further pressures on the English Lakes.

Freshwater Biological Association

The Freshwater Biological Association (FBA) is world renowned for its lake ecology research. Since formation in 1929, it has been housed at a range of sites along Windermere's western shore: from 1931 at Wray Castle, from 1950 at the Ferry Hotel at Claife, and since 2021 at the YMCA's former North Camp.

The FBA has made Windermere one of the world's most-studied bodies of water, accumulating a vast resource of historic data. Its website and publications are a treasure trove for anyone wanting to learn more about the ecosystems of the English Lakes.

A lakeside camp

Camping

In the summer months, the Lake District teems with campsites. These range from large caravan and holiday parks, through slightly pretentious 'glamping' retreats, to simple frill-free fields. Depressingly, the latter are now rare, partly because of economics (hot tubs and cabins attract more affluence) but also because of anti-social behaviour*.

Listed below are a range of campsites, hostels and glamping options alongside, or close to, the English Lakes. Note that waterside campsites sometimes have the verve to charge guests to bring, or launch, their paddlecraft. Most campsites are closed over the winter months. Be mindful that campsite details change more regularly than any other aspect of this guidebook's information: campsites open, campsites close. Also, many of these sites get very busy and are booked up months in advance; you are strongly recommended to call ahead and check what is available before setting off.

Tables of information overleaf.

This is, for example, the reason why Borrowdale's wonderful Stonethwaite campsite closed in 2024.

WILD CAMPING

The author hates this phrase: it's just camping*. But the name is used to distinguish the practice of camping outside formal campsites. There is no legally enshrined right to 'wild camp' in most of England. However, the generally accepted convention within the National Park is that backpackers can discreetly pitch tents on the fells, above the felldykes (the drystone walls separating the upper grazing land from the lower farmland). Of course, that knowledge is of limited use to paddlers!

Outside the summer months, there are potential overnight camp spots alongside some lakes, in some places, for very small groups. Doing this is only appropriate for those with experience of, and equipped for, discreet, lightweight, zero-impact camping. Choose locations away from dwellings and roads. If you arrive and find someone else camped there, then tough luck, move on to prevent crowding. Pitch your tent at sunset and depart very early. Leave *absolutely no trace*; in particular, this means that lighting fires is *never* appropriate. *Not ever.* Should you leave any trace or if you burn things, or if you are indiscreet or cause disturbance, then this is *not* wild camping, this is 'fly camping'. Because of appalling 'fly camping' practises by some, the National Park authorities now disapprove of *all* lakeside camping. In 2025, Public Space Protection Orders (PSPOs) have been imposed at roadside hotspots for fly camping (such as, Windermere's western shores and Coniston Water's eastern shores) and police boats have even patrolled Ullswater.

If wild camping is something that you wish to learn more about, start by looking up the *Wild Camping Code of Conduct* online.

See also 'wild' swimming: it's just swimming.

Camping

Bassenthwaite Lake

Name	Map no.	Grid ref..	Postcode	Tents?	Glamping options?	Beside water?	Charges to launch?	Phone	Website / email	Notes
Herdwick Croft Holiday Park	1	NY 200 323	CA12 4RD	Y	N	N	-	07821 440742	herdwickcroft.co.uk	
Coalbeck Caravan Park	2	NY 207 328	CA12 4RD	N	N	N	-	07821 910249	coalbeck.co.uk	
Irton House Farm	3	NY 203 343	CA13 9ST	Y	N	N	-	017687 76380	irtonhousefarm.co.uk	

Derwent Water

Name	Map no.	Grid ref..	Postcode	Tents?	Glamping options?	Beside water?	Charges to launch?	Phone	Website / email	Notes
Castlerigg Hall	4	NY 281 225	CA12 4TE	Y	Y	N	-	017687 74499	castlerigg.co.uk	
Castlerigg Farm Camping	5	NY 283 224	CA12 4TE	Y	N	N	-	017687 72479	castleriggfarm.com	
Borrowdale Caravan and Motorhome Club Campsite	6	NY 253 187	CA12 5UG	N	N	N	-	017687 77275	caravanclub.co.uk	Caravans and motorhomes only
Hollows Farm	7	NY 249 171	CA12 5UQ	Y	Y	N	-	017687 77298	hollowsfarm.co.uk	
Catbells Camping Barn	8	NY 241 208	CA12 5UE	N	N	N	-	07894 557673	catbellscamping-barn.com	Camping barn for up to eight
YHA Hause End Bunkhouse	9	NY 250 5UE	CA12 5UE	N	N	Y	N	0345 260 3077	yha.org.uk	Bunkhouse, has to be hired whole
Keswick Camping and Caravanning Club Site	10	NY 257 234	CA12 5EP	Y	N	Y	Y	017687 72392	campingandcaravanningclub.co.uk	Members only
Derwentwater Camping and Caravanning Club Site	11	NY 261 232	CA12 5EN	Y	N	N	-	017687 72579	campingandcaravanningclub.co.uk	Members only
YHA Keswick	12	NY 267 235	CA12 5LH	N	N	N	-	0345 371 9746	yha.org.uk	Youth hostel

Thirlmere

Name	Map no.	Grid ref..	Postcode	Tents?	Glamping options?	Beside water?	Charges to launch?	Phone	Website / email	Notes
Thirlspot Farm Camping	13	NY 317 177	CA12 4TN	Y	N	N	-	017687 72551	thirlspotfarm-camping.co.uk	
Fisher-Gill Camping Barn	14	NY 318 184	CA12 4TN	N	Y	N	-	07799 403764	stybeckfarm.co.uk	

Name	#	Grid Ref	Postcode					Phone	Website	Notes
Low Bridge End Farm	15	NY 317 205	CA12 4TS	N	N	N	-	017687 79242	campingbarn.com	Camping barn, sleeps eight
High Bridge End Farm	16	NY 314 193	CA12 4TG	Y	N	N	-	017687 72166		
Ullswater – northern										
Ullswater Holiday Park	17	NY 436 230	CA12 0LR	Y	Y	N	-	017684 86666	ullswaterholiday-park.co.uk	
Cove Caravan and Camping Park	18	NY 430 235	CA11 0LS	Y	N	N	-	017684 86549	cove-park.co.uk	
The Quiet Site	19	NY 430 237	CA11 0LS	Y	N	N	-	017684 86337	thequietsite.co.uk	'Hobbit holes' available!
Waterfoot Park	20	NY 463 246	CA11 0JF	N	Y	N	-	017684 86302	waterfootpark.co.uk	Caravans or glamping only
Waterfoot Carpark Campsite	21	NY 464 244	CA11 0LL	Y	N	N	-		Book via pitchup.com	
Hillcroft Park	22	NY 478 241	CA10 2LT	Y	Y	N	-	017684 86363	hillcroftpark.co.uk	
Park Foot Holiday Park	23	NY 469 238	CA10 2NA	Y	N	Y	N	017684 86309	parkfootullswater.co.uk	Several camping fields, not all are lakeside
Waterside House Campsite	24	NY 464 231	CA10 2NA	Y	Y	Y	N	017684 86332	watersidefarm-campsite.co.uk	
Cross Dormont Camping	25	NY 462 226	CA10 2NA	Y	N	N	-		crossdormont.co.uk	
Ullswater – southern										
Side Farm Campsite	26	NY 396 168	CA11 0NL	Y	N	Y	N	017684 82337	facebook.com – search for their page	Tents and campervans only
The Patterdale Estate	27	NY 389 160	CA11 0PJ	N	N	N	-	017684 82308	the-estate.co.uk	Caravan and Motorhome Club members only
Gillside Farm	28	NY 380 168	CA11 0QQ	Y	Y	N	-	017684 82346	gillsidecara-vanandcamping-site.co.uk	Bunkhouse available

Camping

Name	Map no.	Grid ref.	Postcode	Tents?	Glamping options?	Beside water?	Charges to launch	Phone	Website / email	Notes
Windermere – southern										
Lakes and Fells Caravan Site	29	SD 373 881	LA12 8AX	N	N	N	-	07810 710744	lakesandfells.com	Caravans only
Social District	30	SD 377 884	LA12 8AX	Y	N	Y	N	07507 801944	socialdistrict.co.uk	
Windermere Luxury Glamping Pods	31	SD 405 945	LA23 3JU	N	Y	N	-	07811 528826	barkerknott.co.uk	£££
The Hive Pod Village	32	SD 394 928	LA23 3LN	N	Y	N	-	015394 43751	ghyllhead.org	Camping pods at Ghyll Head Outdoor Education Centre
Park Cliffe Camping and Caravan Park	33	SD 391 910	LA23 3PG	Y	Y	N	-	015395 31344	parkcliffe.co.uk	
Hill of Oaks Caravan & Lodge Park	34	SD 394 899	LA12 8NR	N	Y	Y	Y	015395 31578	hillofoaks.co.uk	Glamping and chalets
Fell Foot Wood	35	SD 383 871	LA12 8NN	Y	N	N	-	015395 31014	fellfootwood.co.uk	Pre-arranged events and private parties only
Windermere – central										
Bowness on Windermere Camping and Caravan Site	36	NY 400 961	LA23 3HB	Y	N	N	-	024 7647 5426	campingandcaravanningclub.co.uk	Members only
Windermere – northern										
YHA Ambleside	37	NY 377 030	LA22 0EU	N	N	Y	N	0345 371 9620	yha.org.uk	Youth hostel
YHA Windermere	38	NY 405 013	LA23 1LA	Y	Y	N	-	0345 371 9352	yha.org.uk	Youth hostel. Tipis and landpods available.
Low Wray Campsite	39	NY 373 017	LA22 0JA	Y	Y	Y	N	015394 32733	nationaltrust.org.uk	Run by the National Trust. Camping pods available.

Name	#	Grid Ref	Postcode					Phone	Website	Notes
Skelwith Fold Holiday Park	40	NY 354 028	LA22 0HY	N	Y	N	-	015394 32277	skelwith.com	
Grasmere										
YHA Grasmere Butharlyp Howe	41	NY 336 077	LA22 9QG	Y	Y	N	-	0345 371 9319	yha.org.uk	Youth hostel. Tipis and landpods available.
Grasmere Glamping	42	NY 336 093	LA22 9RU	N	Y	N	-	015394 35055	theyan.co.uk	Luxury glamping pods £££
YHA Langdale	43	NY 338 053	LA22 9HQ	N	N	N	-	0345 371 9748	yha.org.uk	Youth hostel
Coniston Water – southern										
Water Yeat Campsite	44	SD 291 896	LA12 8DJ	Y	N	Y	N	07780 046112	Book via pitchup.com	Beside Allan Tarn. No large groups.
Crake Valley Holiday Park	45	SD 287 898	LA12 8DL	Y	Y	N	-	07856 977081	crakevalley.co.uk	
Coniston Water – northern										
Shepherd's View Caravan Site	46	SD 283 939	LA21 8BQ	Y	N	N	-	015394 41239	campingandcaravanningclub.co.uk	Members only
The Wilson Arms	47	SD 284 942	LA21 8BB	N	Y	Y	-	015394 41237	thewilsonarms.co.uk	Glamping and campervans
Church House Inn	48	SD 285 942	LA21 8AZ	N	Y	N	-	015394 49159	thechurchouseinn.com	Glamping pods and caravans
Beckstones Glamping Pods	49	SD 287 931	LA21 8BJ	N	Y	N	-	015394 49166	beckstonesglampingpods.co.uk	
Coniston Camping Hoathwaite	50	SD 297 950	LA21 8AX	Y	N	N	-	015394 41873	conistoncamping.co.uk	Lake 600m away by footpath
Coniston Park Coppice	51	SD 297 957	LA21 8LA	Y	Y	N	-	015394 41555	caravanclub.co.uk	Caravan and Motorhome Club membership not needed
Coniston Hall Campsite	52	SD 304 959	LA21 8AS	Y	Y	Y	Y	015394 41223	conistonhallcampsite.co.uk	
YHA Coniston Coppermines	53	SD 289 986	LA21 8HP	N	Y	N	-	0345 371 9630	yha.org.uk	Youth hostel. Whole hostel must be hired.

Camping

Name	Map no.	Grid ref	Postcode	Tents?	Glamping options?	Beside water?	Charges to launch	Phone	Website / email	Notes
YHA Coniston Holly How	54	SD 302 981	LA21 8DD	Y	Y	N	-	0345 371 9511	yha.org.uk	Youth hostel, glamping pods and camping facilities available
Coniston Sports & Social Centre	55	SD 305 978	LA21 8AL	Y	N	N	-	015394 41812	coniston-sports.co.uk	
Pier Cottage Caravan Park	56	SD 310 972	LA21 8AJ	N	N	Y	Y	015394 41252	piercottageconiston.co.uk	Caravans and motorhomes only

Wast Water

Name	Map no.	Grid ref	Postcode	Tents?	Glamping options?	Beside water?	Charges to launch	Phone	Website / email	Notes
Wasdale National Trust Campsite	57	NY 183 076	CA20 1EX	Y	Y	N	-	015394 32733	nationaltrust.org.uk	Lake 750m away via paths. Camping pods and tipis available.
Wasdale Lakeside Pop-up Campsite	58	NY 142 038	CA20 1ET	Y	N	Y	N	07983 142481	facebook.com – search for their page	At Easthwaite Farm. 350m to the lake.
Wasdale Valley View	59	NY 121 044	CA20 1ET	Y	N	N	-			Temporarily closed
Church Stile Farm and Holiday Park	60	NY 126 041	CA20 1ET	Y	Y	N	-	01946 726252	churchstile.co.uk	
Murt Camping Barn	61	NY 131 040	CA20 1ET	N	N	N	-	01946 726044		Camping barn, sleeps eight
YHA Wasdale Hall	62	NY 145 045	CA20 1ET	N	N	Y	N	0345 371 9350	yha.org.uk	Youth hostel

Ennerdale Water

Name	Map no.	Grid ref	Postcode	Tents?	Glamping options?	Beside water?	Charges to launch	Phone	Website / email	Notes
Wild Wool Barn	63	NY 104 163	CA23 3AU	Y	N	N	-	01946 861270	wildwoolbarn.co.uk	Limited tent spots. Camping barn sleeps six.
YHA Ennerdale	64	NY 142 141	CA23 3AX	N	N	N	-	0345 371 9116	yha.org.uk	Youth hostel. Camping barn available.
Low Gillerthwaite Field Centre	65	NY 139 141	CA23 3AX	N	N	N	-	01946 861229	lowgillerthwaite.com	Bunkrooms which can be hired by groups

Low Cock How Farm Camping	66	NY 057 143	CA23 3AQ	Y	N	-	01946 861354	facebook.com/ ennerdalecamping	Bunkhouse also available

Crummock Water

Cragg House Farm Camping Barn	67	NY 174 172	CA13 9XA	N	N	-	017687 70204	cragghousefarm. com	Camping barn for up to eight
Syke Farm Campsite	68	NY 172 170	CA13 9XA	Y	Y	-	017687 70275	sykefarmcamp-site.com	500m walk to Crummock Water, 600m to Buttermere

Loweswater

Holme Wood Bothy	69	NY 123 214	CA13 0RU	N	N	Y	0344 335 1296	nationaltrust. org.uk	Sleeps four
Swallow Barn Camping Barn	70	NY 117 226	CA13 0SU	N	N	-	01946 861465	kathleck@outlook. com	Camping barn sleeping up to eighteen
Askill Farm	71	NY 121 227	CA13 0SU	Y	Y	-	07548 007266	loweswatercamp-site.co.uk	Glamping yurt available

Buttermere

Syke Farm Campsite	72	NY 172 170	CA13 9XA	Y	Y	-	017687 70275	sykefarmcamp-site.com	500m walk to Crummock Water, 600m to Buttermere
Cragg House Farm Camping Barn	73	NY 174 172	CA13 9XA	N	N	-	017687 70204	cragghousefarm. com	Camping barn for up to eight
YHA Buttermere	74	NY 178 168	CA13 9XA	Y	Y	-	0345 371 9508	yha.org.uk	Youth hostel. Landpods available.
Gatesgarth Camping	75	NY 193 149	CA13 9XA	Y	N	-	017687 70256	facebook.com – search for their page	750m to the lake, along bridleways
Dubs Hut	76	NY 209 134	CA12 5XN	N	N	-		mountainbothies. org.uk	Remote, basic bothy
Warnscale Head Bothy	77	NY 205 133	CA12 5XN	N	N	-		mountainbothies. org.uk	Remote, basic bothy

Grasmere and Helm Crag

Further Reading

"To introduce Wordsworth into one's library is like letting a bear into a tulip garden."

Robert Southey, quoted by Thomas De Quincey in 1803

It has been estimated that over 50,000 books have been written about the Lake District. The author hasn't been counting, but thinks that he has made a reasonable dent in that pile; below is an edited selection.

Useful books

36 Islands, Robert Twigger, W&N 2022, ISBN 9781474621632

A Literary Guide to the Lake District, Grevel Lindop, Sigma Leisure 2015, ISBN 9781910758120

An Atlas of the English Lakes, John Wilson Parker, Cicerone 2002, ISBN 1852843551

A Flora of Cumbria, Geoffrey Halliday, University of Lancaster 1997, ISBN 1862200203

A Natural History of the Lakes, Tarns and Streams of the English Lake District, Geoffrey Fryer, Freshwater Biological Association 1991, ISBN 0900386509

Cumbria, the Lake District and its County, John Wyatt, Hale 2004, ISBN 070974409

Derwentwater: In the Lap of the Gods, Ian Hall, Orchard House Books 2019, ISBN 9780992815653

Donald Campbell: The Man behind the Mask, David Tremayne, Bantam Books 2004, ISBN 9780553815115

Ghostly Cumbria, Rob Kirkup, The History Press 2020, ISBN 9780750953125

Grasmere: A History in 55½ Buildings, Grasmere History Group, Grasmere History Group 2019, ISBN 9781916320703

Lake District Mountain Landforms, Peter Wilson, Scotforth Books 2010, ISBN 9781904244561

Lakeland, Derek Ratcliffe, Collins New Naturalist 2002, ISBN 9780007113040

Lake Windermere, Grasmere and Coniston Water Through Time, Gil Jepson, Amberley 2018, ISBN 9781445681931

Radical Wordsworth, Jonathon Bale, William Collins 2020, ISBN 9780008167424

Savage Grandeur and Noblest Thoughts: Discovering the Lake District 1750–1820, Cecilia Powell and Stephen Hebron, Wordsworth Trust 2010, ISBN 9781905256426

The Big Lakes of Lakeland, Alan Smith, Rigg Side Publications 2012, ISBN 9780954467944

The English Lakes, a History, Ian Thompson, Bloomsbury 2010, ISBN 978074759838

The Lake District, Landscape and Geology, Ian Francis, Stuart Holmes and Bruce Yardley, Crowood Press 2022, ISBN 9780719840111

The Last Englishman: the Double Life of Arthur Ransome, Roland Chambers, Faber & Faber 2010, ISBN 9780571222629

The Place Names of Cumbria, Joan Lee, Cumbria Heritage Services 1998, ISBN 090540470X

Thirlmere before the dam, Ian Hall, Orchard House Books 2021, ISBN 9788752570827

Windermere in the Nineteenth Century, Oliver M. Westall (ed.), Centre for North-West Regional Studies 1991, ISBN 0901272884

Historical sources

Exploring the English Lakes by paddlecraft is arguably enhanced by understanding what earlier visitors experienced, and how they viewed this landscape. The following accounts and writings are among those cited in this guidebook and are recommended for those wishing to go further down the rabbit hole. Many are accessible online.

A Complete Guide to the English Lakes, Harriet Martineau, 1855

A Guide through the District of the Lakes, William Wordsworth, 1835

A Guide to the Lakes, in Cumberland, Westmorland, and Lancashire, Thomas West, 1778

A Pictorial Guide to the Lakeland Fells, Alfred Wainwright, 1955–66

Baedecker's Great Britain, 1887

Cumberland and Westmorland, Norman Nicholson, 1949

Ex-Fellwanderer, Alfred Wainwright, 1987

Grasmere Journals, Dorothy Wordsworth, 1800–1803

Journal of A Visit to the Lake District in 1769, Thomas Gray, 1775

Letters from England, Robert Southey, 1807

Observations, relative chiefly to picturesque beauty, made in the year 1772: on several parts of England; particularly the mountains, and lakes of Cumberland, and Westmoreland, William Gilpin, 1786

Swallows and Amazons series, Arthur Ransome, 1930–47

The Complete Tales, Beatrix Potter, 1986

The Lake Counties, W.G. Collingwood, 1902

The Lakers, Norman Nicholson, 1955

The Outlying Fells of Lakeland, Alfred Wainwright, 1974

The Prelude, William Wordsworth, 1850

Walking in the Lake District, H. H. Symonds, 1933

Index of Placenames

A

Abbot's Bay 66
Abbot's Bay House 66
Aira Beck 96
Aira Force 96
Aira Force car park 41, 84, 96
Aira Point 96
Allan Bank 140
Allan Tarn 154
Allithwaite 221
Allonby's Boatyard 143
Ambleside 25, 100, 106, 108, 127, 129
Ambleside Pier 127
Ambleside RUFC 41, 110
Angler's Crag 181, 187
Anna's Nab 154, 155
Another Place 87
Armathwaite Hall 52
Armboth car park 40, 71, 73, 74, 79
Armboth Fell 77
Ash Landing 113, 115, 119, 126
Ash Landing car park 41, 110, 119
Ashness Gate jetty 64
Askham Fell 90
Askill Farm 261
Avon Woods holiday park 117

B

Bailiff Wood 159
Bailiff Wood car park 42, 149, 160
Banerigg 144
Banks Point 39, 50, 51
Barf 55
Barrow Bay 40, 60, 64
Barrow Beck 64
Barrow House 64
Barrow Point 64
Bass Crag 155
Bassenthwaite Lake 18, 19, 22, 26, 33, 37, 39, **47-55**, 213, 218, 219, 237, 256
Bassenthwaite Lakeside Lodges holiday park 52
Bassenthwaite Sailing Club 49, 51

Bass How 135
Bass Rock 135
Beauthorn 87
Beckfoot 159, 185
Beck Leven Foot 159
Beckstones Glamping Pods 259
Beck Wythop 39, 40, 50
Beech Hill car park 41, 110, 117
Beech Hill Hotel 117
Bee Holme 107, 137
Bell Crag 170
Belle Grange 132
Belle Grange Bay 135
Belle Isle 13, 106, 107, 115, 120, 121, 122, 123, 125, 232
Belle View 119
Bellman Landing 116
Belsfield Hotel 124
Birk Fell 97
Birthwaite 231
Bishop of Barf, the 55
Blackstock Point 39, 46, 49, 50, 55, 56
Blackwell 116
Blackwell Bay 116
Blake Fell 199
Blake Holme 118, 125
Blake Holme Nab 117, 118
Bleaberry Fell 77
Bleaberry Tarn 204, 207
Bleach Green 42, 181, 184, 188
Bleach Green car park 184, 185
Blea Water 21
Blelham Beck 137
Blencathra 62, 69
Blowick Bay 98
Blowick House 98
Bluebird Café 162
Bluebird K7 14, 162, 163, 164
Bluebird Wing 162
Boathow Crag 187
Bonscale Tower 90
Boon Beck 42, 150
Borran's Field 138
Borran's Park 138
Borrowdale 21, 61
Borrowdale Caravan and Motorhome Club Campsite 256
Bowness 52, 107, 134, 186
Bowness Bay 22, 49, 52, 123, 125

Bowness Knot 42, 184, 185, 186
Bowness Knott 42, 184
Bowness Knott car park 184
Bowness-on-Windermere 25, 106, 119, 123, 124
Bowness on Windermere Camping and Caravan Site 258
Bowness Plantation 186
Bowness Wood 50, 52
Brackenburn House 66
Braithwaite Bog 54
Brandelhow Bay 40, 60, 66
Brandelhow Park 66
Brandelhow Point 66
Brantwood 14, 159, 160
Brathay Bay 137
Brathay Hall 137
Brathay Neck 138
Brathay Rocks 138
Bridge House 129
Bridges Hole 54
Broad Crag 170
Broad Leys 116
Broad Ness 52
Broadness Farm 52
Brocavum Fort 223
Brock Crag 137
Brockhole 130, 232
Brockle Beck 63
Broken Rib 178
Broomhill Point 63
Brothers Water 19, 37, **101**, 213, 218
Browncove Crags 74
Brown Howe car park 42, 148, 149, 151, 155
Bull Head 115, 126
Burnbank Fell 199
Burnmoor Tarn 21
Burtness Comb 207
Burtness Wood 204, 207, 240
Buttermere 19, 26, 37, 43, 193, 198, **201-209**, 213, 215, 218, 237, 261
Buttermere Dubs 194, 207
Buttermere's north-west beach 43, 201, 203
Buttermere south shore 43, 204
Buttermere village 193, 201, 204, 208

C

Cabin, The 161
Calfclose Bay 40, 60, 64
Calf Rock 152
Calgarth 132
Calgarth Hall 131
Calgarth Park 130, 131
Campbells at Coniston 164
Cannon Crag 115
Cannon Dub 65
Carlew Crag 115
Castle Bay 135
Castle Crag 57, 65, 222
Castle How Fort 51
Castlehows Point 87
Castlerigg Farm Camping 256
Castlerigg Hall 256
Castlerigg Stone Circle 220, 221
Castle Rock 222
Castocks Wood 53
Cat Bells 13, 57, 68
Catbells Camping Barn 256
Cat Gill 64
Causey Pike 57
Char Cottage 206
Char Dub 186
Cherry Holm 98
Chicken Rock 126
Chinese Bridge 65
Church Bay 52
Church Beck 148, 162
Church House Inn 259
Church Stile Farm and Holiday Park 260
Cinderdale Common 43, 192, 196
City, The 75
Claife Heights 115, 119, 135
Claife Viewing Station 14, 115, 119, 230
Clappersgate 138
Clark's Loup 77
Clarkson Memorial 14, 89
Clay Dub 186
Clews Gill 186
Coalbeck Caravan Park 256
Coatlap Point 120, 121
Cockermouth 191
Cockpit stone circle, The 222
Cockshott Point 41, 110, 125
Comb Beck 205, 207
Comb Gill 76
Coniston 148, 228

Coniston Boating Centre 42, 149, 162
Coniston Camping Hoathwaite 259
Coniston Hall 161
Coniston Hall Campsite 259
Coniston Inn 163
Coniston launches piers 162
Coniston Park Coppice 259
Coniston Sailing Club 161
Coniston Sports & Social Centre 260
Coniston village 157, 162
Coniston Water 18, 19, 21, 26, 31, 33, 36, 37, 42, **147-163**, 215, 217, 259
Coniston Water Park 161
Copeland Forest 224
Copperheap Bay 69
Copperheap Hill 67
Cormorant Island 114
Costrells Rocks 113
Cottage Wood 52
Countess Beck 42, 171, 173, 174, 178
Cove Caravan and Camping Park 257
Crabtreebeck House 199
Crag Fell 181, 187
Cragg House Farm Camping Barn 261
Crag Hill 193
Crag Holme 114
Cragwood House 130
Crake Valley Holiday Park 259
Cross Dormont Camping 257
Crosthwaite Church 232
Crow Holme 120
Crow Park 40, 57, 60, 61, 70
Crummock Water 19, 26, 37, 42, **189-195**, 198, 203, 207, 213, 215, 218, 219, 237, 261
Cumbria 17, 22, 221, 223, 224, 225
Cunsey Beck 115
Curlew Crag 125

D

Daffodil Hotel 141, 144
Dale End Farm 143
Dalegarth House 205
Dale Head Hall 77

Dales Wood lay-by 42, 149
Dam Triangle car park 40, 73
Deerbolts Wood 142
Deergarth How Island 74
Derwent Bay 59, 67
Derwent Foot 53
Derwent Isle 57, 59, 61, 62, 64, 226
Derwent Water 18, 19, 20, 21, 22, 26, 31, 32, 33, 36, 37, 40, **57-69**, 213, 218, 219, 228, 232, 237, 256
Derwentwater Camping and Caravanning Club Site 256
Derwent Water Island 67
Derwentwater Marina 70
Devil's Chimney 98
Devoke Water 21
Dob Gill 75
Dob Gill car park 40, 73
Dodd 55, 206
Dodd Wood 49, 55, 228
Dodgson Wood 159
Dodgson Wood car park 42, 149, 152, 161
Dog Nab 117
Dollywaggon Pike 75
Donald Campbell Memorial 14, 99
Dorothy Gate 96
Dove Cottage 14, 139, 144, 230
Dove Nest Bay 129
Dub Beck 200
Dubs Hut 261
Dubwath Beck 51
Dubwath Silver Meadows 51
Duke of Portland boathouse 87
Dunmail Raise 75
Dunmallard 222
Dunmallard car park 40, 83
Dunmallard Hill 82, 87, 88

E

Ecclerigg Crag 130
Ecclerigg House 130
Elter Water 19, 37, **165**, 213, 239
English Lakes, the 17, 25, 27, 39
Ennerdale 228
Ennerdale Water 19, 21, 33, 36, 37, 42, **181-187**, 213, 215, 217, 237, 260
Eply Point 107

Esthwaite Water 19, 37, **166**, 215, 217, 219, 237
Eusemere car park 40, 83
Eusemere House 89

F

Faeryland Grasmere 41, 141, 143
Fairfield 127
Fairfield horseshoe 137
Fairfield Marine 87
Falcon Crag 64
Fallbarrow Park 123
Far Boathouse 87
Fawe Park 69, 70
Fell and Rock Climbing Club 176, 233
Fellborough 115
Fell Foot 106, 107, 111, 117, 118
Fell Foot Country Park 28, 41, 106, 110, 111
Fell Foot Wood 258
Ferry House promontory 120, 126
Ferry Nab 41, 108, 110, 125, 126
Fir Holme 125
Fir Island 148, 159
Fisher Crag 74
Fisher-Gill Camping Barn 256
Fleetwith Edge 204
Fleetwith Pike 13, 193, 204, 205, 206
Floating Island 65
Fountains Abbey 62
Freshwater Biological Association 120, 253
Friar's Crag 59, 63
Friends of the Lake District 233
Furness 227
Furness Abbey 111, 157, 225
Furness Fells 215
Furness forests 18, 227, 240, 248

G

Galava Roman Fort 14, 138, 222
Gale Bay 89
Galemire Bay 69
Gale Naze Crag 138
Gatesgarth Beck 205
Gatesgarth Camping 261
Gatesgarth Farm 206
Geordie's Crag 91
Gill Beck 185

Gillside Farm 257
Glencoyne Bay 100
Glencoyne Beck 93, 100
Glencoyne Bridge 99
Glencoyne Bridge car park 41, 84, 93
Glencoyne Park lay-bys 41, 84
Glencoyne Wood 240
Glenridding 40, 82, 84, 98, 99, 100
Glenridding Beck 99
Glenridding Dodd 99
Glenridding Pier 99
Glenridding Sailing Centre 40, 84, 99
Gnome Garden 174
Goat Crag 205
Goldrill Beck 82, 98
Gondola, Steam Yacht 14, 146, 148, 163
Gosforth 224
Gosforth road 173
Gowbarrow Bay 40, 83, 85
Gowbarrow Hall Farm 85
Gowbarrow Park 40, 83, 85, 96
Gowbarrow Park car park 41, 84
Gowder Crag 65
Grasmere 19, 20, 26, 33, 37, 41, **139-145**, 213, 215, 259
Grasmere Glamping 259
Grasmere Island 143
Grasmere village 140, 141, 144
Grasmoor 196, 199, 207
Grass Holme 114
Graythwaite Estate 166
Great Bay 59, 65
Great Borne 184, 185
Great Gable 175, 176, 193
Great How 77
Great Island 120
Great Langdale Beck 165
Great Wood 63, 238, 240
Greendale Mires 174
Green Holme 165
Green Naze Wyke 115
Greenside 228
Greenside Mine 99
Green Tuft Island 108, 137
Greta Hall 230
Grey Crag 206
Grizedale Forest 148, 151, 159, 228
Grubbins Point 114
Gummer's How 13, 106, 118

H

Hadrian's Wall 223
Hallin Fell 13, 91, 92, 96
Hallinhag Wood 91, 92, 240
Halls Beck 52
Hallsteads 85
Hammer Hole 115
Hanging Rock 100
Harrop Rocks 114
Harrowslack car park 41, 110
Hartley Wife 125
Hassness Crag Wood 43, 204, 205
Hassness Estate 205
Hassness House 205
Hassnesshow Beck 205
Hause Point 43, 75, 77, 192, 193, 195
Haverthwaite and Lakeside Railway 113
Hawes End jetty 67
Hawes How Island 74, 75
Haweswater 18, 19, 37, **101**, 213
Hawkshead 107
Hawse End 67
Haw's Holme 122, 134
Haws How Island 13
Haws Wood 117
Hay Stacks 13, 193, 201, 206
Heald, The 159
Helm Crag 144
Heltondale 89
Helvellyn 74, 76, 99, 127, 213
Helvellyn fells 71, 74
Helvellyn Gill 13, 73, 74, 77
Hen Holme 122, 134
Hen Rock 126
Herdus 185
Herdwick Croft Holiday Park 256
Heron Island 165
Heughscar Hill 88
Hidden Harbour 152
High Bank Ground 159
High Bank Ground Farm 159
High Brandelhow jetty 60
High Bridge End Farm 257
High Crag 193, 206
High Crag Buttress 206
High Ling Crag 195
High Nibthwaite 154
High Peel Near 153
High Seat 77

High Snockrigg 205
High Stile 185, 193, 206
High Street 101, 127, 137, 223
High Street Roman road 90
High Wray Bay 134, 135
Hillcroft Park 257
Hill of Oaks 125
Hill of Oaks Caravan & Lodge Park 117, 258
Hill Top 166
Hind Crag 96
Hive Pod Village, The 258
Hoathwaite Beck 161
Hoathwaite Landing 161
Hodgson Hill 90
Holbeck Point 130
Hollows Farm 256
Holly Howe 159
Holme Beck 200
Holme Crag 108, 129
Holme Islands 13, 194
Holme Wood 13, 198, 199, 200
Holme Wood Bothy 200, 261
Honister 228
Honister Pass 22, 205
Honister Slate Mine 205
Horse Close 207
Horseshoe Cove 114
Houseboat Bay 116
House Holm 97
Howtown 91
Howtown Wyke 40, 90
Hudson Place Farm 200
Hundred Year Stone 14
Hundred Year Stone, The 63

I

Illgill Head 176, 177, 178
Ings, The 63
Innominate Tarn 201
Iron Stone, The 195
Irton House Farm 256
Island, The 13, 140, 143
Isthmus Bay 70

J

Jaws of Borrowdale, the 57, 59, 65
Jenkins Field 129

K

Kailpot Bay 91
Kailpot Crag 91
Kanchenjunga 147, 157
Kathleen Raine Poetry Stones 91
Keldwyth boathouses 132
Kennel Holme 120
Kentmere 137
Keppel Cove 99
Keswick 25, 40, 57, 59, 60, 61
Keswick Camping and Caravanning Club Site 256
Keswick landing stages 57, 59, 61
Kettlewell car park 40, 60, 64, 65
Kirk Fell 175
Kirkstile Inn 200
Kirkstone 127
Kirkstone Beck 101
Kirkstone Pass 100
Kitchen Bay 67
Knoll, the 129

L

Lady Holme 122, 134
Lady's Rake 64
Lake Bank jetty 42, 150, 155
Lake District 17, 18, 49, 51, 221, 230, 231, 235
Lake Head car park 42, 174, 175
Lake Holme 154
Lakeland 227, 228, 231
Lakeland Rowing Club 59
Lake Road 61, 124, 162
Lakes and Fells Caravan Site 258
Lakes Aquarium 113
Lakeside 113
Lakeside Hotel 113
Lakeside Wood 52
Lands Point 161
Lanehead 159
Langdale Chase 130
Langdale Pikes 131, 137, 213, 221
Lanthwaite Hill 196
Lanthwaite Wood 43, 191, 192, 196, 198, 202
Latterbarrow Wood 186
Launchy Gill 74
Laurel House 154

Lazy Bay 114
Leeming House Hotel 87
Lilies of the Valley 122
Lily Bay 137
Lingholm 69
Ling Holme 114, 115
Lingholm Island 69
Lingmell 175
Lingmell Beck 175
Lingmell Gill 175
Lingmell Gill bridge 174
Lingy Holm 98
Little Baswicks 114
Little Crosthwaite 53
Little Isle 165
Little Langdale Beck 165
Lodore Falls 13, 65, 234, 240
Lodore Falls Hotel & Spa 65
Lodore jetty 64
Lodore Wood 240
Longholme 120
Lord Birkett Memorial 90, 91
Lord's Island 59, 63
Loughrigg 13, 142
Loughrigg Fell 137, 142
Low Bank Ground 159
Low Bridge End Farm 257
Low Cock How Farm Camping 261
Lowcrag Wood 64
Lower Gatesgarth 43, 204, 205
Loweswater 19, 37, 43, **197-199**, 203, 213, 218, 261
Loweswater Fell 199
Loweswater village 200
Low Gillerthwaite Field Centre 186, 260
Low Grounds Point 137
Low Ling Crag 195
Low Peel Near 153
Low Peel Near lay-by 42, 150
Lowther Estate 140, 141
Low Wood 178
Low Wood Bay Resort & Spa 129
Low Wood Bay Watersports Centre 41, 110
Low Wray Bay 135
Low Wray Campsite 258
Lyulph's Tower 96

M

Machell Coppice 42, 149, 159
Maggie's Bridge 200
Maiden Castle 222
Maiden Holme 120
Manesty 66
Manesty Park 66
Mardale 101
Mardale Green 101
Mary Mount Hotel 64
Matson Landing 115
Matson Shoal 115
Measand 101
Mellbreak 13, 193, 195, 199
Meregarth 132
Middle Fell 174
Mill Beck 193, 194, 207
Millerground Bay 132
Millerground Landing 41, 110, 132
Mirehouse 53
Mireside 185
Mitchell Wyke 120
Monk Coniston car park 42, 149, 157
Montague Wyke 153
Moor Gill Foot 161
Mossdale Bay 100
Mungrisdale 239
Murt Camping Barn 260
Myrtle Bay 66

N

Nab Cottage 165
Nab, The 165
Nag's Head Inn 76
Napes Needle 175, 176
Narrows, The 85, 125
National Park, The 233
National Trust 232
Near Sawrey 166
Nether Beck 174
Nether How 193
Newby Bridge 111
Newlands Beck 54
Nibthwaite 148
Nibthwaite Quay 154
Nichol End Marine 70
Norfolk Island 13, 82, 97
North Camp 113

O

Oak Isle 154
Octopus lagoon 154
Oldchurch Bay 87
Old Man of Coniston 147, 157, 213
Orchard Wood 52
Orrest Head 132
Otterbield Bay 59, 67, 237
Otterbield Island 67
Otter Island 66
Ouse Bridge 47, 51
Outward Bound Ullswater 85, 91
Oven Bottom 115, 126
Over Beck 174
Overbeck Bridge 174
Overbeck car park 42, 174
Oxen House Bay 151

P

Park Beck 195, 196, 200
Park Cliffe Camping and Caravan Park 258
Park Foot Holiday Park 40, 82, 84, 257
Park Nab 148, 154, 155
Parsonage Bay 125
Parson's Wyke 125
Parson Wyke House 125
Patterdale 96, 98, 100
Patterdale Estate 257
Patterdale's War Memorial 98
Peartree Point 117
Peel 195
Peel Island 13, 21, 147, 148, 152, 153
Peel Wyke 51, 56, 222
Peel Wyke car park 39, 47, 50
Peely Slapehold 87
Pencilmill Beck 87
Penny Rock Beach 41, 141, 142
Penny Rock Wood 41, 139, 141, 142, 144
Penrith 100
Pepperpot, The 121
Pier Cottage 163, 164
Pier Cottage Caravan Park 260
Pike Rigg 205
Pillar. 185
Pillar Rock 185
Pinstones Point 135

Place Fell 83, 96, 97, 241
Pocklington's Island 62
Pooley Bridge 40, 82, 83, 87, 88, 90
Pullwyke 137
Pull Wyke 107, 137
Puppy Holme 120
Purse Point 98

Q

Queen Adelaide's Hill 133
Quiet Site, The 257

R

Raise Beck 75
Rake Beck 186
Ramp Holme 115, 126
Ramps Beck 87
Rampsholme Island 59, 63
Rannerdale 196
Rannerdale Farm 196
Rannerdale Knotts 42, 189, 192, 193, 196
Raven Crag 13, 73, 79
Rawlinson Nab 107, 115
Rayrigg Hall 133
Rayrigg Meadow 41, 110, 133
Rayrigg Wyke 107, 133
Red Nab 135
Red Nab car park 41, 110
Redness Point 54
Red Pike 185, 193, 194, 206
Red Tarn 21, 243
Riddings Bay 113
Rigg, The 101
Ringing Crag 108
River Brathay 13, 138, 165
River Cocker 191, 195, 196
River Crake 103, 154
River Derwent 51, 52, 53, 59, 65, 70
River Eamont 87, 88
River Ehen 182, 183, 184, 185, 188
River Irt 178
River Leven 111, 113, 118, 138
River Liza 183, 186
River Rothay 138, 141, 142, 144, 165
rivers 22, 32
Robin Hood's Chair 187
Rooking 221

Rough Crag 75
Rough Holme 108, 123, 133
Royal Windermere Yacht Club
 123, 232
Ruskin Monument 14, 63
Ruskin Museum 14, 162, 163
Rydal Mount 165
Rydal Water 19, 20, 37, **165**, 213

S

Salmond's Plantation 87
Sandwick 97
Sandwick Bay 91, 92
Sandwick Beck 92, 96
Sandy Nab 115
Sandy Wyke 137
Scafell 175, 176, 213
Scafell Pike 13, 171, 175, 178, 213, 221
Scale Beck 194
Scale Force 13, 194
Scalehow Force 97
Scalehow Wood 97
Scale Island 194
Scales Wood 240
Scarf 206
Scarf Stones, the 64
Scar Ness 49, 52
Scarness Bay 39, 50, 52
Scarth Gap Pass 206
Scoat Fell 185
Screes, The 13, 170, 176, 177
Seamew Crag 137
Seathwaite 21
Seathwaite Tarn 21
Secret Valley 196
Sentinels 205
Shark Bay 130
Sharrow Bay 89
Sharrow Bay Hotel 90
Shepherds Crag 65
Shepherd's View Caravan Site 259
Side Farm Campsite 40, *98*, 257
Side, The 187
Side Wood 186, 187, 240
Silver Bay 13, 97
Silverholme 107, 114
Silver Holme 104, 114
Silver How 143
Silver Point 97
Skelly Neb 85
Skelwith Fold Holiday Park 259

Skelwith Force 165
Skiddaw 54, 55, 56
Skirtful Crags 118
Smithy Beck 186
Snake Holme 125
Social District 258
Solva Holme 114
Sourmilk Gill 204, 207
Sourpool Wyke 126
Sphinx, The 175
Stagshaw Garden 129
Stake Holme 125
Starling Dodd 185
Station Coppice car park 40, 73
St Bega's Church 14, 52, 53, 223
Steam Yacht Gondola 14, 146, 148, 163
Steel End car park 40, 73
Steel Fell 75
Steeple 185
St Herbert's Island 13, 59, 63, 67, 70, 223
St James' Church 201, 208
St John's Beck 77
St Martin's Church 124
Stock Ghyll 129
St Olaf's Church 14, 176
Stoller Campus 113
Storrs Hall 117
Storrs Hall Hotel 116, 117
Storrs promontory 116
Storrs Temple 14, 115, 116
Stott Park Bobbin Mill 113, 227
St Patrick's Boat Landing 98
St Patrick's Church 98
St Patrick's Well 98
Straining Well 76, 77
Strandshag Bay 59, 63
Strawberry Gardens 135
Stybarrow Crag 99, 100
Stybarrow Crag lay-bys 40, 84
Stybarrow Dodd 74
Sunny Bank jetty 42, 149, 151, 161
Swallow Barn Camping Barn 261
Swan Hotel 55
Swarthbeck Gill 90
Swarth Fell 90
Swinburn's Park 85
Syke Farm Campsite 261

T

Tablerock Bay 91
Takodana 75
Tarn Moor tunnel 89
tarns 21
Tent Lodge 159
Theatre by the Lake 61
Thirlmere 18, 19, 22, 26, 32, 33, 36, 37, 40, **71-79**, 213, 215, 256
Thirlmere dam 77, 79
Thirlspot Farm Camping 256
Thompson's Holme 13, 122, 134
Thornthwaite 55
Thornthwaite Forest 228
Thrang Crag 165
Thrang Crag Wood lay-bys 42, 149
Thurston 159
Thwaitehill Bay 90
Thwaitehill Neb 90
Tommy Holme 122
Top o' Selside 151
Torver Back Common 151, 161, 241
Torver Beck 151, 161
Torver Common Wood 161
Torver jetty 161
Tower Wood Outdoor Education Centre 117
Tower Wood Sewage Treatment Works 117
Town Cass 70
Townend 226
Treasure Island 114
Trippet Holme 67
Trout Beck 107, 131, 239
Tuft Rock 133

U

Ullock Pike 54, 55
Ullswater 18, 19, 26, 31, 33, 36, 37, 40, **81-99**, 213, 217, 257
Ullswater Holiday Park 257
Ullswater Marine 87
Ullswater Steamers' Glenridding Pier 99
Ullswater Steamers' pier 87, 90, 96
Ullswater Yacht Club 90

V

Victoria Bay 66

W

Walla Crag 64
Wall Holm 98
Wansfell Pike 129
Warnscale Beck 206
Warnscale Head Bothy 261
Wasdale Hall 178
Wasdale Head 175, 176
Wasdale Head Hall Farm 176
Wasdale Head Hotel 176
Wasdale Lakeside Pop-up Campsite 260
Wasdale National Trust Campsite 260
Wasdale Valley View 260
Wast Water 19, 21, 33, 37, 42, **171-179**, 213, 215, 237, 260
Watbarrow Point 107, 135
Watendlath Beck 64
Waterend 239
Water End 154
Waterfoot Carpark Campsite 257
Waterfoot Park 257
Watergate Farm 43, 199, 200
Waterhead 106, 108, 127, 129, 136
Waterhead Bay 138
Waterhead car park 41, 110, 127
Water Head Pier 163
Water Park Lakeland Adventure Centre 154
Waterside House Campsite 40, 84, 90, 257
Water Yeat Campsite 259
Watson's Dodd 74
West Cumbria Canoe Club 70
Whelpside Gill 76
Whin Rigg 170, 176, 178
White Cross Bay 107, 108, 130, 132
Whiteless Pike 196, 207, 212
White Moss Common 141
White Moss Lower car park 141
White Moss Upper car park 141
Wild Cat Island 117, 147, 152, 153
Wild Ennerdale 13, 181, 183, 184
Wild Wool Barn 260
Wilson Arms, The 259
Windermere 18, 19, 20, 21, 22, 26, 28, 30, 31, 33, 36, 37, 41, **105-137**, 213, 215, 217, 237, 258
Windermere Jetty Museum 14, 108, 113, 124, 133
Windermere Luxury Glamping Pods 258
Windermere Marina Village 126
Windermere Motor Boat Racing Club 108, 116
Windermere Station 231
Windermere Steamboat Museum 126
Withesike Bay 66
Woodend Brow car park 39, 50
Wood House 43, 192, 193
Woodhouse Islands 13, 43, 192, 193
Wood Howe island 101
Wordsworth Point 95
Wordsworth's Island 143
Wray Castle 14, 41, 110, 135, 136, 232
Wray Crag 135
Wray Gill 143
Wyke, The 143
Wythburn 75
Wyth Burn 75, 239
Wythburn Church 14, 76
Wythburn Fells 77
Wythop Wood 56

Y

Yewbarrow 174, 175
Yew Crag 96
Yewdale Beck 162, 163
YHA Ambleside 127, 258
YHA Buttermere 261
YHA Coniston Coppermines 259
YHA Coniston Holly How 260
YHA Ennerdale 260
YHA Grasmere Butharlyp Howe 259
YHA Hause End Bunkhouse 256
YHA Keswick 256
YHA Langdale 259
YHA Windermere 258
YMCA Lakeside 113
Young Wood 239

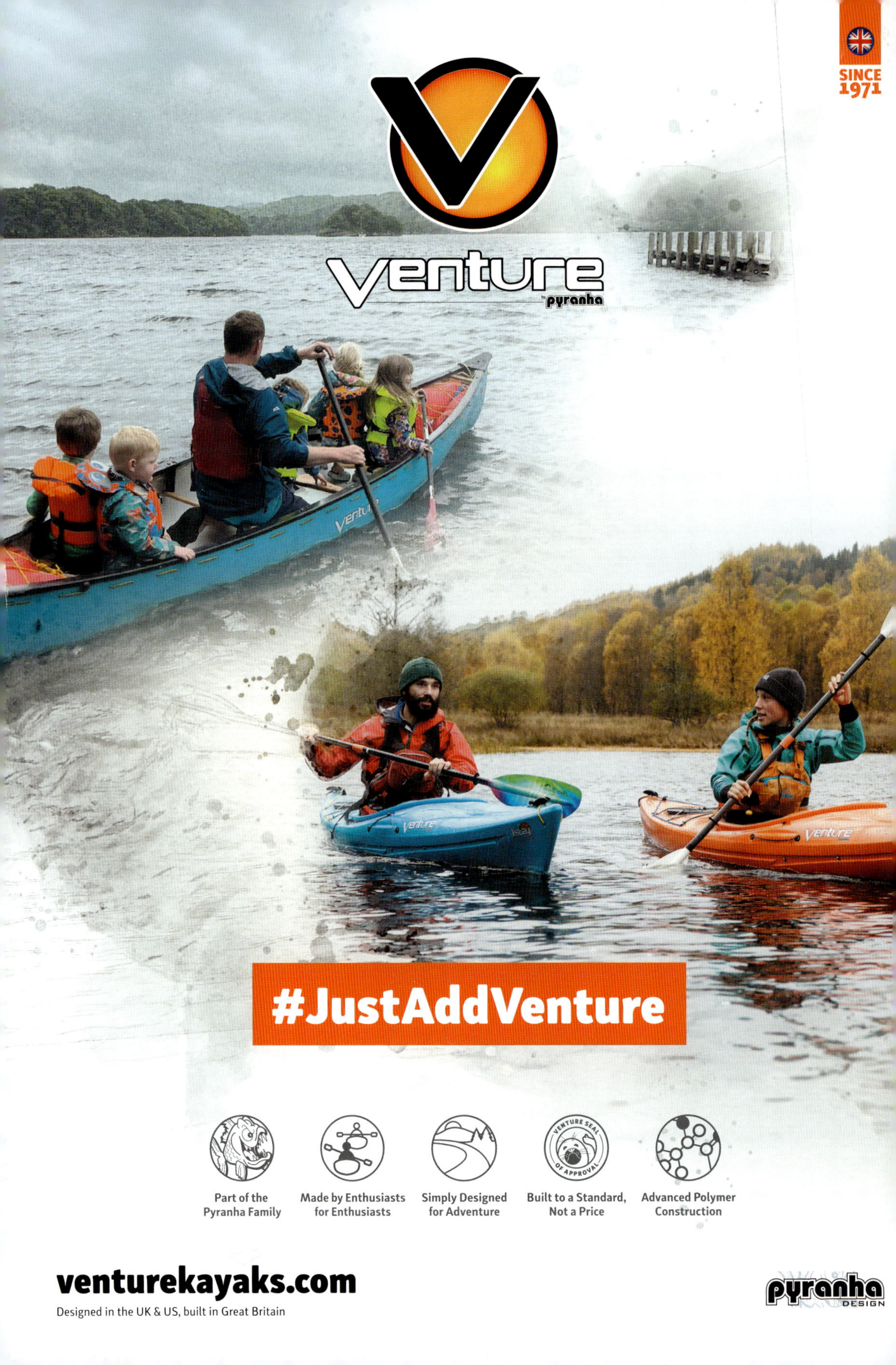

SINCE 1971
venture by pyranha
#JustAddVenture
Part of the Pyranha Family
Made by Enthusiasts for Enthusiasts
Simply Designed for Adventure
Built to a Standard, Not a Price
Advanced Polymer Construction
venturekayaks.com
Designed in the UK & US, built in Great Britain
pyranha DESIGN

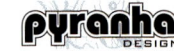